HOME LIFE IN GERMANY

HOME LIFE IN GERMANY

BY

MRS. ALFRED SIDGWICK

NEW YORK
THE MACMILLAN COMPANY
1912

First Published . . May 1908
Second Edition . June 1908
Third Edition 1912

CONTENTS

HOME LIFE IN GERMANY

HOME LIFE IN GERMANY

CHAPTER I

INTRODUCTORY

I WAS once greatly impressed by a story of an officer in the German army, who told his English hostess that he knew the position of every blacksmith's forge in Yorkshire. I wondered at the time how many officers in the English army had learned where to find the blacksmiths' forges in Pomerania. But those are bygone days. Most of us know more about Germany now than we do about our own country.[1] We go over there singly and in batches, we see their admirable public institutions, we visit their factories, we examine their Poor Laws, we walk their hospitals, we look on at their drill and their manœuvres, we follow each twist and turn of their politics, we watch their birth-rate, we write reams about their navy, and we can explain to any one according to our bias exactly what their system of Protection does for them. We are often sufficiently ignorant to compare them with the Japanese, and about once a month we publish a weighty book concerning various aspects of their flourishing empire.

[1] Throughout the book, although I am of German parentage, I have spoken of England as my country and of the English as my country-people. I was born and bred in England, and I found it more convenient for purposes of expression to belong to one country than to both.

Some of these books I have read with ardent and respectful interest; and always as I read, my own little venture seemed to wither and vanish in the light of a profounder knowledge and a wider judgment than I shall ever attain. For I have not visited workhouses and factories, I know little more about German taxes than about English ones, and I have no statistics for the instruction and entertainment of the intelligent reader. I can take him inside a German home, but I can give him no information about German building laws. I know how German women spend their days, but I know as little about the exact function of a Bürgermeister as about the functions of a Mayor. In short, my knowledge of Germany, like my knowledge of England, is based on a series of life-long, unclassified, more or less inchoate impressions, and the only excuse I have for writing about either country I find in my own and some other people's trivial minds.

When I read of a country unknown or only slightly known, I like to be told all the insignificant trifles that make the common round of life. It is assuredly desirable that the great movements should be watched and described for us; but we want pictures of the people in their homes, pictures of them at rest and at play, as well as engaged in those public works that make their public history. For no reason in the world I happen to be interested in China, but I am still waiting for just the gossip I want about private life there. We have Pierre Loti's exquisite dream pictures of his deserted palace at Pekin, and we have many useful and expert accounts of the roads, mines, railways, factories, laws, politics, and creeds of the Celestial Empire. But the book I ask for could not be written by anyone who was not of Chinese birth, and it would probably be written by a woman. It might not have much literary form or value, but it would enter into those minutiæ of life that the masculine traveller either does not see or does not think worth notice. The author of such a small-beer chronicle must have been intimate from childhood with the Chinese point of view, though her home and her friends were in a foreign land. She would probably not know much about her ancestral laws and politics, but she would have known ever since she could hear and speak just what Chinese people said to each other when none but Chinese were by, what they ate, what they wore, how they governed their homes, the relationship between husband and wife, parents and children, master and servant; in what way they fought the battle of life, how they feasted and how they mourned. If circumstances took her over and over again to different parts of China for long stretches of time, she would add to her traditions and her early atmosphere some experience of her race on their own soil and under their own sun. What she could tell us would be of such small importance that she would often hesitate to set it down; and again, she would hesitate lest what she had to say should be well known already to those amongst her readers who had sojourned in her father's country. She would do well, I think, to make some picture for herself of the audience she could hope to entertain, and to fix her mind on these people while she wrote her book. She would know that in the country of her adoption there were some who never crossed their own seas, and others who travelled here and there in the world but did not visit China or know much about its people. She would write for the ignorant ones, and not for any others; and she would of necessity leave aside all great issues and all vexed questions. Her picture would be chiefly, too, a picture of the nation's women; for though they have on the whole no share in political history, they reckon with the men in any history of domestic life and habit.

Germans often maintain that their country is more diverse than any other, and on that account more difficult to describe: a country of many races and various rules held loosely together by language and more tightly of late years by the bond of empire. But the truth probably is, that in our country we see and understand varieties, while in a foreign one we chiefly perceive what is unlike ourselves and common to the people we are observing. For from the flux and welter of qualities that form a modern nation certain traits survive peculiar to that nation: specialities of feature, character, and habit, some seen at first sight, others only discovered after long and intimate acquaintance. It is undoubtedly true that no one person can be at home in every corner of the German Empire, or of any other empire.

There are many Germanys. The one we hear most of in England nowadays is armed to the teeth, set wholly on material advancement, in a dangerously warlike mood, hustling us without scruple from our place in the world's markets, a model of municipal government and enterprise, a land where vice, poverty, idleness, and dirt are all unknown. We hear so much of this praiseworthy but most unamiable *Wunderkind* amongst nations, that we generally forget the Germany we know, the Germany still there for our affection and delight, the dear country of quaint fancies, of music and of poetry. That Germany has vanished, the wiseacres say, the dreamy unworldly German is no more with us, it is sheer sentimental folly to believe in him and to waste your time looking for him. But how if you know him everywhere, in the music and poetry that he could not have given us if they had not burned within him, and in the men and women who have accompanied you as friends throughout life,—how if you still find him whenever you go to Germany? Not, to be sure, in the shape of the wholly unpractical fool who preceded the modern English myth; but, for instance, in some of the mystical plays that hold his stage, in many of his toys and pictures, and above all in the kindly, lovable, clever people it is your pleasure to meet there. You may perhaps speak with all the more conviction of this attractive Germany if you have never shut your eyes and ears to the Germany that does not love us, and if you have often been vexed and offended by the Anglophobia that undoubtedly exists. This Germany makes more noise than the friendly element, and it is called into existence by a variety of causes not all important or political. It flourished long before the Transvaal War was seized as a convenient stick to beat us with. In some measure the Anglicised Germans who love us too well are responsible, for they do not always love wisely. They deny their descent and their country, and that justly offends their compatriots. I do not believe that the Englishman breathes who would ever wish to call himself anything but English; while it is quite rare for Germans in England, America, or France to take any pride in their blood. The second generation constantly denies it, changes its name, assures you it knows nothing of Germany. They have not the spirit of a Touchstone, and in so far they do their country a wrong.

In another more material sense, too, there are many Germanys, so that when you write of one corner you may easily write of ways and food and regulations that do not obtain in some other corner, and it is obviously impossible to remind the reader in every case that the part is not the whole. Wine is dear in the north, but it has sometimes been so plentiful in the south that barrels to contain it ran short, and anyone who possessed an empty one could get the measure of wine it would hold in exchange. Every town and district has its special ways of cooking. There is great variety in manner of life, in entertainments, and in local law. There are Protestant and Catholic areas, and there are areas where Protestants, Catholics, and Jews live side by side. The peasant proprietor of Baden is on a higher level of prosperity and habit than the peasant serf of Eastern Prussia; and the Jews on the Russian frontier, those strange Oriental figures in a special dress and wearing earlocks and long beards, have as little in common with the Jews of Mannheim or Frankfort as with the Jews of the London Stock Exchange. It would, in fact, be impossible for any one person to enter into every shade and variety of German life. You can only describe the side you know, and comment on the things you have seen. So you bring your mite to the store of knowledge which many have increased before you, and which many will add to again.

CHAPTER II

CHILDREN

IN Germany the storks bring the children. " I know the pond in which all the little children lie waiting till the storks come to take them to their parents," says the mother stork in Andersen's story. " The stork has visited the house," people say to each other when a child is born ; and if you go to a christening party you will find that the stork has come too : in sugar on a cake, perhaps, or to be handed round in the form of ice cream. Most of the kindly intimate little jests about babies have a stork in them, and a stranger might easily blunder by presenting an emblem of the bird where it would not be welcome. The house on which storks build is a lucky one, and people regret the disappearance of their nests from the large towns.

When the baby has come it is not allowed out of doors for weeks. Air and sunlight are considered dangerous at first, and so is soap and even an immoderate use of water. For eight weeks it lies day and night in the *Steckkissen*, a long bag that confines its legs and body but not its arms. The bag is lined with wadding, and a German nurse, who was showing me one with great pride, assured me that while a child's bones were soft it was not safe to lift it in any other way. These bags are comparatively modern, and have succeeded the swaddling clothes still used in some parts of Germany. They are bandages wrapping the child round like a mummy, and imprisoning its arms as well as its legs. A German doctor told me that as these *Wickelkinder* had never known freedom they did not miss it ; but he seemed to approve of the modern compromise that leaves the upper limbs some power of movement.

Well - to - do German mothers rarely nurse their children. When you ask why, you hear of nerves and anæmia, and are told that at any rate in cities women find it impossible. I have seen it stated in a popular book about Germany that mothers there are little more than " aunts " to their children ; and the *Steckkissen* and the foster-mother were about equally blamed for this unnatural state of affairs. From our point of view there is not a word to be said in favour of the *Steckkissen*, but it really is impossible to believe that a bag lined with wadding can undermine a mother's affection for her child. Your German friends will often show you a photograph of a young mother holding her baby in her arms, and the baby, if it is young enough, will probably be in its bag. But unless you look closely you will take the bag for a long robe, it hangs so softly and seems so little in the mother's way. It will be as dainty as a robe too, and when people have the means as costly ; for you can deck out your bag with ribbons and laces as easily as your robe. The objection to foster-mothers has reality behind it, but the evils of the system are well understood, and have been much discussed of late. Formerly every mother who could afford it hired one for her child, and peasant women still come to town to make money in this way. But the practice is on the wane, now that doctors order sterilised milk. The real ruler of a German nursery is the family doctor. He keeps his eye on an inexperienced mother, calls when he sees fit, watches the baby's weight, orders its food, and sees that its feet are kept warm.

A day nursery in the English sense of the word is hardly known in Germany. People who can afford it give up two rooms to the small fry, but where the flat system prevails, and rents are high, this is seldom possible. One room is usually known as the *Kinderstube*, and here the children sleep and play. But it must be remembered that rooms are big, light, and high in Germany, and that such a *Kinderstube* will not be like a night nursery in a small English home. Besides, directly children can walk they are not as much shut up in the nursery as they are in England. The rooms of a German flat communicate with each other, and this in itself makes the segregation to which we are used difficult to carry out. During the first few days of a sojourn with German friends, you are constantly reminded of a pantomime rally in which people run in and out of doors on all sides of the stage; and if they have several lively children you sometimes wish for an English room with one door only, and that door kept shut. Even when you pay a call you generally see the children, and possibly the nurse or the *Mamsell* with them. But a typical middle-class German family recognises no such foreign body as a nurse. It employs one maid of all work, who helps the housewife wherever help is needed, whether it is in the kitchen or the nursery. The mother spends her time with her children, playing with them when she has leisure, cooking and ironing and saving for them, and for her husband all through her busy day. Modern Germans like to tell you that young women no longer devote themselves to these simple duties, but if you use your eyes you will see that most women do their work as faithfully as ever. There is an idle, pleasure-loving, money-spending element in Germany as there is in other countries, and it makes more noise than the steady bulk of the nation, and is an attractive target there as here for the darts of popular preachers and playwrights. But it is no more preponderant in Germany than in England. On the whole, the German mother leaves her children less to servants than the English mother does, and in some way works harder for them. That is to say, a German woman will do cooking and ironing when an Englishwoman of the same class would delegate all such work to servants. This is partly because German servants are less efficient and partly because fewer servants are employed.

The fashionable nurses in Germany are either English or peasant girls in costume. It is considered smart to send out your baby with a young woman from the Spreewald if you live in Berlin, or from one of the Black Forest valleys if you live in the duchy of Baden. In some quarters of Berlin you see the elaborate skirts and caps of the Spreewald beside every other baby-carriage, but it is said that these girls are chiefly employed by the rich Jews, and you certainly need to be as rich as a Jew to pay their laundry bills. The young children of the poor are provided for in Berlin, as they are in other cities, by crêches, where the working mother can leave them for the day. Several of these institutions are open to the public at certain times, and those I have seen were well kept and well arranged.

The women of Germany have not thrown away their knitting needles yet, though they no longer take them to the concert or the play as they did in a less sophisticated age. Children still learn to knit either at school or at home, and if their mother teaches them she probably makes them a marvellous ball. She does this by winding the wool round little toys and small coins, until it hides as many surprises as a Christmas stocking, and is as much out of shape; but the child who wants the treasures in the stocking has to knit for them, and the faster she secures them the faster she is learning her lesson. The mother, however, who troubles about knitting is not quite abreast of her times. The truly modern woman flies at higher game; with the solemnity and devotion of a Mrs. Cimabue Brown she cherishes in her children a love of Art. Her watchword is *Die Kunst im Leben des Kindes*, or Art in the Nursery, and she is assisted by men who are doing for German children of this generation what Walter Crane and others did for English nurseries twenty-five years ago. You can get enchanting nursery pictures, toys, and decorations in Germany to-day, and each big city has its own school of artists who produce them: friezes where the birds and beasts beloved of children solemnly pursue each other; grotesque wooden manikins painted in motley; mysterious landscapes where the fairy-tales of the world might any day come true. Dream pictures these are of snow and moonlight, marsh and forest, the real Germany lying everywhere outside the cities for those who have eyes to see. Even the toy department in an ordinary shop abounds in treasures that never seem to reach England: queer cheap toys made of wood, and not mechanical. It must be a dull child who is content with a mechanical toy, and it is consoling to observe that most children break the mechanism as quickly as possible and then play sensibly with the remains. Many of the toys known to generations of children seemed to be as popular as ever, and quite unchanged. You still

find the old toy towns, for instance, with their red
roofed coloured houses and green curly trees, toys that
would tell an imaginative child a story every time they
were set up. It is to be hoped they never will change,
but in this sense I have no faith in Germany. The
nation is so desperately intent on improvement that
some dreadful day it will improve its toys. Indeed, I
have seen a trade circular threatening some such van-
dalism ; and in the last Noah's ark I bought Noah and
his family had changed the cut of their clothes. So
the whole ark had lost some of its charm.

Everyone who is interested in children and their
education, and who happens to be in Berlin, goes to
see the *Pestalozzi Fröbel Haus*, the great model Kindergarten where children of the working classes are received
for fees varying from sixpence to three shillings a month,
according to the means of the parents. There are large
halls in which the children drill and sing, and there are
classrooms in which twelve to sixteen children are
taught at a time. Every room has some live birds or
other animals and some plants that the children are
trained to tend ; the walls are decorated with pictures
and processions of animals, many painted and cut out
by the children themselves, and every room has an
impressive little rod tied with blue ribbons. But the
little ones do not look as if they needed a rod much.
They are cheerful, tidy little people, although many of
them come from poor homes. In the middle of the
morning they have a slice of rye bread, which they eat
decorously at table on wooden platters. They can buy
milk to drink with the bread for 5 pf., and they dine
in school for 10 pf. They play the usual Kindergarten
games in the usual systematised mechanical fashion,
and they study Nature in a real back garden, where
there are real dejected-looking cocks and hens, a real

cow, and a lamb. What happens to the lamb when he becomes a sheep no one tells you. Perhaps he supplies mutton to the school of cookery in connection with the Kindergarten. Some of the children have their own little gardens, in which they learn to raise small salads and hardy flowers. There are carpentering rooms for the boys, and both boys and girls are allowed in the miniature laundry, where they learn how to wash, starch, and iron doll's clothes. The illustration shows them engaged in this business, apparently without a teacher; but, as a matter of fact, the children are always under a teacher's eye, even when they are only digging in a sand heap or weeding their plots of ground. Each child has a bath at school once a week, and at first the mothers are uneasy about this part of the programme, lest it should give their child cold. But they soon learn to approve it, and however poor they are they do their utmost to send a child to school neatly shod and clad.

As a rule German children of all classes are treated as children, and taught the elementary virtue of obedience. *Das Recht des Kindes* is a new cry with some of the new people, but nevertheless Germany is one of the few remaining civilised countries where the elders still have rights and privileges. I heard of an English-woman the other day who said that she had never eaten the wing of a chicken, because when she was young it was always given to the older people, and now that she was old it was saved for the children. If she lived in Germany she would still have a chance, provided she kept away from a small loud set, who in all matters of education and morality would like to turn the world upside down. In most German homes the noisy, spoilt American child would not be endured for a moment, and the little tyrant of a French family would be taught its place, to the comfort and advantage of all concerned. I have dined with a large family where eight young ones of various ages sat at an overflow table, and did not disturb their elders by a sound. It was not because the elders were harsh or the young folk repressed, but because Germany teaches its youth to behave. The little girls still drop you a pretty old-fashioned curtsey when they greet you; just such a curtsey as Miss Austen's heroines must have made to their friends. The little boys, if you are staying in the house with them, come and shake hands at unexpected times,—when they arrive from school, for instance, and before they go out for a walk. At first they take you by surprise, but you soon learn to be ready for them. They play many of the same games as English children, and I need hardly say that they are brought up on the same fairy stories, because many of our favourites come from Germany. The little boys wear sensible carpenters' aprons indoors, made of leather or American cloth; and the little girls still wear bib aprons of black alpaca. Their elders do not play games with them as much as English people do with their children. They are expected to entertain and employ themselves; and the immense educational value of games, the training they are in temper, skill, and manners, is not understood or admitted in Germany as it is here. The Kindergarten exercises are not competitive, and do not teach a child to play a losing game with effort and good grace.

CHAPTER III

SCHOOLS

GERMAN children go to day schools. This is not to say that there are no boarding schools in Germany; but the prevailing system throughout the empire is a system of day schools. The German mother does not get rid of her boys and girls for months together, and look forward to the holidays as a time of uproar and enjoyment. She does not wonder anxiously what changes she will see in them when they come back to her. They are with her all the year round,—the boys till they go to a university, the girls till they marry. Any day in the streets of a German city you may see troops of children going to school, not with a maid at their heels as in Paris, but unattended as in England. They have long tin satchels in which they carry their books and lunch, the boys wear peaked caps, and many children of both sexes wear spectacles.

Except at the Kindergarten, boys and girls are educated separately and differently in Germany. In some rare cases lately some few girls have been admitted to a boys' *Gymnasium*, but this is experimental and at present unusual. It may be found that the presence of a small number in a large boys' school does not work well. In addition to the elementary schools, there are four kinds of Public Day School for boys in Germany, and they are all under State supervision. There is the *Gymnasium*, the *Real-Gymnasium*, the *Ober-Real Schule*, and the *Real-Schule*. Until 1870 the Gymnasiums were the only schools that could send their scholars to the universities; a system that had serious disadvantages. It meant that in choosing a child's school, parents had to decide whether at the end of his school life he was to have a university education. Children with no aptitude for scholarship were sent to these schools to receive a scholar's training; while boys who would have done well in one of the learned professions could not be admitted to a university, except for science or modern languages, because they had not attended a Gymnasium.

A boy who has passed through one of these higher schools has had twelve years' education. He began Latin at the age of ten, and Greek at thirteen. He has learned some French and mathematics, but no English unless he paid for it as an extra. His school years have been chiefly a preparation for the university. If he never reaches the higher classes he leaves the Gymnasium with a stigma upon him, a record of failure that will hamper him in his career. The higher official posts and the professions will be closed to him; and he will be unfitted by his education for business. This at least is what many thoughtful Germans say of their classical schools; and they lament over the unsuitable boys who are sent to them because their parents want a professor or a high official in the family. It is considered more sensible to send an average boy to a *Real-Gymnasium* or to an *Ober-Real Schule*, because nowadays these schools prepare for the university, and any boy with a turn for scholarship can get the training he needs. The *Ober-Real Schule* professedly pays most attention to modern languages;

and it is, in fact, only since 1900 that their boys are received at a university on the classical side. They still prepare largely for technical schools and for a commercial career.

At a *Real-Schule*, the fourth grade of higher school, the course only lasts six years. They do not prepare for the Abiturienten examination, and their scholars cannot go from them to a university. They prepare for practical life, and they admit promising boys from the elementary schools. A boy who has been through any one of these higher schools successfully need only serve in the army for one year; and that in itself is a great incentive to parents to send their children. A *Real-Schule* in Prussia only costs a hundred marks a year, and a *Gymnasium* a hundred and thirty-five marks. In some parts of Germany the fees are rather higher, in some still lower. The headmasters of these schools are all university men, and are themselves under State supervision. In an entertaining play called *Flachsmann als Erzieher* the headmaster had not been doing his duty, and has allowed the school to get into a bad way. The subordinates are either slack or righteously rebellious, and the children are unruly. The State official pays a surprise visit, discovers the state of things, and reads the Riot Act all round. The wicked headmaster is dismissed, the eager young reformer is put in his place, the slackers are warned and given another chance. . . . Blessed be St. Bureaukrazius . . . says the genial old god out of a machine, when by virtue of his office he has righted every man's wrongs. The school in the play must be an elementary one, for children and teachers are of both sexes, but a master at a *Gymnasium* told me that the picture of the official visit was not exaggerated in its importance and effect. There was considerable excitement in Germany

2

over the picture of the evil headmaster, his incompetent
staff, and the neglected children; and I was warned
before I saw the play that I must not think such a
state of affairs prevailed in German schools. The
warning was quite unnecessary. An immoral, idle,
and ignorant class of men could not carry on the
education of a people as it is carried on throughout
the German Empire to-day.

I have before me the Annual Report of a
Gymnasium in Berlin, and it may interest English
people to see how many lessons the teachers in each
subject gave every week. There were thirty teachers
in the school.

SUBJECT	LESSONS PER WEEK
Religion	31
German	42
Latin	112
Greek	72
French	36
History and Geography	44
Mathematics and Arithmetic	56
Natural History	10
Physics	20
Hebrew	4
Law	1
Writing	6
Drawing	18
Singing	12
Gymnasium	27
Swimming	$8\frac{1}{2}$
Handfertigkeit	3

$502\frac{1}{2}$ lessons

The headmaster took Latin for seven hours every
week, and Greek for three hours. A professor who
came solely for religious teaching came for ten hours
every week. But most of the masters taught from
sixteen to twenty-four hours, while one who is down

for reading, writing, arithmetic, gymnastics, German, singing, and *Natur* could not get through all he had to do in less than thirty hours. On looking into the hours devoted to each subject by the various classes, you find that the lowest class had three hours religious instruction every week, and the other classes two hours. There were 407 boys in the school described as *Evangelisch*, 47 Jews, and 23 Catholics; but in Germany parents can withdraw their children from religious instruction in school, provided they satisfy the authorities that it is given elsewhere. The two highest classes had lessons on eight chapters of St. Paul's Epistle to the Romans, on the Epistle to the Philippians, and on the confessions of St. Augustine. Some classes were instructed in the Gospel according to St. John, and the little boys learned Bible History. So Germans are not without orthodox theological teaching in their early years, whatever opinions they arrive at in their adolescence.

Every boy in the school spent two or three hours each week on German composition, and, like boys in other countries, handled themes they could assuredly not understand, probably, like other boys, without a scruple or a hesitation.

" Why does the ghost of Banquo appear to Macbeth, and not the ghost of Duncan ? "

" How are the unities of time, place, and action treated in Schiller's ballads ? "

" Discuss the antitheses in Lessing's Laokoon."

" What can you say about the representation of concrete objects in Goethe's *Hermann and Dorothea ?* "

These examples are taken at random from a list too long to quote completely; but no one need be impressed by them. Boys perform wonderful feats of this kind in England too. However, I once heard a

German professor say that the English boy outdid
the German in *gesunder Menschenverstand* (sound
common sense), but that the German wins in the race
when it comes to the abstract knowledge (*Wissen*) that
he and his countryfolk prize above all the treasures of
the earth. No one who knows both countries can
doubt for a single moment that the professor was
right, and that he stated the case as fairly as it can
be stated. In an emergency or in trying circumstances
the English boy would be readier and more self-
reliant: but when you meet him where entertainment
is wanted rather than resource, his ignorance will make
you open your eyes. This, at any rate, is the kind of
story told and believed of Englishmen in Germany.
A student who was working at science in a German
university had been there the whole winter, and
though the city possessed many fine theatres he had
only visited a variety show. At last his friends told
him that it was his duty to go to the *Schauspielhaus*
and see a play by Goethe or Schiller. " Goethe!
Schiller!" said my Englishman, " *Was ist das?*"

The education of girls in Germany is in a transi-
tion state at present. Important changes have been
made of late years, and still greater ones, so the
reformers say, are pending. Formerly, if a girl was to
be educated at all she went to a *Höhere Töchterschule*,
or to a private school conducted on the same lines, and,
like the official establishment, under State supervision.
When she had finished with school she had finished
with education, and began to work at the useful arts
of life, more especially at the art of cooking. What
she had learned at school she had learned thoroughly,
and it was considered in those days quite as much as
was good for her. The officials who watched and
regulated the education of boys had nothing to do with

girls' schools. These were left to the staff that managed elementary schools, and kept on much the same level. Girls learned history, geography, elementary arithmetic, two modern languages, and a great deal of mythology. The scandalous ignorance of mythology displayed by Englishwomen still shocks the right-minded German. If a woman asked for more than this because she was going to earn her bread, she spent three years in reading for an examination that qualified her for one of the lower posts in the school. The higher posts were all in the hands of men. Of late years women have been able to prepare for a teacher's career at one of the Teachers' Seminaries, most of which were opened in 1897.

More than forty years ago the English princess in Berlin was not satisfied with what was done in Germany for the education of women; and one of the many monuments to her memory is the Victoria Lyceum. This institution was founded at her suggestion by Miss Archer, an English lady who had been teaching in Berlin for some years, and who was greatly liked and respected there. At first it only aimed at giving some further education to girls who had left school, and it was not easy to get men of standing to teach them. But as it was the outcome of a movement with life in it the early difficulties were surmounted, and its scope and usefulness have grown since its foundation thirty-eight years ago. It is not a residential college, and it has no laboratories. During the winter it still holds courses of lectures for women who are not training for a definite career; but under its present head, Fräulein von Cotta, the chief work of the Victoria Lyceum has become the preparation of women for the *Ober Lehrerin* examination. This is a State examination that can only be passed five years after a girl has qualified as *Lehrerin*, and two of these five years must have been spent in teaching at a German school. To qualify as *Lehrerin*, a girl must have spent three years at a Seminary for teachers after she leaves school, and she usually gets through this stage of her training between the ages of fifteen and eighteen. Therefore a woman must have three years special preparation for a subordinate post and eight years for a higher post in a German girls' school.

The whole question of women's education is in a ferment in Germany at present, and though everyone interested is ready to talk of it, everyone tells you that it is impossible to foresee exactly what reforms are coming. There are to be new schools established, *Lyceen* and *Ober-Lyceen*, and *Ober-Lyceen* will prepare for matriculation. When girls have matriculated from one of these schools they will be ready for the university, and will work for the same examinations as men. Baden was the first German State that allowed women to matriculate at its universities. It did so in 1900, and in 1903 Bavaria followed suit. In 1905 there were eighty-five women at the universities who had matriculated in Germany; but there are hundreds working at the universities without matriculating first. At present the professors are free to admit women or to exclude them from their classes; but the right of exclusion is rarely exercised. Before long it will presumably be a thing of the past.

An Englishwoman residing at Berlin, and engaged in education, told me that in her opinion no German woman living had done as much for her countrywomen as Helene Lange, the president of the *Allgemeine deutsche Frauenverein*. Nineteen years ago she began the struggle that is by no means over, the struggle to secure a better education for women and a greater share in its control. In English ears her aim will sound a modest one, but English girls' schools are not entirely in the hands of men, with men for principals and men to teach the higher classes. She began in 1887 by publishing a pamphlet that made a great sensation, because it demanded, what after a mighty tussle was conceded, women teachers for the higher classes in girls' schools, and for these women an academic education. In 1890 she founded, together with Auguste Schmidt and Marie Loeper-Housselle, the *Allegemeine deutsche Lehrerinnen-Verein*, which now has 80 branches and 17,000 members. But the pluckiest thing she did was to fight Prussian officialdom and win. In 1889 she opened *Real-Kurse für Mädchen und Frauen*, classes where women could work at subjects not taught in girls' schools, Latin for instance, and advanced mathematics; for the State in Germany has always decided how much as well as how little women may learn. It would not allow people as ignorant as Squeers to keep a school because it offered an easy livelihood. It organised women's education carefully and thoroughly in the admirable German way; but it laid down the law from A to Z, which is also the German way. When, therefore, Helene Lange opened her classes for women, the officials came to her and said that she was doing an illegal thing. She replied that her students were not schoolgirls under the German school laws, but grown-up women free to learn what they needed and desired. The officials said that an old law of 1837 would empower them to close the classes by force if Helene Lange did not do so of her own accord. After some reflection and in some anxiety she decided to go on with them. By this time public opinion was on her side and came to her assistance; for public opinion does count in Germany even with the officials. The classes went on, and were changed in 1893 to *Gymnasialkurse*. In 1896 the first German women passed the Abiturienten examination, the difficult examination young men of eighteen pass at the end of a nine years' course in one of the classical schools. Even to-day you may hear German men argue that women should not be admitted to universities because they have had no classical training. Helene Lange was the first to prove that even without early training women can prepare themselves for an academic career. Her experiment led to the establishment of *Gymnasialkurse* in many German cities; and even to the admission of girls in some few cases to boys' Gymnasium schools.

To-day Helene Lange and her associates are contending with the schoolmasters, who desire to keep the management of girls' schools in their own hands. She calls the *Höhere Töchterschule* the failure of German school organisation, and she says that the difference of view taken by men and women teachers as to the proper work of girls' schools makes it most difficult to come to an understanding. Consciously or not, men form an ideal of what they want and expect of women, and try to educate them up to it; while women think of the claims life may make on a girl, and desire the full development of her powers. "The Higher Daughter," she says, "must vanish, and her place must be taken by the girl who has been thoroughly prepared for life, who can stand on her own feet if circumstances require it, or who brings with her as housewife the foundations of further self-development, instead of the pretentiousness of the half educated. In one of her many articles on the subject of school reform she points to three directions where reform is needed. What she says about the teaching of history is so characteristic of her views and of the modern movement in Germany, that I think the whole passage is worth translation :—

" All those subjects that help to make a woman a better citizen must be taken more seriously," she says. " It can no longer be the proper aim of history teaching to foster and strengthen in women a sentimental attachment to her country and its national character : its aim must be to give her the insight that will enable her to understand the forces at work, and ultimately play an active part in them. Many branches of our social life await the work of women, civic philanthropy to begin with; and as our public life becomes more and more constitutional, it demands from the individual both a ripe insight into the good of the community and a living sense of duty in regard to its destiny; and, on the other hand, the foundations of this insight and sense of duty must be in our times more and more laid by the mother, since the father is often entirely prevented by his work from sharing in the education of his children. Therefore, both on her own account and in consideration of the task before her, a woman just as much as a man should understand and take a practical interest in public life, and it is the business of the school to see that she does so. Over and over again those who are trying to reform girls' schools insist that history teaching should lead the student to understand the present time ; that it should recognise those economic conditions on which the history of the world, especially in our day, depends in so great a measure ; that it should pay attention not only to dates and events, but also to the living process of civilisation, since it is only from the latter inquiry that we can arrive at the principles of individual effort in forwarding social life."

Nowadays in Germany Helene Lange is considered

one of the " Moderates," but it will be seen from the
above quotation that she has travelled far from the
old ideals which invested women with many beautiful
qualities, but not with the sense and knowledge required of useful public citizens. She proceeds in the
same article to say that scientific and mathematical
teaching should reach a higher standard in girls' schools ;
and thirdly, that certain branches of psychology, phy-
siology, and hygiene should receive greater attention,
because a woman is a better wife and mother when
she fulfils her duties with understanding instead of by
mere instinct. Nor will education on this higher plane
deprive women of any valuable feminine virtues if it
is carried out in the right way. But to this end women
must direct it, and in great measure take it into their
own hands. She would not shut men out of girls'
schools, but she would place women in supreme authority
there, and give them the lion's share of the work.

It seems to the English onlooker that this contest
can only end in one way, and that if the women of
Germany mean to have the control of girls' schools
they are bound to get it. Some of the evils of the
present system lie on the surface. " It is a fact," said a
schoolmaster, speaking lately at a conference,—" it is a
fact that a more intimate, spiritual, and personal relationship is developed between a schoolgirl and her master
than between a schoolgirl and her mistress." This
remark, evidently made in good faith, was received with
hilarity by a large mixed audience of teachers ; and
when one reflects on the unbridled sentiment of some
" higher daughters " one sees where it must inevitably
find food under the present anomalous state of things.
But the schoolmaster's argument is the argument
brought forward by many men against the reforms
desired by Helene Lange and her party. They insist

that girls would deteriorate if they were withdrawn throughout their youth from masculine scholarship and masculine authority in school. They talk of the emasculation of the staff as a future danger. They do not seem to talk of their natural reluctance to cede important posts to women, but this must, of course, strengthen their pugnacity and in some cases colour their views.

Meanwhile many parents prefer to send their daughters to one of the private schools that have a woman at the head, and where most of the teaching is done by women ; or to a *Stift*, a residential school of the conventual type, which may be either Protestant or Catholic. A girl who had spent some years at a well-known Protestant *Stift* described her school life to me as minutely as possible, and it sounded so like the life in a good English boarding-school thirty years ago that it is difficult to pick out points of differences. That only means, of course, that the differences were subtle and not apparent in rules and time-tables. The girls wore a school uniform, were well fed and taught, strictly looked after, taken out for walks and excursions, allowed a private correspondence, shown how to mend their clothes, made to keep their rooms tidy, encouraged in piety and decorum. In these strenuous times it sounds a little old-fashioned, and as a matter of fact a school of this kind fits a girl for a sheltered home but not for the open road. For everyone concerned about the education of women the interesting spectacle in Germany to-day is the campaign being carried on by Helene Lange and her party, the support they receive from the official as well as from the unofficial world, and the progress they make year by year to gain their ends.

CHAPTER IV

THE EDUCATION OF THE POOR

THERE are no people in the world who need driving to school less than the Germans. There are no people in the world who set so high a value on knowledge. In the old days, when they lived with Jove in the clouds, they valued knowledge solely for its own sake, and did not trouble much about its practical use in the world. It is absurd to say, as people often do now, that this spirit is dead in the nation. You cannot be long in the society of Germans without recognising that it survives wherever the stress of modern life leaves room for it. You see that when a German makes money his sons constantly enter the learned and the artistic professions with his full approval, though they are most unlikely to make a big income in this way. You are told by people who work amongst the poor, that parents will make any sacrifices year after year in order to send a boy to one of the higher schools. You know that the Scotsmen who live on oatmeal while they acquire learning have their counterparts in the German universities, where many a student would not dine at all if private or organised charity did not give him a dinner so many days a week. Sometimes you have heard it said of such and such a great German, that he was so poor when he was young that he had to accept these free dinners given in every German university town to penniless students.   The fact would be remembered, but it would never count against a man in Germany.   The dollar is not almighty there.

To say, therefore, that education is compulsory throughout the empire is not to say that it is unpopular. A teacher in an elementary school was once telling me how particular the authorities were that every child, even the poorest, should come to school properly clothed and shod.   "For instance," she said, "if a child comes to school in house-shoes he is sent straight home again." "But do the parents mind that?" I asked from my English point of view, for the teacher was speaking of people who in England would live in slums and care little whether their children were educated or not.   But in Germany even the poorest of the poor do care, and to refuse a child admission to school is an effective punishment.   At any rate, you may say this of the majority.   No doubt if school was not compulsory the dregs of the nation would slip out of the net, especially in those parts of the empire where the prevalent character is shiftless and easy going.   "When you English think that we hold the reins too tight, it is because you do not understand what a mixed team we have to drive," a north German said to me.   "We should not get on, we should not hold together long, if our rule was slack and our attention careless."

At the last census only one in 10,000 could not read or write, and these dunces were all Slavs.   But how even a Slav born under the eye of the Eagle can remain illiterate is a mystery.   In 1905 there were 59,348 elementary schools in the empire, and their organisation is as elaborate and well planned as the organisation of the army.   In Berlin alone there are 280.   All the teachers at these schools have been trained to teach at special seminaries, and have passed State examinations that qualify them for their work. In Germany many men and women, entitled both by class and training to teach in the higher grade schools, have taken up work in the elementary ones from choice. I know one lady whose certificates qualify her to teach in a *Höhere Töchterschule*, and who elects to teach a large class of backward children in a *Volkschule*. Her ambition is to teach those children described in Germany as *nicht völlig normal* : children we should describe as " wanting." She says that her backward children repay her for any extra trouble they give by their affection and gratitude. She knows the circumstances of every child in her class, and where there is real need she can get help from official sources or from philanthropic organisations, because a teacher's recommendation carries great weight in Germany. This lady gets up every day in summer at a quarter past five, in order to be in school by seven. Her school hours are from seven to eleven in summer, and from eight till twelve in winter ; but she has a great deal of work to prepare and correct after school. Her salary is raised with every year of service, and when she is past work she will be entitled to a State pension of thirty pounds.

Children have to attend school from the age of six and to stay till they are fourteen ; and in their school years they are not allowed to work at a trade without permission. They do not learn foreign languages, but they are thoroughly grounded in German, and they receive religious instruction. Of course, they learn history, geography, and arithmetic. In the new schools every child is obliged to have a warm bath every week, but it is not part of a teacher's duties to superintend it. Probably the women who clean the school buildings do so. In the old schools, where there are no bathrooms,

the children are given tickets for the public bathing
establishments.   The State does not supply free food,
but there are philanthropic societies that supply those
children who need it with a breakfast of bread and
milk in winter.   Everyone connected with German
schools says that no child would apply for this if
his parents were not destitute, and one teacher told me
a story of the headmaster's boy being found, to his
father's horror and indignation, seated with the starving
children and sharing their free lunch.   He had brought
his own lunch with him, but it was his first week at
school, and he thought that a dispensation of bread
and milk in the middle of the morning was part of
the curriculum.

School books are supplied to children too poor to
buy them, and it seems that no trouble is given by
applications for this kind of relief by people not entitled
to it.   Gymnastics are compulsory for both boys and
girls in the lower classes, and choral singing is taught
in every school.   Teachers must all be qualified to
accompany singing on the violin.   Most of the elementary schools in Prussia are free.   Some few charge
sixpence a month.   A child can even have free teaching
in its own home if it is able to receive instruction, but
not to attend school.   Medical inspection is rigorously
carried out in German elementary schools.   The doctor
not only watches the general health of the school, but
he registers the height, weight, carriage, state of
nourishment, and vaccination marks of each child on
admission ; the condition of the eyes and ears and
any marked constitutional tendency he can discover.
Every child is examined once a month, when necessary
once a fortnight.   In this way weak or wanting
children are weeded out, and removed to other
surroundings, the short-sighted and the deaf are given

places in the schoolroom to suit them. The system protects the child and helps the teacher, and has had the best results since it was introduced into Prussia in 1888.

Attendance at continuation schools is now compulsory on boys and girls for three years after leaving the elementary school, where they have had eight years steady education. They must attend from four to six hours weekly; instruction is free, and is given in the evening, when the working day is over. Certain classes of the community are free, but about 30,000 students attend these schools in Berlin. The subjects taught are too many to enumerate. They comprise modern languages, history, law, painting, music, mathematics, and various domestic arts, such as ironing and cooking. More boys than girls attend these schools, as girls are more easily exempt. It is presumably not considered so necessary for them as for their brothers to continue their education after the age of fourteen.

One of the most interesting experiments being made in Germany at present is the "open air" school, established for sickly children during the summer months. The first one was set up by the city of Charlottenberg at the suggestion of their *Schulrat* and their school doctor, and it is now being imitated in other parts of Germany. From Charlottenberg the electric cars take you right into the pine forest, far beyond the last houses of the growing city. The soil here is loose and sandy, and the air in summer so soft that it wants strength and freshness. But as far out as this it is pure, and the medical men must deem it healing, for they have set up three separate ventures close together amongst the pine trees. One belongs to the Society of the Red Cross, and here sick and consumptive women come with their children for the day,

and are waited on by the Red Cross sisters. We saw some of them lying about on reclining chairs, and some, less sickly, were playing croquet. The second establishment is for children who are not able to do any lessons, children who have been weeded out by the school doctor because they are backward and sickly. There are a hundred and forty children in this school, and there is a crêche with twenty beds attached to it for babies and very young children. One airy room with two rows of neat beds was for rickety children.

The third and largest of the settlements was the *Waldschule*, open every day, Sundays included, from the end of April to the middle of October, and educating two hundred and forty delicate children chosen from the elementary schools of Charlottenberg. We arrived there just as the children were going to sit down to their afternoon meal of bread and milk, and each child was fetching its own mug hanging on a numbered hook. The meals in fine weather are taken at long tables in the open air. When it rains they are served in big shelters closed on three sides. Dotted about the forest there were mushroom-shaped shelters with seats and tables beneath them, sufficient cover in slight showers; and there were well lighted, well aired class-rooms, where the children are taught for twenty-five minutes at a time.

All the buildings are on the Doecker system, and were manufactured by Messrs. Christoph & Unmark of Niesky. This firm makes a speciality of schools and hospitals, built in what we should call the bungalow style. Of course, this style exactly suits the needs of the school in the forest. There is not a staircase in the place, there is no danger of fire, no want of ventilation, and very little work for housemaids or charwomen. The school furniture is simple and care-

3

fully planned. Some of it was designed by Richard Riemerschmid of Munich, the well-known artist.

Each child has two and a half hours' work each day; all who are strong enough do gymnastics, and all have baths at school. Each child has its own locker and its own numbered blanket for use out of doors on damp or chilly days. The doctor visits the school twice a week, and the weight of each child is carefully watched. The busy sister who superintends the housekeeping and the hygienic arrangements seemed to know how much each child had increased already; and she told us what quantities of food were consumed every day. The kitchen and larder were as bright and clean as such places always are in Germany. When the children arrive in the morning at half-past seven they have a first breakfast of *Griesbrei*. At ten o'clock they have rolls and butter. Their dinner consists of one solid dish. The day we were there it had been pork and cabbage, a combination Germans give more willingly to delicate children than we should; the next day it was to be *Nudelsuppe* and beef. At four o'clock they have bread and milk, and just before they go home a supper like their early breakfast of milk-soup, and bread. 260 litres of milk are used every day, 50 to 60 lbs. of meat, 2 cwts. potatoes, 30 big rye loaves, 280 rolls, and when spinach, for instance, is given, 80 lbs. of spinach. We asked whether the children paid, and were told that those who could afford it paid from 25 to 45 pf. a day. The school is kept open throughout the summer holidays, but no work is done then, and two-thirds of the teachers are away. Although the children are at play for the greater part of the day in term time, and all day in the holidays, the headmaster told us that they gave no trouble. There was not a dirty or untidy child to be seen, nor one with rough manners. They are allowed to play in the light, sandy soil of the forest, much as English children play at the seaside, and we saw the beginning of an elaborate chain of fortresses defended by toy guns and decorated with flowers. We heard a lesson in mental arithmetic given in one of the class-rooms, the boys sitting on one side of the room and the girls on the other ; and we found that these young sickly children were admirably taught and well advanced for their age. To be a teacher in one of these open-air schools is hard work, because the strain is never wholly relaxed. All day long, and a German day is very long, the children must be watched and guarded, sheltered from changes in the weather and prevented from over-tiring themselves. Many of them come from poor cramped homes, and to spend the whole summer in the forest more at play than at work makes them most happy. I met Germans who did not approve of the *Waldschule*, who considered it a fantastic extravagant experiment, too heavy for the rate-payers to bear. This is a side of the question that the rate-payers must settle for themselves ; but there is no doubt about the results of the venture on the children sent to school in the forest. They get a training that must shape their whole future, moral and physical, a training that changes so many unsound citizens into sound ones every year for the German Empire. If the rate-payers can survive the strain it seems worth while.

CHAPTER V

THE BACKFISCH

THE word is untranslatable, though my dictionary translates it. Backfisch, m. fried fish; young girl; says the dictionary. In Germany a woman does not arrive at her own gender till she marries and becomes somebody's *Frau*. Woman in general, girl, and miss are neuter; and the fried-fish girl is masculine. But if one little versed in German wished to tell you that he liked a fried sole, and said *Ich liebe einen Backfisch*, it might lead to misunderstandings. The origin of the word in this application is dubious. Some say it means fish that are baked in the oven because they are too small to fry in pans; but this does not seem a sensible explanation to anyone who has seen white-bait cooked. Others say it means fish the anglers throw back into the water because they are small. At any rate, the word used is to convey an impression of immaturity. A *Backfisch* is what English and American fashion papers call a " miss." You may see, too, in German shop windows a printed intimation that special attention is given to *Backfisch Moden*. It is a girl who has left school but has not cast off her school-girl manners; and who, according to her nation and her history, will require more or less last touches.

Miss Betham-Edwards tells us that a French girl is taught from babyhood to play her part in society, and that the exquisite grace and taste of Frenchwomen are carefully developed in them from the cradle. An English girl begins her social education in the nursery, and is trained from infancy in habits of personal cleanliness and in what old-fashioned English people call "table manners." An Englishwoman, who for many years lived happily as governess in a German country house, told me how on the night of her arrival she tried out of politeness to eat and drink as her hosts did; and how the mistress of the house confided to her later that she had disappointed everyone grievously. There were daughters in the family, and they were to learn to behave at table in the English way. That was why the father, arriving from Berlin, had on his own initiative brought them an English governess; for the English are admitted by their continental friends to excel in this special branch of manners, while their continental enemies charge them with being "ostentatiously" well groomed and dainty. The truth is, that if you have lived much with both English and Germans, and desire to be fair and friendly to both races, you find that your generalisations will not often weigh on one side. The English child learns to eat with a fork rather than with a spoon, and never by any chance to put a knife in its mouth, or to touch a bone with its fingers. The German child learns that it must never wear a soiled or an unmended garment or have untidy hair. I have known a German scandalised by the slovenly wardrobe of her well-to-do English pupil, and I have heard English people say that to hear Germans eat soup destroyed their appetite for dinner. English girls are not all slovens, and nowadays decently bred Germans behave like other people at table. But untidiness is commoner in England than in Germany, and you may still stumble across a German any day who, abiding by old customs, puts his knife in his mouth and takes his bones in his hands. He will not only do these things, but defend them vociferously. In that case you are strongly advised not to eat a dish of asparagus in his company.

Your modern German *Backfisch* may be a person of finish and wide culture. You may find that she insists on her cold tub every morning, and is scandalised by your offer of hot water in it. She has seen Salome as a play and heard Salome as an opera. She has seen plays by G.B.S. both in Berlin and London. She does not care to see Shakespeare in London, because, as she tells you, the English know nothing about him. Besides, he could not sound as well in English as in German. She has read Carlyle, and is now reading Ruskin. She adores Byron, but does not know Keats, Shelley, or Rossetti. Tennyson she waves contemptuously away from her, not because she has read him, but because she has been taught that his poetry is "bourgeois." Her favourite novels are *Dorian Gray* and *Misunderstood*. She dresses with effect and in the height of fashion, she speaks French and English fluently, she has travelled in Italy and Switzerland, she plays tennis well, she can ride and swim and skate, and she would cycle if it was not out of fashion. In fact, she can do anything, and she knows everything, and she has been everywhere. Your French and English girls are ignorant misses in comparison with her, and you say to yourself as you watch her and humbly listen to her opinions, delivered without hesitation and expressed without mistakes: "Where is the German *Backfisch* of yester year?"

"Did you ever read *Backfischchen's Leiden und Freuden?*" you say to her; for the book is in its 55th edition, and you have seen German girls devouring it only last week; German girls of a different type, that is, from your present glittering companion.

"That old-fashioned inferior thing," she says contemptuously. "I believe my mother had it. That is not literature."

You leave her to suppose you could not have made that discovery for yourself, and you spend an amusing hour over the story again, for there are occasions when a book that is not "literature" will serve your purpose better than a masterpiece. The little book has entertained generations of German girls, and is presumably accepted by them, just as *Little Women* is accepted in America or *The Daisy Chain* in England. The picture was always a little exaggerated, and some of its touches are now out of date; yet as a picture of manners it still has a value. It narrates the joys and sorrows of a young girl of good family who leaves her country home in order to live with an aunt in Berlin, a facetious but highly civilised aunt who uses a large quantity of water at her morning toilet. All the stages of this toilet are minutely described, and all the mistakes the poor countrified *Backfisch* makes the first morning. She actually gets out of bed before she puts on her clothes, and has to be driven behind the bed curtains by her aunt's irony. This is an incident that is either out of date or due to the genius and imagination of the author, for I have never seen bed curtains in Germany. However, Gretchen is taught to perform the early stages of her toilet behind them, and then to wash for the first time in her life in a basin full of water. She is sixteen. Her aunt presents her with a sponge, and observes that the civilisation of a nation is judged by the amount of soap it uses. "In much embarrassment I applied myself to this unaccustomed task," continues the ingenuous *Backfisch*, "and I managed it so cleverly that everything around me was soon swimming. To make matters worse, I upset the water-jug, and now the flood spread to the washstand, the floor, the bed curtains, even to my clothes lying on the chair. " If only this business of dressing was over," she sighs as she is about to brush her teeth, with brushes supplied by her aunt. But it is by no means over. She is just going to slip into a dressing-gown, cover her un-brushed hair with a cap, and so proceed to breakfast, when this exacting aunt stops her : actually desires her to plait and comb her hair at this hour of the morning, and to put on a tidy gown. Gretchen's gown is extremely untidy, and on that account I will not admit that the portrait is wholly lifelike. In fact, the author has summed up the sins of all the *Backfisch* tribe, and made a single *Backfisch* guilty of them. But caricature, if you know how to allow for it, is instructive. Mr. Stiggins is a caricature, yet he stands for failings that exist among us, though they are never displayed quite so crudely. " Go and brush your nails," says the aunt to the niece when the girl attempts to kiss her hand ; and the *Backfisch* uses a nail-brush for the first time in her life.

Then the two ladies sit down to breakfast. Gretchen fills the cups too full, soaks her roll in her coffee, and drinks out of her saucer. Her aunt informs her that " coffee pudding " is not polite, and can only be allowed when they are by themselves ; also that she must not drink out of the saucer. " But we children always did it at home," says Gretchen. " I can well believe it," says the aunt. " *Everything is permitted to children.*" The italics are mine.

An aunt who has such ideas about the education of the young is naturally not surprised when at dinner-time she has to admonish her niece not to wipe her mouth with her hand, not to speak with her mouth full, to eat her soup quietly, to keep her elbows off the table, not to put her fingers in her plate or her knife in her mouth, and not to take her chicken into her hands on ceremonial occasions.

" My treasure," says the aunt, " as you know, we are going to dinner with the Dunkers to-morrow. Be good enough not to take your chicken into your hands. Here at home I don't object to it, but the really correct way is to separate the meat from the bone with the knife and fork."

The docile *Backfisch* says *Jawohl, liebe Tante*, and feels that this business of becoming civilised is full of pitfalls and surprises. Never in her life has she eaten poultry without the assistance of her fingers. When she gets to the dinner-party she is fortunate enough to sit next to her bosom friend, who starts in horror and whispers " With a knife, Gretchen," when Gretchen is just about to dip her fingers in the salt. The *Backfisch* is truly anxious to learn, but she feels that the injunctions of society are hard, and says it is poor sport to eat your chicken with a knife and fork, because the best part sticks to the bones. Then her friend stops her from drinking fruit syrup out of her plate, and her neighbour on the other side, a stout guzzler who has not been taught by his aunt to eat properly, encourages Gretchen to drink too much champagne.

After these early adventures the education of the *Backfisch* proceeds quickly. She has to learn at her aunt's tea-parties not to fill cups to overflowing in sheer exuberance of hospitality; and she is also instructed not to press food on people. " In good society," says the aunt, " people decline to eat because they have had enough, and not because they require pressing." She is obliged also to discourage Gretchen

from waiting too attentively on the young men who
visit at the house; and Gretchen, who does not care
about young men, but only yearns to be serviceable,
devotes herself in future to the old ladies, their foot-
stools, their knitting, and their smelling bottles. This
touch is one of many that makes the book, in spite of
its obvious shortcomings, valuable as a picture of
German character and manner. It is impossible to
imagine Gretchen in a French or English story of the
same class. The French girl would be more adroit
and witty; the English girl would expect young men
to wait on her; and neither of them would gush as
Gretchen did about her old ladies. " My readiness
to serve them knew no bounds. To arrange their
seats to their liking, to give them stools for their feet
and cushions for their backs, to rush for their shawls
and cloaks, to count the rows in their knitting, to help
them pick up their stitches, to thread their needles, to
wind silk or wool, to peel fruit, to run for smelling
bottles and cold water,—all these things I did with
delight the instant my watchful eye discovered the
smallest wish, and I was always cordially thanked."

Tastes differ. Some old ladies would be made quite
uncomfortable by such fussy attentions. The *Backfisch*
goes on to say that she was equally assiduous in
waiting on the old gentlemen. She picked up anything
they dropped, polished their spectacles for them, and
listened to their dull stories when no one else would.
I consider the portrait of Gretchen in this story a
literary triumph. I can see the girl; I can hear her
voice and laugh. I know exactly how she behaved
and what the old ladies and gentlemen said to her, how
she dressed and how she did her hair; not because the
author tells me just these things, but because her type
is as true to life to-day as it was thirty years ago. As

a contrast to her, a fine young lady from the city presently joins the household, and the aunt does not have to provide her with a tooth-brush. The new arrival wears blue satin slippers, drinks her chocolate in bed, and cannot dress without the help of a maid. In this way the author shows you that girls brought up in cities are superfine rather than savage, and that you are not to suppose the ordinary German *Backfisch* is like her little heroine from the provinces.

The truth of the matter is, that no one nowadays has such manners as the *Backfisch* had when she first came from the wilds; at least, no one of her class, even if they have grown up in Hinter-Pommern. But if you travel in Germany next week and stay in small towns and country places, you will still meet plenty of people who take their poultry bones in their fingers and put their knives in their mouths. If they are men you will see them use their fork as a dagger to hold the meat while they cut it up; you will see them stick their napkins into their shirt collars and placidly comb their hair with a pocket comb in public; if they are women and at a restaurant, they will pocket the lumps of sugar they have not used in their coffee. But if you are in private houses amongst people of Gretchen's type you will see none of these things. A German host still pulls the joint close to him sometimes or stands up to carve, and a German hostess still presses you to eat, still in the kindness of her heart piles up your plate. But this embarrassing form of hospitality is dying out. As Gretchen's aunt said, people in good society recognise that a guest refuses food because he does not want it. Some years ago, when you had satisfied your hunger and declined more, your German friends used to look offended or distressed, and say *Sie geniren sich gewiss*. This is a difficult phrase to translate, because the idea is

one that has never taken root in the English mind,
Sich geniren, however, is a reflective verb, a corruption
of the French verb *se gêner*, and what they meant was
that you really wanted a third potato dumpling but did
not like to say so. Whether your reluctance was
supposed to proceed from your distrust of your host's
hospitality or shame at your own appetite, is not clear ;
in either case it was taken, is even to-day still often taken,
for artificial. To accept a portion of an untouched dish
was considered a sign that you came from "a good
house" where no one grudged or wished to save the
food put on the table; and formerly you could not
refuse sugar in your tea without being commended for
your economy. You are still invited to eat tarts and
puddings in Germany with what we consider the
insufficient assistance of a tea-spoon, but I have never
been in a private house where salt-spoons were not
provided. You never used to find them in inns of a
plain kind, and unless you were known to be English
and peculiar you were not provided with more than one
knife and fork for all the courses of a *table d'hôte*
You would see your German neighbours putting theirs
aside as a matter of course when their plates were
removed.

On the whole, then, the celebrated picture of the
Backfisch, though it is overloaded, bears some relation to
the facts of life in Germany : not only in the episodes
that make the early chapters entertaining, but all
through the story in atmosphere, in the little touches that
give a story nationality. When the excellent Gretchen
has been civilised she spends a great deal of time in the
kitchen, and soon knows all the duties of the complete
housekeeper ; while, when the frivolous Eugenie becomes
Braut she cannot cook at all. But frivolous as she is,
she recognises that marriage is unthinkable without

cooking, and straightway sets to work to learn. Then, too, the *Backfisch* is the ideal German maiden, cheerful, docile, and facetious; and constantly on the jump (*springen* is the word she uses) to serve her elders. Middle-aged Germans used to have a most tiresome way of expecting girls to be like lambs in spring, always in the mood to frisk and caper: so that a quiet or a delicate girl had a bad time with some of them. *Ein junges Mädchen muss immer heiter sein,* they would say reproachfully. But it does not follow that you are always *heiter* just because you are not twenty yet; especially in Germany, where girls are often anæmic and have headaches. However, perhaps the modern German maiden does not allow her elders to be so silly.

There are some other ways, too, in which my *Backfisch* of thirty years ago is typical of German womanhood both then and now. She is as good as gold, she is devoted to duty not to pleasure, and she is as guileless as a child. You know that when she marries she will be faithful unto death; you know that her husband and her children will call her blessed. These things come out quite naturally, almost unconsciously, in the little story that is "not literature," and which for all that is so truly and deeply German in its quality and tone. This Gretchen of the schoolroom, this caricature of the country cousin, is akin in her simplicity, sweetness, and depth of nature to that other Gretchen whose figure lives for ever in the greatest of German poems. Just as the women of Shakespeare and the women of Miss Austen are subtly kin to each other, inasmuch as they are English women, so Goethe's girl and the girl of the poor little schoolroom story are German in every pulse and fibre. And this national essence, the honesty, goodness, and sweetness of the girl, are the real things, the things to remember about her. Those little matters of the toilet and the table will soon be out of date, are out of date already in the greater part of Germany. As a picture of forgotten manners they will always be amusing, just as it is amusing to read an eighteenth-century English story of school life, in which the young ladies fought and bit and scratched each other and were whipped and sent to bed.

CHAPTER VI

THE STUDENT

WHEN an English lad goes to the university he usually goes there from a public school, where out of school hours he has been learning for years past to be a man. In these strenuous days he may have learned a little in school hours too, but that is a new departure. Cricket and character are what an English boy expects to develop at school, and if there is stuff in him he succeeds. He does not set a high value on learning. Even if he works and brings home prizes he will not be as proud of them as of his football cap, while a boy who is head of the school, but a duffer at games, will live for all time in the memory of his fellows as a failure. But the German boy goes to school to acquire knowledge, and he too gets what he wants. The habit of work must be strong in him when at the age of eighteen he goes to one of his many universities. But when he gets there he is free for the first time in his life, and the first use he for the most part makes of his freedom is to be thoroughly, happily idle. This idleness, if he has a backbone and a call to work, only lasts a term or two; and no one who knows how a German boy is held to the grindstone for twelve years of school life can grudge him a holiday. But the odd fact is, that the Briton who leaves school a man is more under control at Oxford or Cambridge than the German at Heidelberg who leaves school a boy.

A German university is a teaching institution which prepares for the State examinations, and is never residential. There are no old colleges. The professors live in flats like other people, and the students live in lodgings or board with private families. There is one building or block of buildings called the *Universität* where there are laboratories and lecture-rooms. The State can decline a professor chosen by the university; but this power is rarely exercised. The teachers at a German university consist of ordinary professors, extraordinary professors, and *Privatdocenten*—men who are not professors yet, but hope to be some day. An Englishman in his ignorance might think that an extraordinary professor ought to rank higher than an ordinary one; but this is not so. The ordinary professors are those who have chairs; the extraordinary ones have none. But all professors have a fixed salary which is paid to the day of their death, though they may cease work when they choose. The salaries vary from £240 to £350, and are paid by the State, but this income is increased by lecturing fees. Whether it is largely increased depends on the popularity of the lecturer and on his subject. An astronomer cannot expect large classes, while a celebrated professor of Law or Medicine addresses crowds. I have found it difficult to make my English friends believe that there are professors now in Berlin earning as much as £2500 a year. The English idea of the German professor is rudely disturbed by such a fact, for his poverty and simplicity of life have played as large a part in our tradition of him as his learning. The Germans seem to recognise that a scholar cannot want as much money as a man of affairs; therefore,

when one of their professors is so highly esteemed by
the youth of the nation that his fees exceed £225, half
of the overflow goes to the university and not to him
at all. In this way Berlin receives a considerable
sum every year, and uses it to assist poorer professors and to attract new men. As a rule a German
professor has not passed the State examinations. These
are official, not academic, and they qualify men for
government posts rather than for professorial chairs.
A professor acquires the academic title of doctor by
writing an original essay that convinces the university
of his learning. The title confers no privileges. It is
an academic distinction, and its value depends on the
prestige of the university conferring it.

Germans say that our English universities exist to
turn out gentlemen rather than scholars, and that the
aim of their own universities is to train servants for the
State and to encourage learning. I think an Englishman would say that a gentleman is bred at home, but
he would understand how the German arrived at his
point of view. When a German talks of an English
university he is thinking of Oxford and Cambridge,
and he knows that, roughly speaking, it is the sons of
well-to-do men who go there. Perhaps he does not
know much about the Scotch and Irish and Welsh
universities, or London, or the north of England;
though it is never safe to build on what a German
does not know. I once took for granted that a man
talking to me of some point in history would no more
remember all the names and dates of the Kings of
Scotland than I remember them myself. But he knew
every one, and was scandalised by my ignorance. So
perhaps the average German knows better than I do
what it costs a man to graduate at Edinburgh or at
Dublin. Anyhow, he knows that three or four years

4

at Oxford or Cambridge cost a good deal; and he knows that in Berlin, for instance, a student can live on sixty pounds a year, out of which he can afford about five pounds a term for academic fees. If he is too poor to pay his fees the authorities allow him to get into their debt, and pay later in life when he has a post. There are cases where a man pays for his university training six years after he has ended it. But a German university comes to a man's help still more effectively when there is need for it, and will grant him partial or even entire support. Then there are various organisations for providing hungry men with dinners so many days a week; sometimes at a public table, sometimes with families who arrange to receive one or more guests on certain days every week. The Jewish community in a university always looks after its poor students well, and this practice of entertaining them in private houses is one that gives rises to many jests and stories. The students soon find out which of their hosts are liberal and which are not, and give them a reputation accordingly.

A German comparing his universities with the English ones will always lay stress on the fact that his are not examining bodies, and that his professors are not crammers but teachers. A student who intends to pass the State examinations chooses his own course of reading for them, and the lectures that he thinks will help him. He does not necessarily spend his whole time at the same university, but may move from one to the other in pursuit of the professors he wants for his special purpose. He is quite free to do this; and he is free to work night and day, or to drink beer night and day. He is under no supervision either in his studies or his way of life.

English people who have been to Germany at all

have invariably been to Heidelberg, and if they have been there in term time they have been amused by the gangs of young men who swagger about the narrow streets, each gang wearing a different coloured cap. They will have been told that these are the "corps" students, and the sight of them so jolly and so idle will confirm their mental picture of the German student, the picture of a young man who does nothing but drink beer, fight duels, sing *Volkslieder* and *Trinklieder*, and make love to pretty low-born maidens. When you see a company of these young men clatter into the Schloss garden on a summer afternoon, and drink vast quantities of beer, when you observe their elaborate ceremonial of bows and greetings, when you hear their laughter and listen to the latest stories of their monkey tricks, you understand that the student's life is a merry one, but except for the sake of tradition you wonder why he need lead it at a seat of learning. Anything further removed from learning than a German corps student cannot be imagined, and the noise he makes must incommode the quiet working students who do not join a corps. Not that the quiet working students would wish to banish the others. They are the glory of the German universities. In novels and on the stage none others appear. The innocent foreigner thinks that the moment a young German goes to the Alma Mater of his choice he puts on an absurd little cap, gets his face slashed, buys a boarhound, and devotes all his energies to drinking beer and ragging officials. But though the "corps" students are so conspicuous in the small university towns, it is only the men of means who join them. For poorer students there is a cheaper form of union, called a *Burschenschaft*. When a young German goes to the university he has probably

never been from home before, and by joining a *Corps*
or a *Burschenschaft* he finds something to take the
place of home, companions with whom he has a
special bond of intimacy, and a discipline that carries
on his social education; for the etiquette of these
associations is most elaborate and strict. The
members of a corps all say "thou" to each other, and
on the *Alte Herren Abende*, when members of an older
generation are entertained by the young ones of to-day,
this practice still obtains, although one man may be a
great minister of State and the other a lad fresh from
school. The laws of a "corps" remind you of the
laws made by English schoolboys for themselves,—
they are as solemnly binding, as educational, and as
absurd. If a Vandal meets a Hessian in the street he
may not recognise him, though the Hessian be his
brother; but outside the town's boundary this prohibition is relaxed, for it is not rooted in ill feeling but in
ceremony. One corps will challenge another to meet
it on the duelling ground, just as an English football
team will meet another—in friendly rivalry. All
the students' associations except the theological require
their members to fight these duels, which are really
exercises in fencing, and take place on regular days of
the week, just as cricket matches do in England.
The men are protected by goggles and by shields and
baskets on various parts of their bodies, but their
faces are exposed, and they get ugly cuts, of which
they are extremely proud. As it is quite impossible
that I should have seen these duels myself, I will
quote from a description sent me by an English friend
who was taken to them in Heidelberg by a corps
student. "They take place," he says, "in a large
bare room with a plain boarded floor. There were
tables, each to hold ten or twelve persons, on three

sides of the room, and a refreshment counter on the fourth side, where an elderly woman and one or two girls were serving wine. The wine was brought to the tables, and the various corps sat at their special tables, all drinking and smoking. The dressing and undressing and the sewing up of wounds was done in an adjoining room. When the combatants were ready they were led in by their seconds, who held up their arms one on each side. The face and the top of the head were exposed, but the body, arms and neck were heavily bandaged. The duellists are placed opposite each other, and the seconds, who also have swords in their hands, stand one on each side, ready to interfere and knock up the combatant's sword. They say '*Auf die Mensur*,' and then the slashing begins. As soon as blood is drawn the seconds interfere, and the doctor examines the cut. If it is not bad they go on fighting directly. If it needs sewing up they go into the next room, and you wait an endless time for the next party. I got awfully tired of the long intervals, sitting at the tables, drinking and smoking. While the fights were going on we all stood round in a ring. There were only about three duels the whole morning. There was a good deal of blood on the floor. The women at the refreshment counter were quite unconcerned. They didn't trouble to look on, but talked to each other about blouses like girls in a post office. The students drove out to the inn and back in open carriages. It is a mile from Heidelberg. The duels are generally as impersonal as games, but sometimes they are in settlement of quarrels. I think any student may come and fight on these occasions, but I suppose he has to be the guest of a corps."

A German professor lecturing on university life constantly used a word I did not understand at first.

The word as he said it was *Commang*, with a strong accent on the second syllable. The word as it is written is *Comment*, and means the etiquette set up and obeyed by the students. The Germans have taken many French words into their language and corrupted them, much as we have ourselves: sometimes by Germanising the pronunciation, sometimes by conjugating a French verb in the German way as they do in *raisonniren* and *geniren*. The *Commang*, said the professor, was a highly valuable factor in a young man's education, because it helped more than anything else to turn a schoolboy into a man of the world. So when I saw a little book called *Der Bier Comment* for sale I bought it instantly, for I wanted to know how beer turned a schoolboy into a man of the world. It began with a little preface, a word of warning to anyone attempting to write about the morals, customs, and characteristics of the German nation. No one undertaking this was to forget that the Germans had an amazing *Bierdurst*, and that they liked to assuage this thirst in company, to be cheerful and easy, and to sing while they were drinking. Then it goes on to give the elaborate ceremonial observed at the *Kneiptafel*. One of my dictionaries, although the German-English part has 2412 pages, translates *Kneipe* as " any instrument for pinching." I never yet found anything I wanted in those 2412 pages. Another dictionary, one that cost ninepence, and is supposed to give you all words in common use, does not include *Kneipe* at all. As an instrument for pinching, *Kneipe* is certainly not common, except possibly amongst people who use tools. As a word for a sort of beer club it is as common as beer. It is not only students who go to the *Kneipe*. In some parts of Germany men spend most of the evening drinking beer and smoking with their friends, while the womenfolk are by themselves or with the children at home. But the beer *Commang* that the professor thought had such educational value is the name for certain intricate rites practised by university students at the *Kneiptafel.* Those who sit at the table are called Beer Persons, and they are of various ranks according to the time of membership and their position in the Kneipe. Every Beer Person must drink beer and join in the songs, unless he has special permission from the chairman. The Beer Persons do not just sit round the table and drink as they please. If they did there would be no *Comment,* and I suppose no educational value. They have to invite their fellows to drink with them, and the quantity drunk, the persons who may have challenged, and the exact number of minutes that may elapse before a challenge is accepted and returned, is all exactly laid down. Then there are various festive and ingenious ways of drinking together, so as to turn the orgy into something like a game. For instance, the glass " goes into the world," that is, it circulates, and any Beer Person who seizes it with a different hand or different fingers from his neighbour is fined. Or the glasses are piled one on the top of another while the Beer Persons sing, and some one man has to drink to each glass in the pile at the word of command. Or the president orders a " Beer Galop " with the words " *Silentium für einen Biergalopp : ich bitte den nötigen Stoff anzuschaffen.*" At the word of command everyone, beginning with the president, passes his glass to his left-hand neighbour and empties the one he receives. Then the glasses are refilled, passed to the right, and emptied again as soon as possible. The president, it seems, has to exercise a good deal of discretion and ingenuity, for if the *Kneipe* seems flat it lies with him to order the moves in the game that will make it lively and stimulate beer, song, and conversation. There are various fines and punishments inflicted according to strict rule on those who transgress the code of the *Kneipe*, but as far as I can make out they all resolve themselves into drinking extra beer, singing extra songs, or in really serious cases ceasing to be a Beer Person for whatever length of time meets the offence. An Englishman who was present at some of these gatherings in Heidelberg, told me that the etiquette was most difficult for a foreigner to understand, and always a source of anxiety to him all the evening. He was constantly invited to drink with various members, and the German responsible for him explained that he must not only respond to the invitation at the moment, but return it at the right time: not too soon, because that would look like shaking off an obligation, and not too late, because that would look like forgetting it.

A *Kommers* is a students' festival in which the professors and other senior members of a university take part, and at which outsiders are allowed to look on. The presiding students appear *in vollem Wichs*, as we should say in their war paint, with sashes and rapiers. Young and old together drink beer, sing songs, make speeches, and in honour of one or the other they "rub a Salamander,"—a word which is said to be a corruption of *Sauft alle mit einander*. This is a curious ceremony and of great antiquity. When the glasses are filled, at the word of command they are rubbed on the table; at the word of command they are raised and emptied; and again at the word of command every man rubs his glass on the table, the second time raises it and brings it down with a crash. Anyone who brought his glass down a moment earlier or later than the others would spoil

the *Salamander* and be in disgrace. In *Ekkehardt*
Scheffel describes a similar ceremonial in the tenth
century. "The men seized their mugs," he says,
"and rubbed them three times in unison on the
smooth rocks, producing a humming noise, then they
lifted them towards the sun and drank; each man
set down his mug at the same moment, so that it
sounded like a single stroke."

A *Kommers* is not always a gay festival. It may
be a memorial ceremony in honour of some great
man lately dead. Then speeches are made in his
praise, solemn and sacred music is sung, and the
Salamander, an impressive libation to the dead man's
Manes, is drunk with mournful effect.

In small university towns—and it must be remembered that there are twenty-two universities in
Germany—the students play a great part in the social
life of the place. German ladies have often told me
that the balls they looked forward to with most
delight as girls were those given by students, when
one "corps" would take rooms and pay for music,
wine, and lights. For supper, tickets are issued on
such occasions, which the guests pay themselves.
The small German universities seem full of the
students in term time, especially in those places
where people congregate for pleasure and not for
work. Even in a town as big as Leipsic they are
seen a good deal, filling the pavement, occupying
the restaurants, going in gangs to the play. But
in Berlin the German student of tradition, the beer
person, the duellist, the rollicking lad with his big dog,
is lost. He is there, you are told, but if you keep to
the highway you never see him; and, to tell the truth,
in Germany you miss him. He stands for youth and
high spirits and that world of ancient custom most

of us would be loth to lose. In Berlin, if you go to the *Universität* when the working day begins, you see a crowd of serious, well-mannered young men, most of them carrying books and papers. They are swarming like bees to the various lecture-rooms; they are as quiet as the elderly professors who appear amongst them. They have no corps caps, no dogs, no scars on their scholarly faces. By their figures you judge that they are not Beer Persons. They have worked hard for twelve years in the gymnasiums of Germany, they have no idle habits, no interests so keen as their interest in this business of preparing for the future. They are the men of next year's Germany, and will carry on their country's reputation in the world for efficiency and scholarship.

CHAPTER VII

RIEHL ON WOMEN

NOT long ago I heard a German professor say that anyone who wanted to speak with authority about the German family must read *Die Familie* by W. H. Riehl. He said that, amongst other things, this important work explained why men went to the *Kneipe*, because they were fond of home life; and also what was the sphere of women. I thought it would be useful to have both these points settled; besides, I asked several wise Germans about the book, and they all nodded their heads and said it was a good one. So I got it, and was surprised to find it came out in 1854. I thought ideas about women had advanced since then, even in Germany, though a German friend had warned me just before my last visit not to expect much in this way. She made a movement with her lips as if she was blowing a bit of thistledown from her. "Remember," she said, "that is what you will be directly you get there . . . nothing at all." But I had been to Germany so often that I was prepared to be "nothing at all" for a time, and not to mind it much. What I wanted to discover was how far German women had arrived at being "something" in the eyes of their men. In my eyes they had always been a good deal: admirable wives and mothers, for instance, patient, capable, thrifty, and self-sacrificing. At first I thought that my friend was wrong, and that women of late years had made great strides in Germany. I met single women who had careers and homes of their own and were quite cheerful. When you are old enough to look back twenty or thirty years, and remember the blight there used to be on the "old maid," and the narrow gossiping life she was driven to lead, you must admit that these contented bachelor women have done a good deal to emancipate themselves. In England they have been with us for a long time, but formerly I had not come across them in Germany. On the contrary, I well remember my amazement as a girl at hearing a sane able-bodied single woman of sixty say she had naturally not ventured on a summer journey to Switzerland till some man who looked after her money affairs, but was in no way related, had given her his consent. I did once hear a German boast of having struck his wife in order to bring her to submission. He was not a navvy either, but a merchant of good standing. He was not a common type, however. German men, on the whole, treat their womenfolk kindly, but never as their equals. Over and over again German women have told me they envied the wives of Englishmen, and I should say that it is impossible for an English woman to be in Germany without feeling, if she understands what is going on around her, that she has suddenly lost caste. She is "nothing at all" because she is a woman: to be treated with gallantry if she is young and pretty, and as a negligible quantity if she is not. That perhaps is a bitter description of what really takes place, but after reading Herr Riehl, and hearing that his ideas are still widely accepted in Germany, I am not much afraid of being unjust. His own arguments convict the men of the nation in a measure nothing I could say would. They are in extreme opposition to the ideas fermenting amongst modern women there, and the strange fact that they are not regarded as quite out of date makes them interesting.

Herr Riehl's theory, to put it in a nutshell, is that the family is all-important, and the individual, if she is a woman, is of no importance at all. He does not object to her being yoked to a plough, because then she is working for the family, but he would forbid her, if he could, to enter any profession that would make her independent of the family. She is not to practise any art, and if she "commences author" it is a sure sign that she is ugly, soured, and bitter. In any country where they are allowed to rule, and even in any country where they distinguish themselves in art and literature, civilisation as well as statecraft must be at a standstill. Queen Elizabeth and Maria Theresa were evidently awkward people for a man laying down this theory to encounter, so he goes out of his way to say that they were not women at all, but men in women's clothes. Moreover, he has no doubt that the Salic law must ultimately prevail everywhere.

A woman has no independent existence: he says she is taught from childhood to be subordinate to others; she cannot go out by herself with propriety; she is not a complete creature till she finds a mate. The unlucky women who never find one (more than 400,000 in Germany) are not to make any kind of career for themselves, either humble or glorious. Each one is to search carefully for relatives who will give her a corner in their house, and allow her to work for them. If no one wants her she may live with other women and bring up poor children. He would allow women some education. Far be it from him to think that women are to remain in compulsory ignorance. But their education is to be "womanly," and carried on in the family. Women teachers in public schools he considered a danger to the State, and he would send all girls till they reach their twelfth or fourteenth year to the elementary schools, where they would be taught by men and associate with bare-footed children. Woman, in short, is to learn how to be woman at home, and how not to be superwoman in school. She may even have some instruction in art and science, but only a limited instruction that will not encroach on her duty to the family.

The fate of lonely single women is much on Herr Riehl's mind. What are we to do with them? he asks despairingly. "What is to become of the army of innocent creatures, without means, without a craft, doomed to an aimless, disappointed life. Shall we shut them up in convents? Shall we buy them into Stifts? Shall we send them to Australia? Shall we put an end to them?" Quite in the manner of Dogberry, he answers his own questions. Let them go their ways as before, he says. He knows there is no short cut to social regeneration, and he will not recommend one, not even extirpation. He points out that the working women of Germany have never asked to be on an equality with men. The lower you descend in the social scale the less sharply women are differentiated from men, and the worse time women have in consequence. The wife of a peasant is only his equal in one respect: she works as hard as he does. Otherwise she is his serf. The sole public position allowed to a woman in a village is that of gooseherd; while those original minds who in other circumstances would take to authorship or painting have to wait, if they are peasants, till they are old, when they can take to fortune-telling and witchcraft. Herr Riehl admits that the lot of women when they are peasants is not a happy one. He does not make the admission because he thinks it of much consequence, but because it illustrates his argument that the less " feminine " women are the less power they exercise. He has no great fault to find with the peasant's household, where the wife is a beast of burden in the field and a slave indoors, bears children in quick succession, is old before her time, and sacrifices herself body and soul to the family. But he points out that on a higher social plane, where women are more unlike men, more distinctively feminine, the position they take is more honourable. Yet it is these same " superfeminine " women who are foolishly claiming equality with men.

Herr Riehl's views expressed in English seem a little behind the times, here and there more than a little brutal. He speaks with sympathy of suttee, and he quotes the Volga-Kalmucks with approval. This tribe, it seems, " treat their wives with the most exquisite patriarchal courtesy; but directly the wife neglects a household duty courtesy ceases (for the *genius* of the house is more important than the personal dignity of the wife), and the sinner is castigated (*wird tüchtig durchgepeitscht*). The whip used, the household sword and sceptre, is handed down from generation to generation as a sacred heirloom." I have translated this passage instead of alluding to it, because I thought it was an occasion on which Herr Riehl should literally speak for himself.

It is, however, fair to explain that modern men as well as modern women come under his censure. All the tendencies and all the habits of modern life afflict him, and he lashes out at them without discrimination, and with such an entire lack of prophetic insight that I have found him consoling. For this book was published sixteen years before the Franco-Prussian War, when Germany, the world must admit, proved that it was not decadent. Yet every page of it is a Jeremiad, an exhortation to his countryfolk to stop short on the road to ruin. He does not see that the whole nation is slowly and patiently girding its loins for that mighty effort; he believes it is blind, weak, and flighty. If he had lived in England, and a little later, he would certainly have talked about the Smart Set, Foreign Financiers, and the Yellow Press. As he lived in Germany fifty years ago, he scolds his countryfolk for living in flats. He wants to know why a family cannot herd in one room instead of scattering itself in several. As for a father who cannot endure the cry of children, that man should never have been a father, says Herr Riehl. He cannot approve of the dinner hour being put off till two o'clock. Why not begin work at five and dine at eleven in the good old German way? He praises the ruinous elaborate festivals that used to celebrate family events, and considers that the police help to destroy family life by fining people who in their opinion spend more than they can afford on a wedding or a christening. He objects to artificial Christmas trees, and points out that other nations set a tree in the drawing-room, but that Germans have it in the nursery, the innermost sanctum of family life. He arrives at some curious conclusions when he discusses the German's habit of turning the beer-house into a sort of club that he calls his *Kneipe*. Other races can drink, he says; *aber bloss die germanischen können kneipen*—only the Germanic peoples can make themselves at home in an inn. What does the *Stamm-gast*, the regular guest, ask but the ways of home?

the same chair every night, the same corner, the same glass, the same wine; and where there is a *Stammtisch* the same companions. He sees that family life is more or less destroyed when the men of the household spend their leisure hours, and especially their evenings, at an inn, but he says that the homelike surroundings of the *Kneipe* prove the German's love of home. In fact, he suggests that even the habitual drunkard is often a weak, amiable creature cut out for family life; only, he has sought it at the public-house instead of on his own hearth.

Herr Riehl is, in fact, deeply concerned to see amongst his countryfolk a gradual slackening of family ties, a widespread selfish individualism amongst women, an abdication of duty and authority amongst men. His views about women sound outrageous to-day, chiefly because he wants to apply them to all women without distinction; and also because they display a total want of consideration for the welfare and the wishes of women themselves. But his position is interesting, because with some modifications it is the position still taken by the majority of German men; naturally, not by the most advanced and intelligent, but by the average German from the Spree to the Danube. He thinks that woman was made for man, and that if she has board, lodging, and raiment, according to the means of her menfolk, she has all she can possibly ask of life. When her menfolk are peasants, she must work in the fields; when they belong to the middle or upper classes, her place is in the kitchen and the nursery. Unless he is exceptionally intelligent he does not understand that this simple rule is complicated by modern economic conditions, and by the enormous number of women thrown on their own resources. He would send them as Herr Riehl did, to the kitchens and nurseries of other people; or he would give up the problem in despair, as Herr Riehl did, admitting with a sigh that modern humanitarianism forbids the establishment of a lethal chamber for the superfluous members of a weaker sex.

The most modern German women are in direct opposition to Herr Riehl, and it must be said that some of their leaders are enthusiastic rather than sensible. They are drunk with the freedom they claim in a country where women are not even allowed to attend a political meeting except with the express consent of the police. In their ravings against the tyranny of men they lose all historical sense, just as an American does when he describes a mediæval crime as if it had been committed by a European with a twentieth-century conscience. They charge men with keeping half humanity in a degrading state of slavery, and attribute all the sins of civilisation to the enforced ignorance and helplessness of women. Their contempt for their masters is almost beyond the German language to express, eloquently as they use it. They demand equality of education and opportunity, but they do not want to be men. Far be such a desire from their minds. They mean to be something much better. To what a pass have men brought the world, they ask? How much better would manners and morals and politics be in the hands of women! They repel with indignation the taunt that women have no right to govern the State because their bodies are too weak to defend it. They point out with a gleam of sense and justice that the mother of children does serve the State in a supremely important way; and for that matter they are willing to take many State duties on their shoulders, and to train for them as arduously and regularly as men train for the wretched business of killing each other. They will not mate with those poor things—modern men—under the existing marriage

laws. They refuse to be household beasts of burden a
day longer. Life, life to the dregs with all its joys
and all its responsibilities, is what they want, and love
if it comes their way. But not marriage. Young
Siegfrieds they ask for, young lions. Here one be-
wildered reader rubbed her eyes ; for she had just heard
Siegfried and the Götterdämmerung again, and sometimes she reads in the *Nibelungenlied* ; and if ever a
man won a woman with his club, by muscle seemingly,
by magic really, but anyhow by sheer bodily strength,
was not that man Siegfried ? and was not the woman
Brünnhilde ? And what does the Siegfried of the Lied
say when his wife has failed to keep a guard on her
tongue—

> "Man soll so Frauen ziehen," sprach Siegfried, "der Degen,
> Das sie üppig Reden lassen unterwegen.
> Verbiet es deinem Weibe ; der meinen thu' ich's auch.
> Ich schäme mich, wahrlich um solchen übermüthigen Brauch."

And then, just as if he was one of those Volga-
Kalmucks admired by Herr Riehl, he beats poor
Kriemhilde black and blue.

> "Das hat mich bald gereuet," so sprach das edle Weib ;
> " Auch hat er so zerblaüet deswegen meinen Leib !
> Dass ich es je geredet, beschwerte ihm den Muth :
> Das hat gar wohl gerochen der Degen tapfer und gut."

Yet here is the last development in women, the
woman who refuses as an outrage both the theory of
masculine superiority and the fact so evident in Germany
of masculine domination, here is the self-constituted
superwoman calling as if she was Eve to the primæval
male. It may be perverse of me, but my imagination
refuses to behold them mated.

CHAPTER VIII

THE OLD AND THE NEW

GERMANY stands midway between France and England in its care for its womenfolk. French parents consider marriage the proper career for a woman, and with logical good sense set themselves from the day of a girl's birth to provide a dowry for her. When she is of a marriageable age they provide the husband. They will make great sacrifices to establish a daughter in prosperity, and they leave nothing to chance. We leave everything to chance, and the idea of marriage made by bargain and without love offends us. Such marriages are often enough made in England, but they are never admitted. Some gloss of sentiment or of personal respect is considered decent. But on the whole in this country a girl shifts for herself. If she marries, well and good; if she remains single, well and good too, provided she can earn her living or has means. When she has neither means nor craft and fails to marry, she is one of the most tragic figures in our confused social hierarchy, difficult to help, superfluous. She sets her hand to this and that, but she has no grip on life. To think of her is to invoke the very image of failure and incompetence. She flocks into every opening, blocking and depressing it; as a "help" she becomes a byword, for she has grown up without learning to help herself or anybody else. If she is a Protestant she has no haven. Only people who have set themselves to help poor ladies know the difficulties of the undertaking, and the miseries their protégées endure.

Even in the Middle Ages the conscientious German was doing more for this helpless element of his population than England and America are doing to-day. He saw that some of his daughters would remain unmarried, and that if they were gently bred he must provide for their future, and he did this by founding *Stifte*. The old *Stift* was established by the gentlemen of some one district, who built a house and contributed land and money for its maintenance, so that when they died their unmarried daughters should still have a suitable home. Some of these old *Stifte* are very wealthy now, and have buildings of great dignity and beauty, they still admit none but the descendants of the men who founded them, and when they have more money than they need to support the *Stift* itself, they use it to pension the widows and endow the brides belonging to their group or families. In Hesse-Cassel, for instance, there is an ancient *Stift* formed by the *Ritterschaft* of the Duchy and it is so well off that it can afford to pension every widow and fatherless child, and buy an outfit for every bride whose name either by marriage or descent entitles her to its protection. The example set by the noble families of the Middle Ages was followed in time by other classes, and *Stifte* were established all over Germany for the daughters of the bourgeoisie. They grew in number and variety; some had a school attached to their endowment and some an orphanage. In some the rule was elastic, in others binding. There are *Stifte* from which a woman may absent herself for the greater part of the year, and yet draw an income from its funds and have a room or rooms appointed

to her use; there are others where residence is compulsory. Some are only open to descendants of the
founders; some sell vacancies. A woman may have
to wait year after year for a chance of getting in; or
she may belong to one that will admit her at a certain
age. In many there is a presiding lady, the Domina
or Abbess; and when the present Emperor visited a
well-known *Stift* lately he gave the Abbess a shepherd's
crook with which to rule her flock. Some are just sets
of rooms with certain privileges of light and firing
attached. Their constitution varies greatly, according
to the class provided for and the means available. But
you cannot be much amongst Germans without meeting
women who have been educated, endowed, helped in
sickness, or supported in old age by one of these
organisations. You come across girls of gentle birth
but with no means who have been brought up in a
Stift, or you hear of well-to-do girls whose parents
have paid high for their schooling in one. You know
the elderly unmarried daughter of an official living on
his pension, and you find that though she has never
been taught to earn her bread she looks forward to old
age with serenity, because when she was a child her
relations bought her into a *Stift* that will give her at
the age of fifty free quarters, fire, light, and an income
on which, with her habits of thrift, she can live comfortably. Another woman engaged in private teaching
and a good deal battered by the struggle for life, comes
to you some day more radiant than you have ever seen
her, and you find that influential friends have put her
case before a *Stift*, and that it has granted her two
charming rooms with free fire and light. I heard of a
cook the other day who, after many years of faithful
service, left her employers to spend her old age in a
Stift. No social stigma attaches to the women living

in one, and they are as free, in some cases as well placed and well born, as the English women living at Hampton Court. Some friction and some gossip is presumably inevitable wherever women herd together in an unnatural segregation from men and children. But at any rate the German *Stift* saves many a woman from the tragic struggle with old age and poverty to which the penniless incapable spinster is condemned in our country. It may not be a paradise, but it is a haven. As I said at the beginning, the Frenchman dowers and marries his girl, the German buys her a refuge, the Englishman leaves her to fate.

On the whole, the German believes that the woman's province is within the limits of the household. He wants her to be a home-maker, and in Germany what "he" wants her to be still fixes the standard. But as the census reveals the existence of large numbers of single women, and as "he" often has a thoughtful and benevolent mind, more and more is done there every year to prepare those women who must earn their living to earn it capably. It has been understood for some time past that Herr Riehl's plan of finding a family roof for every woman without one presents difficulties where there are 400,000 odd women to provide for in this way. One of the people who first saw this clearly, and supported every sensible undertaking that came to the assistance of women, was the Empress Frederick ; and one of the institutions that she encouraged and esteemed from the beginning was the *Lette-Verein* in Berlin.

The *Lette-Verein*, named after its originator, Dr. A. Lette, was founded, says its prospectus, to further the education of women and to increase the efficiency of women dependent on themselves for support. What it actually does is to train for housekeeping and office

work, and for some trades. Its interest lies in the
ordered and thoughtful provision it makes both for the
woman who means to devote herself body and soul to
the family; and for the woman who prefers, or who is
driven, to stand in the market-place and compete with
men. The *Lette-Verein* does not train servants or
admit servants to its classes. It occupies a large block
of buildings in the west of Berlin, for its various schools
and hostels require a great deal of room. Students
who live in the city can attend daily classes; but those
who come from a distance can have board and residence
for £1 a week or less. Once a week strangers are
allowed to see the *Lette-Haus* at work, and when I
went there we were taken first to the kitchens, where
the future housewives of Germany were learning to
cook. The stoves were the sensible low closed-in ones
used on the continent, and the vessels were either
earthenware or metal, kept brightly polished both
inside and out. The students were preparing and
cooking various dishes, but the one that interested me
was the *Leipziger Allerlei*, because I compared it with
the " herbage " an English plain cook throws into water
and sends up half drained, half cold, and often enough
half clean. I could not stop to count the vegetables
required for *Leipziger Allerlei*, but there seemed to be
at least six varieties, all cooked separately, and after-
wards combined with a properly made sauce. The
Englishman may say that he prefers his half-cooked
cabbage, and the English woman, if she is a plain cook,
will certainly say that the cabbage gives her as much
trouble as she means to take; but the German woman
knows that when she marries her husband will want
Leipziger Allerlei, so she goes to the *Lette-Haus* and
learns how to make it. Even the young doctors of
Berlin learn cooking at the *Lette-Haus*. Special

classes for invalid cookery are held on their behalf, and are said to be popular and extremely useful. Certainly doctors whose work is amongst the poor or in country places must often wish they understood something about the preparation of food. The girls who go to the *Lette-Haus* are taught the whole art of housekeeping, from the proper way to scour a pan or scrub a floor to fine laundry work and darning, and even how to set and serve a table. An intelligent girl who had been right through the courses at the *Lette-Haus* could train an inexperienced servant, because she would understand exactly how things ought to be done, how much time they should take, and what amount of fatigue they involve. If her servants failed her she would be independent of them. Some students at the *Lette-Haus* do, as a matter of fact, form a household that is carried on without a single servant, and is on this account the most interesting branch of the organisation. The girls are from fourteen to sixteen years of age, and they pay £25 a year for instruction, board, and lodging. Some of them are the daughters of landed proprietors, and some will eventually earn a living as " supports of the housewife," an honourable career shortly referred to by Germans as *eine Stütze*. They were a happy, healthy looking lot of girls. They wear neat serviceable gowns while they are at work, aprons, linen sleeves to protect their stuff ones, and pretty blue handkerchiefs tied like turbans over their hair. Some of them were busy at the wash-tub, and this seemed heavy work for girls of that age. The various kinds of work are done in turn, and the student when her washing week comes round is employed in this way three hours every morning. On alternate days she mangles clothes, and in the afternoons she sews. Our guide would not admit that three hours at the wash-tub could be too great a strain on a half-developed girl, and it is a question for medical wisdom to decide. The cooking and ironing looked hot work, but these young German girls were cheerfully and thoroughly learning how to do them, and whether they marry or stay single their knowledge of these arts will be of inestimable use in later years. I heard of an able-bodied Englishwoman the other day who took to her bed in tears because her maids left her suddenly. She could not have roasted a leg of mutton or made the plainest pudding. This is the school of the future, said our enthusiastic guide when we went to see the " children " at work at the *Lette-Haus* ; and I, remembering my helpless Englishwoman, agreed with her. The children's afternoons are mostly given to needlework, and they are instructed in the prospectus not to bring new clothes with them, because it is desired that they should learn how to mend old ones neatly and correctly. They are taught to darn and patch so finely that the repair cannot easily be discovered ; they make sets of body linen for themselves, three finely sewn men's linen shirts, a gown for work-days, and some elaborate blouses. In another part of the *Lette-Haus*, where students were being trained as expert embroiderers and dressmakers, we were shown pieces of flowered brocade into which patches had been so skilfully inserted that you could only find them by holding them up to the light. In the bookbinding department there were amateur and professional students. The professionals apprentice themselves for three years, and from the first receive a small weekly wage. The length of their apprenticeship is determined by the length of time prescribed for men, and not by what is necessary for their training. I asked if they easily found regular work later, and was told that at present the demand for expert women bookbinders exceeded the supply. The *Lette-Haus* trains women to be photographers, printers, and clerks. In fact, with German thoroughness and foresight it docs all one big institution can to save the women of the nation from the curse of incompetence. It turns them out efficient housewives or efficient craftswomen, according to their needs.

The German woman of to-day has travelled far from the ideal set up by Herr Riehl, and still upheld by his disciples. Women have found that the realities of life clash with that particular ideal, and rudely upset it. Just like any man, a woman wants bread when she is hungry, and when there is no man to give it to her she must raven for it herself. She has been driven from a family hearth that has no fire on it, and from a family roof that cannot afford her shelter. On the whole, if I may judge from personal observation, it has done her good. The traditional old maid is dying out in Germany as assuredly as she is dying out in England, and who shall regret her? Her outlook was narrow, her temper often soured. She had neither self-reliance nor charm. She was that sad, silly spectacle, a clinging plant without support. Now that she is learning to grow on her own account, she finds that there is a good deal in life a sensible plant can enjoy without clinging. The German "old maid" of the twentieth century has, like her English sister, transformed herself into a "bachelor," a person who for this reason or that has not married, and who nevertheless has a cheerful time. She has her own work, she often has her own flat, and if she lives in one of the big cities she has her own club.

There are at present three Ladies' Clubs in Berlin all flourishing. The subscription to the *Berliner Frauenklub* is only six marks a year, yet it provides the members with comfortably furnished rooms and well cooked meals at low prices. A member of this club can dine for ninepence, and have a hot dish from fourpence to sevenpence. She has access to a library of 1300 volumes, to the leading papers and reviews, and to magazines in four languages. She can entertain women at the club, but not men; though she can meet men there at certain hours of the day. Social gatherings of various kinds are arranged to meet the various needs and ages of the members; and one night a week four or five card-tables are set out, so that the older members can have a quiet game of skat or whist. We wonder what Herr Riehl would say if he could see them.

Another German Ladies' Club in Berlin is the *Deutscher Frauenklub*, and it is nicknamed the Millionaire's Club because the subscription is twenty-five shillings. It is a rather smarter club than the other, and has a charming set of rooms. There are about 450 members. The Third Club is a branch of the London Lyceum, and it has aroused great interest and attention in Berlin, not only because it is on a more magnificent scale than the other clubs, but because of the brave effort it makes to unite the women of all nations and help them. Most of the women distinguished in art and literature have joined it.

I began this chapter by saying something of the *Stift*, the refuge for unmarried women that Germany established in the Middle Ages and still preserves. I end it with the Lyceum Club, that latest manifestation of a modern woman's desire to help her own sex. The character of these institutions and their history are both significant. In other days men helped women; in these days women try to help themselves. The *Stift* gives a woman bread and shelter in idleness; the aim of the Lyceum Club is not to give, but to bring women together and to encourage good work. The *Stifte* are still crowded and the Lyceum flourishes, for in our time the old woman jostles the new. But the new woman has arrived, and is making herself felt ; with amazing force and swiftness, you must admit when you reflect on the position of women in Germany thirty or forty years ago.

CHAPTER IX

GIRLHOOD

IN the *Memoiren einer Idealistin,* those genuine and interesting Memoirs that have been so widely read in Germany of late, Malvida von Meysenbug, the daughter of a highly placed official at a small German Court, describes her confirmation day and the long period of preparation and the spiritual struggle that preceded it.

" During a whole year my sister and I went twice a week to the pastor's house to be instructed in the dogma of the Protestant Church," she says. . . . " The ceremony was to be on Sunday. The Friday before we had our last lesson. Our teacher was deeply moved ; with tears in his eyes he spoke to us of the holiness and importance of the act we were about to perform. . . . According to the German custom amongst girls of the better classes, we put on black silk dresses for the first time for our confirmation, and this ceremonial attire calmed me and did me good. Our maid took special pains with our toilet, as if we were going to a worldly entertainment, and chattered more than usual. It jarred on me, but it helped to distract my thoughts. When it was time to start I said Good-bye to my mother with deep emotion, and asked her to forgive me my faults. My sister and I were to go to the pastor's house on our way to church.

There we found everything strewn with flowers. Our teacher received us in his priestly robes, and spoke to all of us so lovingly and earnestly that the most indifferent were moved. When the church bells began to peal our procession set out, the pastor at its head, and we following two by two. The way from the rectory to the church was strewn with flowers, and the church was decked with them. The Choral Society of the town, to which some of our best friends belonged, received us with a beautiful hymn. I felt on wings, I prayed to God that this hour might be blessed to me throughout my life. The sermon preached by the voice that had so often affected me made me calm. When the preacher required us to make our confession of faith, I uttered my 'Yes' with firm assurance. Then I knelt before him with the rest to receive his blessing. He put his hands on our heads, accepted us as members of the Protestant Church, and blessed each one separately, and with a special verse from the Bible. To me he said, 'Be thou faithful unto death, and I will give thee a crown of life.' My heart echoed the solemn vow: Faithful unto death. The choir greeted the young Christians with a song of victory. We did not return to the seats reserved for candidates, but sat with our parents and relatives waiting with them until everyone had left the church, except those who wished to partake of the Holy Communion."

Malvida von Meysenbug is too much absorbed in her intense spiritual experiences to describe the lighter side of confirmation in Germany, which celebrates it with presents and a gathering of friends. A girl gets her first black silk gown for the occasion, and both boys and girls get as many presents as they do at Christmas or on a birthday. These are all set out for the inspection of the friends who assemble at the house after the religious ceremony, to congratulate the parents and the youngest member of their church.   There is an entertainment of coffee, chocolate, and cakes ; and a few days later both boys and girls return these visits of congratulation in the company of their parents.   Some years ago, when a girl had been confirmed, she was considered officially grown up and marriageable, and entered straight away into the gaieties that are supposed to lead to marriage.   But the modern tendency in Germany is to prolong girlhood, and the wife of sixteen is as rare there amongst the educated classes as it is here.

Amongst the Jews in Germany marriages are still arranged for the young people by their elders; often, as in France, through the intervention of friends, but also by the business-like office of the marriage broker. It need hardly be said, perhaps, that the refined and enlightened Jews refuse to marry in this way.   They insist on choosing their own mate, and even on overlooking some disparity of fortune.   Unorthodox Jews marry Christian women, and the Jewish heiress constantly allies herself and her money with a title or a uniform. In the latter case, however, the nuptials are just as business-like as if the *Schadchan* had arranged them and received his commission.   The Graf or the Major gets the gold he lacks, and the rich Jewess gets social prestige or the nearest approach to it possible in a Jew-baiting land.   An ardent anti-Semite told me that these mixed marriages were not fertile, and that if only everyone of Jewish blood would marry a Christian, the country would in course of time be cleared of a race that, she solemnly assured me, is as great a curse to it, and as inferior as the negro in America.   But as she was an anti-Semite with a sense of humour she admitted that the remedy was a slow one and difficult to enforce.

As a matter of fact, the Jews marry mostly amongst themselves in Germany, and men are still living in Frankfurt and other large cities who have made comfortable fortunes by the brokerage they charged on their matchmaking. Formerly a prosperous unmarried Jew used to be besieged by offers from these agents; and so were men who could give their daughters a good dowry. The better-class Jews do not employ them nowadays, but their marriages are suggested and arranged much as marriages are in France. A young merchant of Berlin thinks it is time to settle down, or perhaps wants a little capital to enlarge his business. He consults an uncle in Frankfurt. The uncle tells his old friend, the father of several daughters, that the most handsome, industrious, and accomplished man the world has ever seen, his own nephew, in fact, thinks of marriage, and that his conditions are this and that; he tells his nephew that the most beautiful and amiable creature in Germany, a brilliant musician, a fluent linguist, a devoted daughter, and a person of simple housewifely tastes, lives next door to him, the uncle. Except for the housewifely tastes, it sounds, and in fact is, rather like a courtship in the *Arabian Nights* so far. The prince hears of the princess, and without having seen her sets out to seek her hand. The young merchant pays a flying visit to Frankfurt, is presented to the most beautiful creature in Germany, finds her passable, has a talk to her father as business-like as a talk between two solicitors, proposes, is accepted, and at once becomes the most ardent lover the world has ever seen.

Amongst Christians marriages are certainly not arranged for girls in this matter-of-course way, and so " old maids " abound. Girls without money have far less chance of marriage in Germany than in England,

6

where young people mate as they please and where a
man expects to support his wife entirely; while the
spectacle, quite common here, of girls with a good deal
of money remaining single from various reasons, sometimes actually from want of opportunity to marry, this
every-day occurrence amongst the English better
classes is unknown on the continent. In her powerful
novel *Aus guter Familie*, Gabrielle Reuter describes
the life of a German girl whose parents cannot give
her a dowry, and who is doomed in consequence to old
maidhood and to all the disappointments, restrictions,
and humiliations of unsought women. While women
look to marriage and nothing else for happiness, there
must be such lives in every monogamous country,
where they outnumber the men; but in England a
woman's marriage is much more a matter of chance
and charm than of money. If she is poor and misses
her chance she is worse off than the German, for she
has no *Stift* provided for her; but if she is attractive
she is just as likely to marry without a fortune as with
one. Those German women who consider their ideas
"progressive" have taken up a new cry of late, a cry
about every woman's "right" to motherhood; but they
do not seem to have found a satisfactory way of
securing this right to the 400,000 women who outnumber the men. One learned professor wrote a
pamphlet advocating polygamy, but his proposal did
not have the success he no doubt felt it deserved.
The women who discuss these questions, in magazines
they edit and mostly write themselves, said that his
arguments were all conducted from the man's point
of view, and were most reprehensible. Their own chief
aim at present is to protect the mothers of illegitimate
children, and this seems a natural and proper thing for
the women of any community to do. Otherwise they

are not a united body. There are moderates and
immoderates amongst them, and as I am a moderate
myself in such matters, I think those who go all lengths
are lunatics. It makes one open one's eyes to go to
Germany to-day with one's old-fashioned ideas of the
German Frau, and hear what she is doing in her desire
to reform society and inaugurate a new code of morals.
She does not even wait till she is married to speak with
authority. On the contrary, she says that marriage is
degrading, and that temporary unions are more to the
honour and profit of women. " Dear Aunt S.," I heard
of one girl writing to a venerable relative, " I want you
to congratulate me on my happiness. I am about to
be united with the man I love, and we shall live
together (*in freier Ehe*) till one of us is tired of it."
A German lady of wide views and worldly knowledge
told me a girl had lately sent her a little volume of
original poems that she could only describe as unfit
for publication ; yet she knew the girl and thought her
a harmless creature. She was presumably a goose who
wanted to cackle in chorus. This same lady met
another girl in the gallery of an artist who belonged to
what Mr. Gilbert calls the " fleshly school." " Ah ! "
said the girl to my friend, " this is where I feel at
home." One of these immoderates, on the authority
of Plato, recommended at a public meeting that girls
should do gymnastics unclothed. Some of them are
men-haters, some in the interests of their sex are all
for free love. None of them accept the domination of
men in theory, so I think that the facts of life in their
own country must often be unpleasantly forced on
them. I discussed the movement, which is a marked
one in Germany at present, with two women whose
experience and good sense made their opinion valuable.
But they did not agree. One said that the excesses

of these people were the outcome of long repression, and would wear out in time. The other thought the movement would go on and grow ; which was as much as to say that she thought the old morals were dead. Undoubtedly they are dead in some sets in Germany to-day. You hear of girls of good family who have asserted their " right to motherhood " without marriage ; and you hear of other girls who refuse to marry because they will not make vows or accept conditions they consider humiliating. These views do not attract large numbers ; probably never will. But they are sufficiently widespread to express themselves in many modern essays, novels, and pamphlets, and even to support several magazines. The women holding them are of various types and quality, and are by no manner of means agreed with each other ; while those women who are working steadily and discreetly for the progress of their sex condemn the extreme party, and consider them a check on all real advancement.

The German girl, then, is not always the simple creature tradition paints her. At any rate she reads novels and sees plays that would have been forbidden to her mother. Nevertheless she is as a rule just as happy as a girl should be when the man of her dreams asks her to marry him. In other days a proposal of marriage was a ceremonial in Germany. A man had to put on evening dress for the occasion, and carry a bouquet with him. " Oh yes," said a German friend of mine, " this is still done sometimes. A little while ago a cousin of mine in Mainz was seen coming home in evening dress by broad daylight carrying his bouquet. The poor fellow had been refused." But in these laxer times a man is spared such an ordeal. It is more usual in Germany than in England to speak to a girl's father before proposing to her, but even this is not invariable nowadays. Young people make their own opportunities. "Last year my brother proposed to his present wife in the woods near Baden while they gathered Waldmeister," said a young German to a girl he ardently admired. "It will be in flower next week, and your parents have just arranged that I may meet them at the *Alte Schloss* in time for dinner. After dinner we will walk in the woods—*nicht wahr?*" But the girl, as it happened, did not wish to receive a proposal of marriage from this young man, so she took care not to walk in the woods and gather Waldmeister with him. It is often said that the sexes herd separately in Germany, and do not meet each other much. But this always seems to me one of the things said by people who have looked at Germans and not lived amongst them. A nation that has such an intimate home life, and is on the whole poor, receives its friends in an intimate informal way. Young men have different occupations and interests from girls, but when they are admitted to a family they are often admitted on terms of easy friendship. In London you may ask a young man with others to dinner at intervals, and never get to know him; in Berlin you ask him without others to supper, and soon get to know him very well. Besides, a German cannot endure life long without an *Ausflug* or a *Landpartie*, and when the family plans one it includes one or two of its friends.

When two Germans do get engaged they let their world know of it. A betrothal there is not the informal flimsy contract it often is with us. They begin by publishing the event in their newspapers, and sending round printed forms announcing it to their friends. In the newspaper the announcement is rather bare compared with the advertisement of other family events. "Engaged. Frl. Martha Raekelwitz mit Hrn.

Ingenieur Julius Prinz Dresden-Hamburg" is considered sufficient. But the printed intimations sent round on gilt-edged paper or cardboard to the friends of the contracting parties are more communicative. On one side the parents have the honour to announce the engagement of their daughter Anna to Mr. So-and-So, and on the other side Mr. So-and-So announces his engagement to Miss Anna. Here is a reproduction of such a form, with nothing altered except the actual names and addresses. On the left-hand side of the double sheet of cartridge paper the parents of the *Braut* have their say—

" Die Verlobung ihrer Tochter Pauline mit Herrn Referendar Dr. jur. Heinrich Schmidt in Berlin beehren sich ergebenst anzuzeigen.

Geh. Regierungsrat Dr. EUGEN BRAND
Königl. Gymnasialdirektor und
FRAU HELENE, geb. ENGEL

STUTTGART, *im Juni* 1906

Tiergarten 7 "

Then on the opposite page the future bridegroom speaks for himself—

"Meine Verlobung mit Fräulein Pauline Brand, Tochter des Königl. Gymnasialdirektors Herrn Geh. Regierungsrat Dr. Eugen Brand und seiner Frau Gemahlin Helene, geb. Engel, in Stuttgart, beehre ich mich ergebenst anzuzeigen.

Dr. jur. HEINRICH SCHMIDT
Referendar

BERLIN, *im Juni* 1906

Kurfürstendamm 2000 "

Directly these forms have been circulated, all the friends who have received one and live near enough pay a visit of congratulation to the bride's parents, and soon after the betrothed couple return these visits with some ceremony.   It is quite impossible, by the way, to talk of Germans who are officially engaged without calling them the bride and bridegroom.   They plight their troth with the plain gold rings that will be their wedding rings, and this stage of their union is celebrated with as much ceremony and merrymaking as the actual wedding.   The Germans are giving up so many of their quaint poetical customs that the girl of to-day probably wears a fine diamond engagement ring instead of the old-fashioned gold one.   But the ring with which her mother and grandmother plighted their troth was the ring with which they were wedded, and when Chamisso wrote *Du Ring an meinem Finger* he was not writing of diamonds.   All the tenderness and poetry of Germany go out to lovers, and the thought of a German bride and bridegroom flashes through the mind with thoughts of flowers and moonlight and nightingales. At least, it does if you can associate them with the poems of Heine and Chamisso, with the songs of Schumann, and with the caressing intimate talk of the German tongue unloosed by love.   But your experience is just as likely to play you the unkindest trick, and remind you of German lovers whose uncouth public endearments made everyone not to the manner born uncomfortable.

When the bride and bridegroom live in the same town, and know a large number of people, they are overdone with festivities from the moment of betrothal to the day of marriage.   The round of entertainments begins with a gala dinner given by the bride's father, and this is followed by invitations from all the relatives and friends on either side. When you receive a German *Brautpaar* they should be the guests of honour, and if you can hang garlands near them so much the better. You must certainly present the *Braut* with a bouquet at some stage of the proceedings, and you will give pleasure if you can manufacture one or two mottoes in green stuff and put them in conspicuous places. For instance, I knew of a girl who got engaged away from home. Do you suppose that she was allowed to return to a bare and speechless front door as her English cousin would? Nothing of the kind. The whole family had set to work to twine laurel wreaths and garlands in her honour, and she was received with *Wilkommen du glückseliges Kind* done in ivy leaves by her grandmother. It was considered very *rührend* and *innig*. At some time during the engagement the betrothed couple are sure to get photographed together, and anyone who possesses a German family album will bear me out that the lady is nearly always standing, while her bearded lover is sitting down. When they are both standing they are arm in arm or hand in hand. I remember a collection possessing two photographs of a married daughter with her husband. One had been taken just before the wedding in the orthodox pose; he in an easy chair and she standing meekly by his side: the other represented them a year after marriage, when Heaven had sent them twins. They were both standing then, and they each had a baby in a *Steckkissen* in their arms.

If the bridegroom is not living in the same town with his bride her life is supposed to run rather quietly in his absence. She is not expected to dance with other men, for instance; but rather to spend her time in embroidering his monogram on every conceivable object he might use: on tobacco pouches, or slippers, on letter cases, on braces, on photograph frames, on luggage straps, on fine pocket handkerchiefs. If she is expert and possesses the true sentiment she will embroider things for him with her hair. In these degenerate days she does not make her own outfit. Formerly, when a German girl left school she began to make stores of body and house linen for future years. But in modern cities the *Braut* gets everything at one of the big " white " shops, from her own laces and muslins to the saucepan holders for the kitchen, and the bread bags her cook will hang outside the flat for the baker's boy. In Germany it is the bride, or rather her parents, who furnish the house and provide the household linen ; and the linen is all embroidered with her initials. This custom extends to all classes, so that you constantly hear of a servant who is saving up for her *Aussteuer*, that is, the furniture and linen of a house as well as her own clothes. If you ask whether she is engaged you are told that the outfit is the thing. When the money for that is there it is easy to provide the bridegroom. In higher spheres much more is spent on a bride's trousseau than in England, taking class for class. Some years ago I had occasion to help in the choice of a trousseau bought in Hamburg, and to be often in and out of a great " white ware " business there. I cannot remember how many outfits were on view during those weeks, but they were all much alike. What some people call " undies " had been ordered in immense quantities, sometimes heavily trimmed with Madeira work, sometimes with a plain scollop of double linen warranted to wash and wear for ever. The material was also invariably of a kind to wear, a fine linen or a closely woven English longcloth. How any one woman could want some six dozen " nighties " (the silly slang sounds especially silly when I think of those

solid highly respectable German garments) was a
question no one seemed to ask. The bride's father
could afford six dozen ; it was the custom to have six
dozen if you could pay for them, and there they were.
The thin cambric garments French women were beginning to wear then were shown to you and tossed
contemptuously aside as only fit for actresses. But
this has all been changed. If you ask for " undies "
in Berlin to-day, a supercilious shoplady brings you
the last folly in gossamer, decolletée, and with elbow
sleeves ; and you wonder as you stare at it what a
sane portly German housewife makes of such a garment. In this, as in other things, instead of abiding
by his own sensible fashions, the German is imitating
the French and the Americans ; for it is the French
and the Americans who have taught the women
of other nations to buy clothes so fragile and so
costly that they are only fit for the purse of a Chicago
packer.

When the outfit is ready and the wedding day near,
the bride returns all the entertainments given in her
honour by inviting her girl friends to a Bride-chocolate
or a Bean-coffee. This festivity is like a *Kaffee-Klatsch*,
or what we should call an afternoon tea. In Germany,
until quite lately, chocolate and coffee were preferred to
tea, and the guests sat round a dining-table well spread
with cakes. At a Bean-coffee the cake of honour had
a bean in it, and the girl who got the bean in her slice
would be *Braut* before the year was out. Another
entertainment that takes place immediately before the
marriage is given by the bride's best friend, who invites
several other girls to help her weave the bridal wreath
of myrtle. The bride does not help with it. She
appears with the bridegroom later in the afternoon
when the wreath is ready. It is presented to her with

great ceremony on a cushion, and as they bring it the
girls sing the well-known song from the *Freischütz*—

> "Wir winden dir den Jungfernkranz
> Mit veilchenblauer Seide;
> Wir führen dich zu Spiel und Tanz
> Zu Glück und Liebesfreude!
>
> Lavendel, Myrt' und Thymian
> Das wächst in meinen Garten;
> Wie lang bleibt doch der Freiersmann?
> Ich kann es kaum erwarten.
>
> Sie hat gesponnen sieben Jahr
> Den goldnen Flachs am Rocken;
> Die Schleier sind wie Spinnweb klar,
> Und grün der Kranz der Locken.
>
> Und als der schmucke Freier kam,
> War'n sieben Jahr verronnen:
> Und weil sie der Herzliebste nahm
> Hat sie den Kranz gewonnen."

The bridegroom receives a buttonhole, but no one
sings him a song. In the opera he is not on the stage
during the bridesmaids' chorus. I have not been able
to find out whether the quaint pretty verses are by
Friedrich Kind, who founded the libretto of the opera
on a story by August Apel, or whether he borrowed
them from an older source. German brides wore
myrtle and their friends wove a wedding wreath for
them long before 1820, when *Der Freischütz* appeared.

CHAPTER X

MARRIAGES

" HE was a pompous, stiff-jointed man," said my friends, "an official in a small town, who would go to the stake rather than break the letter of the law. But when he came to Berlin to attend a niece's marriage he thought he would have some fun. He arrived late on *Polterabend,* and he brought with him an enormous earthenware crock. Instead of ringing he hurled the crock against the outside door of the flat, so that it smashed to atoms with a noise like thunder. The inhabitants of that flat came forth like a swarm of bees, but they were not laughing at the fun, because it was not their *Polterabend.*" He had broken crockery on the wrong floor.

In cities this ancient German custom of breaking crockery at the bride's door on *Polterabend* (the night before the wedding) has died out, but it has not long been dead. I have talked with people who remembered it in full force when they were young. I believe that the idea was to appease the *Poltergeist,* who would otherwise vex and disturb the young couple. My dictionary, the one that has 2412 pages, says that a *Poltergeist* is a "racketing spectre," probably what we who are not dictionary makers would call a hobgoblin. In Brands' *Antiquities* I find reference to this old custom at the marriage of a Duke of York in Germany, when great quantities of glass and china were smashed at the palace doors the night before the wedding.

Polterabend is still celebrated by Germans, although they no longer consider it polite to smash crockery. There is always a large entertainment, sometimes at the bride's house, sometimes at the house of a near relative; there are theatricals with personal allusions, or recitations of home-made topical poetry, some good music, and the inevitable evergreens woven into sentiments of encouragement and congratulation. The bride's presents are set out much as they are in England, and perhaps class for class more valuable presents are given in Germany than in England. Electro-plate, for instance, was considered impossible a few years ago. A wedding present, if it was silver at all, must he real silver. But it is not so much the custom as with us to give presents of money.

The civil marriage takes place either the day before or early on the same day as the religious ceremony. The bride used to wear black silk, and still wears a dark plain costume for this official function. Her parents go with her and the necessary witnesses. The religious ceremony often used to take place in the house, but that is no longer customary. The anonymous author of *German Home Life*, a book published and a good deal read in 1879, says that marriage is a troublesome and expensive ceremony in Germany, and that this accounts for the large number of illegitimate children. Mr. O. Eltzbacher, the author of *Modern Germany* published in 1905, confirms what was said in 1877 as to the number of illegitimate children born in Germany and Austria, for he says that in Germany itself they are 9 per cent., while in those districts of Austria where the Germans form about nine-tenths of the population, from 20 per cent. to 40 per cent. of the children are born out of wedlock. In France statistics give 9 per cent., in Scotland 7.4 per cent., and in

England and Wales 4.2 per cent. Nevertheless in modern Germany children are not illegitimate because their parents are too poor to pay their marriage fees. The civil marriage is obligatory everywhere, and costs nothing. The religious ceremony need cost nothing at all. In the porch of every church in Prussia there is a notice stating on which days *Freie Trauungen* are conducted. Several couples are married at the same time, but they have the full liturgy and the marriage sermon. A small charge is made for the organist and for the decoration of the church. A friend whose husband has a large poor parish in Berlin tells me that the Social Democrats object to the religious ceremony, and will stand guard outside the house on the day of the civil marriage, to make sure that the newly made husband and wife do not leave together to go to church. Sometimes an artisan will wait a fortnight after the civil ceremony before he ventures to have the religious one. Every artisan in Berlin has to belong to the *Sozialdemokratischer Verband*, because if he did not his fellow-workmen would destroy his tools and ruin his chances of work. Apparently they interfere with his private affairs as well.

The marriage service is not to be found in the prayer-book Germans take to church, but I have both read it and listened to it. The vows made are much the same as here; but in Germany great importance is attached to the homily or marriage sermon. This is often long and heavy. I have heard the pastor preach to the young couple for nearly half an hour about their duties, and especially about the wife's duty of submission and obedience. His victims were kept standing before him the whole time, and the poor little bride was shaking from head to foot with nervousness and excitement. In some cities the carriage used by a well-to-do bride

and bridegroom is as big as a royal coach, and upholstered with white satin, and on the wedding day
decorated inside and out with garlands of flowers.
The bridegroom fetches his bride in this coach, and
enters the church with her. When a pretty popular
girl gets married all her admirers send flowers to the
church to decorate it. The bride and bridgroom
exchange rings, for in Germany men as well as women
wear a plain gold wedding ring, and it is always worn
on the right hand. The bridegroom and all the male
guests wear evening dress and silk hats. The women
wear evening clothes too, and no hats. The bride
wears the conventional white silk or satin and a white
veil, but her wreath must be partly of myrtle, for in
Germany myrtle is the bride's emblem.

After the wedding dinner the bride slips away
unnoticed and changes her gown, and is presently
joined by the bridegroom, but not by any of the guests.
No rice and no old slippers are thrown in Germany,
and no crowd of friends assembles to see the young
pair start. The bride bids her parents farewell, and slips
away with her husband unseen and unattended. After
the wedding dinner there is often dancing and music.

A hundred years ago wedding festivities lasted for
many days after the wedding, and the bride and bridegroom did not go till they were over. When the
celebrated and much married Caroline Schlegel married
her first husband, George Böhmer, in 1784, the ceremony
took place at her own home in Göttingen, where her
father was a well-known professor. "It would be unnatural if a young wife did not begin with an account
of her wedding day," she says in one of her letters.
"Mine was delightful enough. Böhmer breakfasted
with me, and the morning hours passed gaily, and yet
with quietness. There was no trepidation—only an

intercourse of souls. My brother came. We were together till four, and when he left us he gave us his blessing with tears. . . . Lotte and Friederike wove the bridal wreath. . . . Then I had a talk with my father and dressed myself. . . . Meanwhile those dear Meiners sent me a note, with which were some garters they had embroidered themselves. Several of my friends wrote to me, and last of all I got a silhouette, painted on glass, of Lotte and Friederike weaving my bridal wreath. When I was dressed I was a pretty bride. The room was charmingly decorated by my mother. Soon after four o'clock Böhmer arrived, and the guests, thirty-eight in number. Thank Heaven, there were no old uncles and aunts, so the company was of a more bearable type than is usual on such occasions. I stood there surrounded by my girl friends, and my most vivid thought was of what my condition would be if I did not love the man before me. My father, who was still far from well, led me to the clergyman, and I saw myself for life at Böhmer's side and yet did not tremble. During the ceremony I did not cry. But after it was over and Böhmer took me in his arms with every expression of the deepest love, while parents, brothers, sisters, and friends greeted me with kind wishes as never a bride was greeted before, my brother being quite overwhelmed—then my heart melted and overflowed out of sheer happiness."

A week later Caroline and her husband are still at Göttingen, and still celebrating their marriage. At one house, under pretence of the heat, the bride was led into the garden, and beheld there an illuminated motto: "Happy the man who has a virtuous wife: his life will be doubly long." Another friend arrayed her son as Hymen, and taught him to strew flowers in Caroline's path, leading her thus to an arbour where there was a throne of moss and flowers, with high steps ascending to it, a canopy and a triumphal arch. Concealed behind a bush were musicians, who sang an appropriate song, while the bride and bridegroom mounted the throne and sank in each other's arms before a crowd of sympathising and tearful spectators.

This took place more than a hundred and twenty years ago, but I have in my possession what I can only describe as the "literature" of a marriage celebrated three years ago between a North and a South German, both belonging to commercial families of old standing; and it supplies me, if I needed it, with documentary evidence that Germans enjoy now what they enjoyed then. The marriage took place in winter and from a flat, so that the bride's friends could not build grottoes or hide musicians behind a bush; but for weeks before both sides of the family must have been busy composing the poems sung at the wedding feast, the music that accompanied them, and the elaborate humorous verses containing allusions to the past history of the bride and bridegroom. To begin with, there is a dainty book of picture postcards, the first one giving portraits of a very handsome and dignified bridegroom with his dainty bride. Then there is a view of Dresden where the bridegroom was born, another of the Rhenish town in which he found his bride, and one of Berlin where she used to stay with a married sister and deal "baskets" right and left to would-be admirers. In Germany, when a girl refuses a man she is said to give him a "basket," and a favourite old figure in the cotillon used to put one in a girl's hands and then present two men to her. She danced with the one she liked best, and the rejected man had to dance round after them with the basket.

Besides the book of postcards, each guest at this wedding was presented with printed copies of the

7

Tafel-Lieder composed by members of the family.
One of these has eight verses and each verse has eight
lines. It relates little events in the life of the bridegroom
from babyhood onwards. You learn that he was a clever
child, that he lived at home with his mother instead of
going abroad to learn his work, that when he was young
he ardently desired to go on the stage, that he is a fine
gymnast and musician, but that he needs a wife because
he is a dreamy person capable of putting on odd boots.
Another *Tafel-Lied* describes the courtship step by step,
and even the assistance given by the poet's wife to bring
the romance to its present happy conclusion.

> "At last Frau Sophie stirred in the affair,
> Her eyes had piercèd to his heart's desire,
> With fine diplomacy she coaxed Miss Clare
> To own her maiden heart was set on fire.
> On all the words and sighs there follow deeds:
> He comes, he woos her, and at last succeeds."

The songs are not all sentiment. They are jocular,
and contain puns and play upon names. Three out
of the five end with an invitation to everyone to raise
their glasses with a *Hoch* to the married pair. This is
done over and over again at German weddings, and as
all the guests want to clink glasses with the bride and
bridegroom, there is a good deal of movement as well
as noise. Besides the *Tafel-Lieder*, each of which made
a separate booklet with its own dedication and illustration, every guest received an elaborate book of
samples: samples of the various straws used that
summer for ladies' hats. The bridegroom's family had
manufactured hats for many generations; they were
wealthy, highly considered people, and extremely proud
of their position in their own industry. I am sure that
when an Englishman in the same trade and of the same
standing gets married, the last thing that would be

mentioned at his wedding would be hats. It would be
considered in the highest degree indecorous. But the
German is still guileless enough to be satisfied with his
station in life when it is sufficiently honourable and
prosperous, and for this wedding two little nieces had
prepared this card of samples and composed a rhyme
for each different colour—

> "Wie ist doch der Onkel hoch beglückt
>   Das Tantchen heute der 'Brautkranz' schmückt"

went with " myrtle green."

> "Liebe Gäste, mit Genuss,
>   Wollet alle Euch erheben—
>   Hoch das Brautpaar—
>   Es soll leben ! "

went with the " champagne " straw at the end ; and one
accompanying the " silver " straw contained an allusion
to the " silver " wedding twenty-five years hence, when
the bride's golden hair would be silver-grey.

Here is the *menu*, mostly in French, to which all the
Tafel-Lieder were sung, and all the toasts drunk and
congratulatory speeches made. You will observe that
it is none of your light cup, cake, and ice entertainments
that you have substituted for the solid old wedding
breakfast in this country.

HOCHZEITS-TAFEL.

Caviar-Schnitten	Patisserie
Potage Douglas	Fruits & Dessert
Saumon-S^{ce} Bernaise	Fromage
Pommes Naturelles	——
Selle de Chevreuil	Scharzberger Mousseux
à la Chipolata	1900er Caseler
Ris de Veau en demi Deuil	1896er St. Emilion
Poularde	
Salade & Compote	1890er Schloss Johannisberg
Asperges en Branches	
S^{ce} Mousseline	Moet et Chandon
Glace Napolitaine	White Star

And that no guest should depart hungry—

| Kaltes Abendbrot | Bier |

Germans celebrate both silver and golden weddings with as much ceremony and rejoicing as the first wedding. The husband and wife receive presents from all their friends, and entertain them according to the best of their circumstances. Children will travel across the world and bring grandchildren with them to one of these anniversaries, and they are of course a great occasion for the topical poetry, theatricals, and tableaux that Germans enjoy. If the grandmother by good luck has saved a gown she wore as a girl, and the grandchild can put it on and act some little episode from the old lady's youth, everyone will applaud and enjoy and be stirred to smiles and tears. There is as much feasting as at a youthful wedding, and perhaps more elaborate performances. Silver-grey is considered the proper thing for the silver bride to wear.

It seems like a want of sentiment to speak of divorce in the same breath with weddings; but as a matter of fact, divorce is commoner in Germany than in England, and more easily obtained. Imprisonment for felony is sufficient reason, and unfaithfulness without cruelty, insanity that has lasted three years, desertion, ill treatment or any attempt on the other's life. You hear divorce spoken of lightly by people whose counterparts in England would be shocked by it; people, I mean, of blameless sequestered lives and rigid moral views. Some saintly ladies, who I am sure have never harboured a light thought or spent a frivolous hour, told me of a cousin who played whist every evening with her present husband and his predecessor. My friends seemed to think the situation amusing, but not in any way to be condemned. At the same time, I have heard Germans quote the saying—" *Geschiedene Leute scheiden fort und fort*," and object strongly to associate with anyone, however innocent, who had been connected with a matrimonial scandal.

A woman remains in possession of her own money after marriage even without marriage settlements; but the husband has certain rights of use and investment. Her clothes, jewels, and tools are her own, and the wages she earns by her own work. A man's creditors cannot seize either these or her fortune to pay his debts. Both in Germany and England the wife must live in the house and place chosen by the husband, but in Germany she need not follow him to *unwirtlichen* countries against her will. He can insist on her doing the housework and helping him in his business when he has no means to pay substitutes; but she can insist on being maintained in a style proper to their station in life. He is responsible for her business debts if he has consented to her undertakings; but he can forbid her to carry on a business if he prefers that she should be supported by him and give her time and strength to the administration of their home. When they are legally separated he must make her an allowance, but it need only be enough for the bare necessaries of life if the separation is due to her misconduct. The father and mother have joint control of the children, but during the father's lifetime his rule is paramount. When he is dead or incapacitated parental authority remains in the mother's hands. It is her right and duty to care for the child's person, to decide where it shall live, and to superintend its education. She can claim it legally from people who desire to keep it from her. A child born in wedlock is legitimate unless the husband can prove otherwise, and he must establish proof within a year of the birth coming to his knowledge. But a woman is not allowed to prove that a child born in wedlock is illegitimate.

If a man dies intestate and leaves children or grandchildren, his widow inherits a fourth of his property; if he only has more distant relatives, half; if he has none, the whole. A man cannot cut his wife off with a shilling. He must leave her at least half of what would come to her if he died intestate. All the laws relating to husband and wife are to be found in the *Bürgerliches Gesetzbuch*, which can be bought for a mark. As far as the non-legal intelligence can grasp them, they seem according to our times to be just to women, except when they give the use of her income to the husband. This is a big exception, however. I remember hearing a German say that his sister's quarterly allowance, which happened to be a large one, was always sent to her husband, as it was right and proper that important sums of money should be in the man's hands and under his control. This undoubtedly is the general German view. After the moonshine, the nightingales, the feasting, the toasts, and the family poetry come the realities of life: and the realities in German make the man the predominant partner.

CHAPTER XI

THE HOUSEHOLDER

RENTS are high in Germany. At least, the Germans say so, and so do the people whose books about Germany are crammed with soul-satisfying statistics and elaborate calculations. Over-crowding, too, is said to be worse in Germany than in English cities. But I have always seen the rent and the crowding judged by the number of rooms and not by their size. This is really misleading, because you could put the whole of a small London flat into many a German middle-class dining-room or *Wohnzimmer*. You could bring up a family in a single room I once had for a whole summer in Thüringen for 5s. a week. It was as big as a church, and most light and airy. One camped in bits of it. I think rent for rent rooms in Germany are quite twice as large as in London. In Berlin, where rent is considered wickedly high, you can get a flat in a good quarter for £80, and for that sum you will have four large rooms, three smaller ones, a good kitchen, an attic that serves as a lumber-room, and a share in a laundry at the top of the house. There will even be a bathroom with a trickle of cold water, but it is only in the very newest and most expensive German flats that you find hot and cold water laid on. Your drawing and dining-rooms will be spacious, and one of them is almost sure to have a balcony looking on the street and the pleasant avenue of trees with which it is planted. For this rent you must either make yourself happy on the third or fourth floor in a house without a lift, or you must find one of the delightful "garden" dwellings behind the *Hof*; but you will have a better home for your money than you could get in a decent part of London. In fact, it comes to this, in spite of all the statistics in favour of London. If you can only spend £80 on your rent you can live in a good quarter of Berlin, near enough to the Tiergarten, close to the Zoological Gardens, and within a tram-ride of the delightful woods at Halensee. In London you can get a small house for £80, but it will either be in an unattractive quarter or in a suburb. A flat, wherever it is, must always seem a dwelling place rather than a home, but the Germans have elected to live in flats and accept their disadvantages. In and around all the great cities there are villas, but their number hardly counts in comparison with the masses of tall white houses, six storeys high for the most part, and holding within their walls all degrees of wealth and poverty. The German villa is florid, and likes blue glass balls and artificial fountains in its garden. It is often a villa in appearance and several flats in reality. Its most pleasant feature is the garden-room or big verandah, where in summer all meals are served. Outside Hamburg, on the banks of the Elbe, the merchant princes of the city have built themselves palaces surrounded by splendid park-like gardens. But Hamburg, though it does not love the English, is always accused by the rest of Germany of being English. It certainly has beautiful gardens. So have other German cities in some instances, but well kept gardens are not the matter of course in Germany that they are here. You see more bare and artificial ones and more neglected overgrown ones in an afternoon's walk than you do all the year round in England. But I wish we could follow the German fashion of planting all our streets with double avenues of healthy trees. Berlin in spring seems to be set in a wood; it is so fresh and green. The flowering shrubs, on the other hand, are not to be compared with ours. Everyone rushes to see a few lilac bushes, and Gueldres roses trimmed to a stiff snowball of flowers, and everyone says *Wie Herrlich!* but you miss the profusion of lilac, hawthorn, and laburnum that runs riot all about London in every residential road and every garden. Above all, you miss the English lawns. In Berlin wherever grass is grown it looks either thin or coarse. The majority of Germans do not dream of wanting a garden. They are content with a few palms in their sitting-room or window boxes on their balcony. They are proud of their window-gardening in Berlin, but I think London windows in June are gayer and more flowery. The palms kept in German rooms attain to a great size and number, and a palm is a favourite present. Nursery gardeners undertake the troublesome business of repotting them every spring, so the owners have nothing to do but water them and keep them from draughts. There are usually so many windows in a German sitting-room that those near the plants need never be opened in winter; and even when the temperature sinks several degrees below zero outside, the air of the flat is kept artificially warm, so warm that English folk gasp and flag in it. At the first sign of winter the outside windows, removed for the summer, are brought back again. Our windows are unknown on the continent, and disliked by continentals who see them here. They call them guillotine windows, and consider them dangerous. Theirs all open like doors, so that you have four doors to each window, and until you get used to them you find they make a pretty clatter whenever you set them wide. But in winter they are only opened for a few minutes every morning when the room is " aired." It is considered extravagant to open them at other times, because the heat would escape and more fuel would be required. I suppose everyone in England understands that our open fireplaces are almost unknown in Germany. They have enclosed stoves of iron or porcelain that make little work or dirt and give no pleasure. There is no gathering round the hearth. You sit about the room as you would in summer, for it is evenly heated. All the beauty and poetry of fire are wanting ; you have nothing but an atmosphere that will be comfortable or asphyxiating, according to the taste of your hosts. Years ago in South Germany you burnt nothing but logs of wood in the old-fashioned iron stoves, and there was some faint pleasure in listening to their crackle. You could just see the flames too, if you stooped low enough and opened the little stove door. But the wood burnt so quickly that it was most difficult to keep a big room warm. Nowadays you always find the porcelain stove that Mark Twain says looks like the family monument. In some of these coal is burnt, or a mixture of coal and peat. Some burn anthracite, and are considered economical. A *Füllofen* of this kind is kept burning night and day during the worst of the winter. It requires attention two or three times in twenty-four hours ; it is easily regulated, and if the communicating doors are left open it warms two or three rooms. A friend who has a large flat in Berlin told me that there was one of these stoves in her husband's study, and that her drawing-room which opens out of it, and which they constantly use, had only had a fire in it five times last winter. I find on look-

ing at this friend's budget that she spends £16 a year
on turf and other fuel, and this seems high for a flat
where so few fires were lighted. But fuel is dear in
German towns. Briquettes are largely used in cities,
small slabs of condensed coal that cost one pfennig each.
It takes about twenty-four slabs to keep a stove in
during the day. The great advantage of the *Füllofen*
over the ordinary stove is that it keeps in all night.
There are dangerous variations of temperature in a
German flat that is kept as hot as an oven all day, and
allowed to sink below zero during the night. But you
hear complaints on all sides in Germany, both of incon-
siderate English people who waste fuel by opening
windows in cold weather; and of the sufferings endured
by Germans who have been in England in winter. They
do not like our open fireplaces at all, because they say
they wish to be warm all over and not in bits. " In
England," they tell you solemnly, " you can be warm
either in front or at the back ; but you cannot be warm
on both sides as we are here. Besides, your fireplaces
make dirt and work and are extravagant. They
would not suit us." In fact, they imply that for the
French and the English they are well enough, but not
for the salt of the earth. The German kitchen stoves
are certainly more practical and economical than ours,
and I never can understand why we do not fetch a few
over and try them. They are entirely enclosed, and
much lower than ours. The Berlin kitchener has one
fire that is lighted for a short time to roast a joint, and
another using less fuel that heats water and does light
cooking. The sweep, who is bound by the etiquette of
his trade to wear a tall hat in Germany, does not come
into your flat at all. You hear him shout through the
courtyard that he will visit the house next day, and he
works from the garrets and cellars. The police regulate

his visits as they regulate everything else in Germany. Chimneys must be swept every six weeks in summer, and every four weeks in winter in Berlin. Dustbins are emptied every day, and in some towns the police make most troublesome regulations with regard to them. The householder has to set his outside to be emptied, and the police insist on this being done at a certain hour, neither earlier nor later, so that if your servant happens to be careless or unpunctual you will be repeatedly fined.

Staircases vary greatly according to the date and rent of the house. The most modern houses in Berlin have broad front staircases with thick carpets, and in some cases seats of " Nouveau Art " design on the landings. In such houses you are always met on the threshold by printed requests to wipe your feet and shut the door gently. They don't tell you to do as you're bid. That is taken for granted, or the police will know the reason why. There is always an uncarpeted back staircase for servants and trades-people, and for the tenants who inhabit the poorer parts of the building. In houses where all the tenants belong to the poorer classes, you find notices that forbid children to play in the Hof, and command people not to loiter or to make any noise on the stairs. Carpet-beating and shaking, which is constantly and vigorously carried on, is only allowed on certain days of the week and at certain hours. When there is a house porter he is not as important and conspicuous as the French concierge. In my experience he has usually gone out and thoughtfully left the front door ajar. He is not a universal institution even in Berlin.

Taxes vary in different parts of Germany. In Saxony a man spending £500 a year pays altogether £60 for Income tax, Municipal rates, Water, School, and Church rates. In Berlin the Income tax is not an Imperial (Reichs) tax, but a *Landes* tax, and amounts to £15 on an income of £500. Smaller incomes pay less and larger ones more, in proportion varying from about 2 to 4 per cent. Besides this *Staats* tax there is a municipal tax of exactly the same amount in Berlin and Charlottenberg. But there are towns in Prussia where it is less; others, mostly in the Western Provinces, where it is more, considerably more in some cases. The water rate is paid by the house owners, and the tenant pays it in his rent. There are no school taxes. The church tax is compulsory on members of the *Landeskirche*. When a man has no capital his income tax is levied on his yearly expenses; but the man whose income is derived from capital pays a higher tax than the man who has none. The German, too, pays a great deal to the State indirectly; for nearly everything he requires is taxed. But the three things he loves best, tobacco, beer, and music, he gets cheap—cheaper than he can in a Free Trade country; so he pays for everything else as best he can, and tries to look pleasant. " But the burden is almost more than we can bear," said one thoughtful German to me when I told him how greatly English people admired their municipal enterprise, and the admirable provision made in Berlin for the very poor.

Last time I went to Germany I actually made the acquaintance of one German who did not smoke, and on various occasions I was in the society of others who did not smoke for some hours. In the Berlin tramcars smoking is strictly forbidden, but I did not observe that this rule was strictly enforced. In fact, my attention was drawn to it one day by finding my neighbour's cigar unpleasantly strong. One cigar in a tramcar, however, is nothing at all, and should not be mentioned. It is when a railway carriage beautifully upholstered with crimson velvet holds you, six Germans, and one Englishman, for eight hours on a blazing summer day, that you begin to wonder whether, after all, you do mind smoke. To be sure, you might have travelled in a *Nichtraucher* or a *Damen-Coupé*, but changes are a nuisance on a journey. Besides, you know that a *Damen-Coupé* is always crowded, and that the moment you open a window someone will hold a handkerchief tearfully to her neck and say, "*Aber ich bitte meine Dame: es zieht!*" and all the other women in the carriage will say in chorus, "*Ja! ja! es zieht!*" and if you don't shut the window instantly the conductor will be summoned, and he will give the case against you. So you travel all day long with seven cigars, most of them cheap strong ones, that their owners smoke very slowly and replace directly they are finished. And after a time the conversation turns on smoking, and your neighbour admits that he always lights his first cigar when he gets up in the morning and smokes it while he is dressing. His wife dresses in the same room and does not like it, but . . . It is unnecessary to say more. Five cigars out of six are in sympathy with him, while you amuse yourself by wondering what revenge a wife could take in such circumstances. A bottle of the most offensive scent in the market suggests itself, but you look at your neighbour's profile, and see that he is the kind of man to pitch scent he did not like out of the window. You have heard of one German husband who did this when his wife brought home perfumes that did not please him. And then your memory travels back and back along the years, arriving at last at the picture of an English nursery, in the household where a German guest had arrived the night before. The nurses and the children are sitting peacefully at breakfast, when there enters to them a housemaid, scornful, scandalised, out of breath with her hurry to impart what she had seen.

"He's a-smoking in bed," she says, "that there Mr. Hoggenheimer! He's a-smoking in bed!"

"Some of them do," says nurse, who is a travelled person, and refuses to be taken by surprise.

"Well, of all the nasty . . ."

"Sh!" says nurse, pointing to the children, all eyes and ears.

So that is all you can remember about the housemaid and Mr. Hoggenheimer. But you remember him—a little dark man who sent you books you could not read at Christmas, and brought you enchanting gingerbreads covered with hundreds and thousands. You thought him rather funny, but you liked him, and if he wanted to smoke in bed why not? You liked toys in bed yourself, and you would have taken the dog there if only it had been allowed. Then you come back again to the present hour, nearly all the years of your life later, and you are in a railway carriage with six German householders who, like Mr. Hoggenheimer, want cigars in and out of season.

"To-morrow," you say to your Englishman; "to-morrow I shall travel in a *Nichtraucher*."

"But then I can't smoke," he says quite truly.

"We shall not travel together."

"But that is so unsociable."

"I would rather be unsociable than suffocated," you explain. "I have suffered tortures to-day."

"Have you? But you always say you don't mind smoke."

"In reason. Seven cigars and one woman are not

reasonable. Never again will I travel with seven cigars."

" I thought we had a pleasant journey," says the Englishman regretfully. " That little man next to you——"

" Mr. Hoggenheimer——? "

" Was that his name?—I couldn't understand all he said, but he had an amusing face."

" A face can be misleading," you say; " that man bullies his wife."

" How do you know ? "

" He told us so. He smokes before breakfast . . . while he is dressing, . . . and he has no dressing room. . . ."

The Englishman looks calm.

" They do take one into their confidence," he remarks. " My neighbour told me that he never could eat mayonnaise of salmon directly after roast pork, because it gave him peculiar pains. I was afraid you'd hear him describe his symptoms; but I believe you were asleep."

" No, I wasn't," you confess; " I heard it all, and I shut my eyes, because I knew if I opened them he'd address himself to me. I shut them when he began talking to you about your *Magen* and what you ought to do to give it tone. You seemed interested."

" It's quite an interesting subject," says the Englishman, who makes friends with every German he meets. " He is not in the least like an Englishman," they say to you cordially,—" he is so friendly and amiable."

CHAPTER XII

HOUSEWIVES

" FRENCHWOMEN are the best housewives in Europe," said a German lady who knew most European countries well; "the next best are the English; Germans come third." The lady speaking was one whose opinions were always uttered with much charm, but *ex-cathedra*; so that you found it impossible to disagree with her . . . until you got home. But to hear the supreme excellence of the *Hausfrau* contested takes the breath away; to see her deposed from the first place by one of her own countrywomen dazzles the eyes. It was a new idea to me that any women in the world except the Germans kept house at all. If you live amongst Germans when you are young you adopt this view quite insensibly and without argument.

" My son is in England," you hear a German mother say. " I am uneasy about him. I fear he may marry an Englishwoman."

" They sometimes do," says her gossip, shaking her head.

" It would break my heart. The women of that nation know nothing of housekeeping. They sit in their drawing-rooms all day, while their husband's hard-earned money is wasted in the kitchen. Besides . . . *mein armer Karl*—he loves *Nudelsuppe* and *Küken mit Spargel*. What does an Englishwoman know of such

8

things? She would give him cold mutton to eat, and he would die of an indigestion. I was once in England in my youth, and when I got back we had a *Frikassee von Hähnchen mit Krebsen* for dinner, and I wept with pleasure."

"Perhaps," says the gossip consolingly, "your Karl will remember these things and fetch himself a German wife."

"Poor girl!" says Karl's not-to-be-consoled mother, "she would have to live in England and keep house there. It happened to my niece Greta Löhring. She had a new cook every fortnight, and each one was worse than the one before. In England when a cook spoils a pudding she puts it in the fire and makes another. Imagine the eggs that are used under such circumstances."

I remember this little dialogue, because I was young and ignorant enough at the time to ask what a German did when she spoilt a pudding, and was promptly informed that in Germany such things could not happen. A cook was not allowed to make puddings unless her mistress stood by and saw that she made them properly; "unless she is a *perfekte Köchin*," added Karl's mother, "and then she does not spoil things."

A German friend, not the travelled one, but a real home-baked domestic German, took me one hot afternoon this summer to pay a call, and at once fell to talking to the mistress of the house about the washing of lace curtains. There were eight windows in front of the flat, and each window had a pair of stiff spotless lace curtains, and each curtain had been washed by the lady's own hands. My friend had just washed hers, and they both approached the subject as keenly as two gardeners will approach a question of bulbs or Alpines. There are different ways of washing a white curtain, you know, and different methods of rinsing and drying it, and various soaps. Starch is used too at some stage of the process; at least, I think so. But the afternoon was hot and the argument involved. The starch I will not swear to, but I will swear to ten waters—ten successive cleansings in fresh water before the soul of the housewife was at rest.

" And how do you wash yours ? " said one of them, turning to me.

" Oh—I ! " I stammered, taken aback, for I had been nearly asleep; " I send a post-card to Whiteley's, and they fetch them one week and bring them back the next. They cost 1s. a pair."

The two German ladies looked at each other and smiled. Then they politely changed the subject.

This trivial story is not told for its intrinsic merits, but because it illustrates the difference of method between English and German women. The German with much wear and tear of body and spirit washes her own lace curtains. She saves a little money, and spends a great deal of time over them. The English-woman, when she possibly can, likes to spend her time in a different way. In both countries there are admirable housekeepers, and middling housekeepers, and extremely bad ones. The German who goes the wrong way about it sends her husband to the *Kneipe* by her eternal fussing and fidgeting. She is not his companion mentally, but the cook's, for her mind has sunk to the cook's level, while her temper through constant fault-finding is on a lower one. The English-woman sends her husband to the club or the public house, according to his social station, because she is incapable of giving him eatable food. But the English belief that German housewives are invariably dull and stodgy is not a whit more ignorant and untrue than the German belief that all Englishwomen are neglectful, extravagant housekeepers. The Englishwoman keeps house in her own way, and it is different from the German way, but it is often admirable. The comfort, the organisation, and the unbroken peace of a well-managed English household are not surpassed, in some details not equalled, anywhere in the world.

The German ideal (for women) is one of service and self-sacrifice. Let her learn betimes to serve, says Goethe, for by service only shall she attain to command and to the authority in the house that is her due.

> "Dienen lerne bei Zeiten das Weib nach ihrer Bestimmung,
> Denn durch Dienen allein gelangt sie endlich zum Herrschen
> Zu der verdienten Gewalt, die doch ihr im Hause gehöret,
> Dienet die Schwester dem Bruder doch früh, sie dienet den Eltern;
> Und ihr Leben ist immer ein ewiges Gehen und Kommen,
> Oder ein Heben und Tragen, Bereiten und Schaffen für Andre;
> Wohl ihr, wenn sie daran sich gewöhnt, dass kein Weg ihr zu sauer
> Wird, und die Stunden der Nacht ihr sind wie die Stunden des Tages:
> Dass ihr niemals die Arbeit zu klein und die Nadel zu fein dünkt,
> Dass sie sich ganz vergisst, und leben mag nur in Andern!"

She is to serve her brothers and parents. Her whole life is to be a going and coming, a lifting and carrying, a preparing and acting for others. Well for her if she treads her way unweariedly, if night is as day to her, it no task seems too small and no needle too fine. She is to forget herself altogether and live in others.

It is a beautiful passage, and an unabashed magnificent masculine egotism speaks in every line of it. Whenever I read it I think of the little girl in *Punch* whose little brother called to her, "Come here, Effie. I wants you." And Effie answered, "Thank you, Archie, but I wants myself!" Herr Riehl quotes the passage at the end of his own exhortations to his countrywomen, which are all in the same spirit, and were not needed by them. German women have always been devoted to their homes and their families, and they are as subservient to their menfolk as the Japanese. They do not actually fall on their knees before their lords, but the tone of voice in which a woman of the old school speaks of *die Herren* is enough to make a French, American, or Englishwoman think there is something to be said for the modern revolt against men. For any woman with a spice of feminine perversity in her nature will be driven to the other camp when she meets extremes; so that in Germany she feels ready to rise against overbearing males; whilst in America she misses some of the regard for masculine judgment and authority that German women show in excess. At least, it seems an excess of duty to us when we hear of a German bride who will not go down to dinner with the man appointed by her hostess till she has asked her husband's permission; and when we hear of another writing from Germany that, although in England she had ardently believed in total abstention, she had now changed her opinion because her husband drank beer and desired her to approve of it. But it was an Englishwoman who, when asked about some question of politics, said quite simply and honestly, " I think what Jack thinks."

The truth is, that the women of the two great Germanic races are kin. There are differences, chiefly those of history, manners, and environment. The likeness is profound.

" Par une rencontre singulière," says M. Taine, " les femmes sont plus femmes et les hommes plus hommes ici qu'ailleurs. Les deux natures vont chacune à son extrême ; chez les uns vers l'audace, l'esprit d'entreprise et de resistance, le caractère guerrier, impérieux et rude ; chez les autres vers la douceur, l'abnégation, la patience, l'affection inépuisable ; chose inconnue dans les pays lointains, surtout en France, la femme ici se donne sans se reprendre et met sa gloire et son devoir à obeir, à pardonner, à adorer, sans souhaiter ni pretendre autre chose que se fondre et s'absorber chaque jour davantage en celui qu'elle a volontairement et pour toujours choisi.   C'est cet instinct, un antique instinct Germanique, que ces grands peintres de l'instinct mettent tous ici en lumière ! . . . L'âme dans cette race, est à la fois primitive et serieuse.   La candeur chez les femmes y subsiste plus longtemps qu'ailleurs. Elles perdent moins vite le respect, elles pèsent moins vite les valeurs et les caractères : elles sont moins promptes à deviner le mal et à mesurer leurs maris. . . . Elles n'ont pas la netteté, la hardiesse d'idées, l'assurance de conduite, la précocité qui chez nous en six mois font d'une jeune fille une femme d'intrigue et une reine de salon.   La vie enfermée et l'obéissance leur sont plus faciles.   Plus pliantes et plus sédentaires elles sont en même temps plus concentrées, plus intérieures, plus disposées à suivre des yeux le noble rêve qu'on nomme le devoir. . . ."

I cannot imagine what M. Taine means by saying that Englishwomen lead a more sedentary and sequestered life than Frenchwomen, but the rest of his description presents a well-known type in England and Germany.   "Voir la peinture de ce caractère dans toute la littérature anglaise et allemande," he says in a footnote.   "Le plus grand des observateurs, Stendhal tout imprégné des moeurs et des idées Italiennes et françaises, est stupéfait à cette vue.   Il ne comprend rien à cette espèce de dévouement, ' à cette servitude, que les maris Anglais, sous le nom de devoir, ont eu l'esprit d'imposer à leurs femmes.'   Ce sont ' des moeurs de sérail.' "

Here the "greatest of all observers" seems to talk nonsense, for marriage in the seraglio does not hinge on the submission of one wife to one husband, but on a plurality of wives that English and German women have only endured in certain historic cases. In both western countries marriage has its roots in the fidelity of one man and one woman to each other. A well-known English novelist once said quite truly that an Englishman very rarely distrusts his wife, and never by any chance distrusts the girl who is to become his wife; and just the same may be said of the German of the better classes. In both countries you will find sections of society above and below where morals are lax and manners corrupt. German professors write sketches of London in which our busy grimy city is held up to a virtuous Germania as the modern Sodom and Gomorrah; and the Continental Anglophobe likes nothing better than to entertain you with pictures of our decadent society, pictures that really do credit to the vividness and detail of his imagination. Meanwhile our press assures the respectable Briton that Berlin is the most profligate city in Europe, and that scurrilous German novels about the German army will show him what the rotten state of things really is in that much over-rated organisation. But these national amenities are misleading. The bulk of the nation in both countries is sound, and family life still flourishes both here and there. The men of the race, in spite of Herr Riehl's prognostications, still have the whip hand, as much as is good for them in England, a little more than is good for them in Germany. If you go to Germany you must not expect a man to open a door for you, or to wait on you at afternoon tea, or to carry a parcel for you in the street. He will kiss your hand when he greets you, he will address you as gracious lady or gracious miss, he will put his heels together and make you beautiful bows, he will pay you compliments that are manifestly, almost admittedly, artificial. That at least is one type of man. He may leave out the kisses and the bows and the compliments and be quite undisguisedly bearish; or he may be something betwixt and between, kindly, concerned for your pleasure and welfare. But whatever he is he will never forget for a moment that you are "only a woman." If you marry him he will expect to rule everywhere except in the kitchen, and as you value a quiet life you had better take care that the kitchen produces what pleases him. On occasion he will assert his authority with some violence and naïveté. No one can be long amongst Germans, or even read many German novels, without coming across instances of what I mean. For example, there was once a quarrel between lovers that all turned upon a second glass of champagne. The girl did not want it, and the man insisted that she should drink it whether she wanted it or not. What happened in the end is forgotten and does not matter. It is the comment of the historian that remains in the memory.

" Her family had spoilt her," said he. " When they are married and my friend gets her to himself she will not behave so."

" But why should she drink a second glass of champagne if she did not want it? " I asked.

" Because he commanded her to," said this Petruchio, beginning to bristle at once; and he straightway told me another story about a man who threw his lady-love's dog into a pond, not because the dog needed a bath, but in assertion of his authority. The lady had wished to keep her dog out of the water.

" Did she ever forgive the man? " said I.

" Forgive!—What was there to forgive? The man

wished to put the dog in the pond. A man must know how to enforce his will . . . or he is no man."

I nearly said " Lor! " like Mr. Tweddle in *The Tinted Venus*, but in Germany it's a serious matter, a sort of *lèse majesté*, to laugh at the rightful rule of man. You must expect to see them waited on hand and foot, and to take this service as a matter of course. I have known Englishmen embarrassed by this state of affairs.

" They will get me chairs," complained one, " and at table the daughters jump up and wait on me. It's horrid."

" Not at all," said I. " It's your due. You must behave as if you were used to it."

" I can't. The other day I got the daughters of the house to sit still while I handed about cups of tea, and if some of the old boys didn't jump down their throats and tell them they'd no business to let me forget my dignity. Bless my dignity . . . if it's such a tender plant as that. . . ."

" Sh! " I said. " They must have been old-fashioned people. In some houses young men hand cups."

" They look jolly self-conscious while they're doing it, . . . as if they didn't half like it. You bet, they take it out of their womenfolk when they get home. Look at that chap Müller! "

" Where is he? "

" In Dresden, where I lived last winter. He stormed the house down because his wife took up his glass of beer and drank before he did. Nearly had a fit. Said his dignity as a husband was damaged. Then he turned to me and asked whether even in England a wife would be so bold and bad? "

" What did you say? "

" I didn't say anything. I looked sick."

"That's no use. You should say a great deal, and wave your arms about and hammer on the table. You don't know how to show emotion."

"I should hope not," says the Englishman. "But German women are always telling me they envy the women in our country."

"That's their politeness," I assure him. "They don't mean it. They're as happy as the day is long. Besides, Germans don't get drunk and beat their wives with pokers. You know perfectly well that most Englishmen——"

But, of course, whatever you say about German women of the present day can be contradicted by anybody who chooses to describe one at either end of the scale, for the contrasts there are violent. You will find in the same street a woman who exercises a profession, lives more or less at her club, and is as independent as her brother; and women who are household drudges, with neither leisure nor spirit for any occupation that would enrich their minds.

CHAPTER XIII

HOUSEWIVES (*Continued*)

IN Germany the home is furnished by the bride's parents, and the household linen forms part of her trousseau and is marked by her monogram. In describing the furniture of a German flat, you must first decide whether you are going to choose one furnished to-day by a fashionable young woman in Berlin or Hamburg; or one furnished by her parents twenty to twenty-five years ago. Modern German furniture is quite easily suggested to the English imagination, because some of it looks as if the artist had visited our Arts and Crafts Exhibitions and then made his own designs in a nightmare; while some has accepted English inspiration and adapted itself wisely and cleverly to German needs. To-day a German bride will have in her bedroom a wardrobe with a big mirror, a toilet table or chest, a marble-topped washstand and two narrow bedsteads, all of fumed wood. If she has money and understanding the things have probably come from England, not from an emporium, but from one of our artists in furniture whom the Germans know better and value more highly than we do ourselves. But if she has money only she can buy florid pretentious stuff that outdoes in ugliness the worst productions of our "suite" sellers. Her mother, however, probably did without any kind of toilet table or glass in her wardrobe. Twenty years ago you occasionally saw such things in the houses of rich people, but they were quite unusual. A small hanging glass behind the washstand was considered enough for any *ordentliche Frau*. Nowadays in rare cases the *ordentliche Frau* actually has silver brushes and powder pots and trinket boxes. But as a rule she still does without such things; she brushes her beautiful hair with an ivory or a wooden brush, and leaves paint and powder to ladies who are presumably not *ordentlich*. At one time narrow brass or iron bedsteads were introduced from England, and were used a great deal in Germany. I remember seeing one all forlorn in a vast magnificent palace bedroom where a fourposter hung with brocade or tapestry would have looked more at home. But the real old-fashioned bedstead, still much liked and formerly seen everywhere was always of wood, single and with deep sides to hold the heavy box mattress. In Mariana Starcke's *Travels in Europe*, published in 1833, she says of an inn in Villach, "tall people cannot sleep comfortably here or in any part of Germany; the beds, which are very narrow, being placed in wooden frames or boxes, so short that any person who happened to be above five feet high must absolutely sit up all night supported by pillows; and this, in fact, is the way in which the Germans sleep."

I think this is a statement that will be as surprising to any German who reads it as the statements made by Germans about England have often been to me. It is true, however, that tall people do find the old-fashioned German bedsteads short; and it is true that the big square downy pillows are supported by a wedge-shaped bolster called a *Keilkissen*. But the *Plumeau* is what the German loves, and the Briton hates above all things : the mountain of down or feathers that tumbles off on cold nights and stays on on hot ones. You hate it all the year round, because in winter it is too short and in summer it is an oppression. Sometimes the sheet is buttoned to it, and then though you are a traveller you are less than ever content. At the best you never succumb to its attractions. Every spring the good German housewife takes her maid and her *Plumeaux* to a cleaner and sits there while the feathers are purified by machinery and returned to their bags. In this way she makes sure of getting back her own feathers both in quality and quantity. Except for the *Plumeaux* and the want of a dressing-table and proper mirror, an ordinary German bedroom is very comfortable and always very clean. However plain it is you can use it partly as a sitting-room, because a sofa and a good sized table in front of it are considered an indispensable part of its furniture. When Germans come to England and have to live in lodgings or poorly furnished inns, the bedrooms seem to them most comfortless and ill provided. The poor Idealist who lived as an exile in London in the early Victorian age describes her forlorn room with nothing in it but a " colossal " bed, a washstand, and a chest of drawers, and though she does not describe them, you who know London from that side can see the half-dirty honey-combed counterpane, the untempting cotton sheets, the worn uncleanly carpet, the grained or painted furniture with doors and drawers that will not shut ; and if you know Germany too you must in honesty compare with it the pleasant rooms you have inhabited there for less rent than she paid her Mrs. Quickly,—rooms with cool clean painted floors, solid old dark elm cupboards, and bedsteads that when you had pitched the *Plumeau* on the floor or the sofa were inviting because they were made with spotless home-spun linen.

What we call the drawing-room used to be extremely chill and formal in Germany, but it has never been as hideously overloaded as English drawing-rooms belonging to people who do not know better. The " suite " of furniture covered with rep or brocade was everywhere, and the rep was frequently grass-green or magenta. There was invariably a sofa and a table in front of the sofa, and a rug or a small carpet under the table. Even in these days this arrangement prevails and must continue to do so while the sofa is considered the place of honour to which the hostess invites her leading guest. If you go to Germany in ignorance of the social importance attached to the sofa, you may blunder quite absurdly and sit down uninvited or when your age or your sex does not entitle you to a seat there. I was once present when an English girl innocently chose a corner of the sofa instead of a chair, though there were older women in the room. The hostess promptly and audibly told her to get up, for she knew it was not an affair to pass off as a joke. In England the question of precedence comes up chiefly at the dinner-table. The host and hostess must send the right people together and place them correctly too. In Germany you have to know as hostess who is to sit on the sofa ; and your decision may be complicated by the absurd titles of your guests. For instance, one Frau Direktor may be the wife of a post office official who had a university education, and in Germany a university education counts ; while another Frau Direktor, though she can afford better clothes, is merely the wife of the man who manages the factory in the next village. I have heard a story of a Frau Kreisrichter and a Frau Actuar that ended in a life-long feud, and it all turned on a *Kaffee Klatsch* and the wrong woman on the sofa. It it not easy to know what to do about these ridiculous titles in Germany, because some people insist on them and some laugh at them as much as we do. I once asked a lady who had the best right to know, about using military titles instead of names: Herr Lieutenant, Herr Major, and so on. She was quite explicit. "*Mir ist es ein Greuel*," she said, and went on to tell me that it was only done as one might expect by people who did not know better, and of course by servants. All the same, it is well to be careful and study the individual case. I know of an American who addressed his professor as Professor Lachs.

"Where are your manners, mein Herr?" said the professor in a fury, "I am Herr Professor Dr. Lachs to every student in this laboratory."

But when it comes to Mrs. Tax-Collector and Mrs. Organist and Mrs. Head Master, and it does come to this quite seriously, it is difficult for the foreigner to appraise values. The length of the titles, too, is a stumbling-block. You may marry a harmless Herr Braun, and in course of time become Frau Wirklicher-geheimeroberregierungsrath. In this case I don't think your friends would use the whole of your title every time they addressed you; but you would undoubtedly have a seat on the sofa before all the small fry.

On the table in front of the sofa there used always to be a heavy coloured cloth, and then put diamond-wise a light embroidered or lace one. A vase of artificial or real flowers, according to taste, stood exactly in the middle, and a few books in ornamental bindings on either side. There would be very few ornaments, but these few would be good of their kind, though probably hideous. Luckily the family did not assemble here on State occasions. For every-day use there was a *Wohnzimmer* soberly furnished with solid well made chairs and cupboards. Here the mistress of the house kept her palms, her work-table, and her pet birds. Here her husband smoked his after-dinner cigar and drank his coffee before going to his work again. Here the elder children did their lessons for next day's school, and here at night the family sat round one lamp,—the father smoking, the mother probably mending, the children playing games. For German fathers do not live at the *Kneipe*. They are occasionally to be found with their families. When the flat was not large enough to furnish a third sitting-room, the dining-room was used in this way. A modern German family still lives in any room rather than the drawing-room, but it has learned how to make a drawing-room attractive. The odious "suite" has been abolished or dispersed, and a lighter, less formal scheme of decoration is making its way. You see charming rooms in Germany nowadays, but they are never quite like English ones, even when your friends point to a wicker chair or an Eastern carpet and tell you that they love everything English and have furnished in the English fashion. In the first place, you do not see piles of magazines and papers or of library books in a German drawing-room. They would be considered scandalously untidy, and put away in a cupboard at once. If there are cut flowers they are not arranged as they are here. On ceremonial occasions and anniversaries great quantities of flowers are presented, but they are mostly wired and probably arranged in a fanciful shape. The favourite shape changes with the season and the fashion of the moment. One year those who wish to honour you and have plenty of money, will send you lyres and harps made of violets, pansies, pinks, cornflowers, any flower that will lend itself meekly to popular design. The favourite design in Berlin one spring was a large flat sofa cushion of Guelder roses with tall sprays of roses or carnations dancing from it. On ordinary occasions market bunches are put into water as an English cottager puts in his flowers, level and tightly packed. But on a festive occasion in a rich man's house you hear of a long dinner table strewn with branches of pink hawthorn and peonies. In fact, a riot of flowers is now considered correct by wealthy people, but you do not find them here and there and everywhere, whether people are wealthy or not, as you do in England. That is partly because there are so few private gardens.

The extreme tidiness of German rooms is a constant source of surprise. They are as guiltless of "litter" as the showrooms of a furniture emporium. You would think that the people who live in them were never employed if you did not know that Germans were never idle. Every bit of embroidery has its use and its own corner. The article now being embroidered is neatly folded inside the work-basket or work-table when it is not in the lady's hands. The one book she is reading will be near. Any other books she possesses will be on shelves, and probably behind glass doors. Each chair has its place, each cushion, each ornament. Even where there are children German rooms never look disarranged. I can truly say I have only once seen a German room untidy and dusty, and that was in a house with no one but a " Mamsell " in charge; and she apologised and explained that it was to be spring cleaned next day. There is, by the way, a curious litter of things kept on a German sideboard in many houses,—coffee machines, silver, useful and ornamental glass, great blue beer jugs, and suchlike; but they are kept there with intention and not by neglectful accident. Then the narrow corridor of a German flat is often uncomfortably choked with articles of household use: lamps, for instance, and a refrigerator, and the safe in which the mistress locks her food; spare cupboards too, and neat piles of papers and magazines. It will be inelegant, but it will be orderly and clean.

It is the way in this country to laugh at the German *Hausfrau*, and pity her for a drudge; and it is the way with many Germans to talk as if all Englishwomen were pleasure loving and incompetent. The less people know of a foreign nation the greater nonsense they talk in general, and the more cocksure they are about their own opinions. A year ago, when I was in Germany, I asked a friend I could trust if there really was much Anglophobia abroad except in the newspapers. She reflected a little before she answered, for she was honest and intelligent.

"There is none amongst people like ourselves," she said,—"people who know the world a little. But you come across it?" She turned to her husband.

"There are others like G.," she said. "He turns green if anyone speaks of England, and he says Shakespeare is *dumm*. You see, he has never been out of Germany, and has never met any English people."

So I told her about my English cook, who snorted with scorn when I assured her Germans considered rabbits vermin and would not eat them.

"H . . . ph!" she said, "I shouldn't have thought foreigners were so particular."

The average German housewife has to keep the house going on exceedingly small means and with inefficient help. It is her pride and pleasure to make a little go a long way, and she can only achieve this by working with her hands. Probably her servant cannot cook, but she can, and it would never occur to her to let her husband and children eat ill-prepared food because servants do not like ladies in the kitchen. A German lady, like a princess of ancient Greece, considers that it becomes her to do anything she chooses in her own house, and that the most convenient household workshop is the kitchen. The Idealist from whom I have quoted before was the daughter of a well-known German diplomatist, and she had been used since childhood to the atmosphere of Courts. She was an accomplished well-born woman of the world, but she had not been a week in her sordid London lodgings with the woman she calls Mrs. Quickly, before she blundered in her innocent German way—into the lodging-house kitchen. Figure to yourself the stupe-faction and the indignation of Mrs. Quickly, probably engaged, though the Idealist does not say so, in dining off the foreign woman's beef. " I went down to the kitchen," says Fräulein von Meysenbug, "with a muslin gown on my arm to ask for an iron so that I could iron my gown there. The kitchen was Mrs. Quickly's true kingdom ; here she alone reigned at the hearth, for the servant was not allowed to approach the saucepans. Mrs. Quickly looked at me with uncon-cealed astonishment as I came in, but when I proffered my request her astonishment turned to wrath. ' What ! ' she shrieked, ' a lady ironing in the kitchen ? That is impossible.' And with the mien of offended majesty she snatched the gown from me, and ordered the little maid servant to put an iron in the fire and to iron the gown ; then she turned to me and said with tragic emphasis, ' You are a foreigner. You don't understand our English ways : we consider it extremely unladylike for a lady to enter the kitchen, and worse still if she wants to iron her own gown. No, ma'am, please to ring the bell when you require anything; otherwise you will ruin my servants.' Much ashamed of my ignorance on this higher plane of English custom," continues the Idealist, " I crept back to my parlour and laughed heartily as I looked round the dirty, wretchedly furnished room, and reflected on the abyss set by prejudice between the ground-floor and the basement."

" How do you like your new German governess ? " I once asked an English friend who lived in the country and had just engaged a German lady for her only daughter.

" Oh ! I like her," said my friend without enthusiasm. " She is a brilliant musician and a fine linguist and all that. But she has such odd ideas about what a girl ought to know. The other day I actually caught her teaching Patricia to *dust*."

" If you don't watch her," I said, " she'll probably teach Patricia to cook."

My friend looked anxious first, and then relieved.

" I don't see how she could do that," she said. " The cook would never have them in the kitchen for five minutes. But now you mention it, I believe she can cook. When things go wrong she seems to know what has been done or not done."

" That might be useful," I suggested.

" I don't see it. I expect my cook to know her work, and to do it and not to rely on me. I've other fish to fry."

But the German housewife expects to have her fingers literally in every pie even when by rights they should be employed elsewhere. You hear, for instance, of a great Court functionary whose wife is so devoted to cooking that though she has a large staff of servants

she cannot be persuaded to spend the day anywhere
but in her kitchen. Mistresses of this kind breed incapable servants, and you find, in fact, that German maids
cannot compare with our English ones in qualities
of self-reliance, method, and initiative. They mostly
expect to be told from hour to hour what to do, and
very often to lend a hand to the ladies of the household rather than to do the thing themselves. Indeed,
though the servants are on duty from morning till
night more than English servants are, in some ways
they have an easier time of it than ours, because they
are used so much to run errands and go to market.
Everyone who has been in German towns can remember
the hordes of servants with baskets and big umbrellas
strolling in twos and threes along the streets in the
early morning. They are never in any hurry to get
home to work again, and a good many doubtless know
that what they leave undone will be done by their
mistress. The German kitchen with its beautiful
cleanliness and brightly polished copper pans I have
described, but I have not said anything yet about the
fidgety housewife who carries her *Tüchtigkeit* to such a
pitch that she ties every wooden spoon and twirler with
a coloured ribbon to hang by against the wall. In
England you hear of ladies who tie every bottle of
scent on the toilet table with a different ribbon, and
that really has more sense in it, because it must be trying to a cook's nerves to use spoons tied with delicate
ribbons that must not be spoiled. Every housewife
has dainty little holders for the handles of saucepans
when they are hot. You see them, all different shapes
and sizes, on view with the piles of kitchen cloths and
the various aprons that form part of every lady's
trousseau, and if you have German friends they
probably present you with a few from time to time.

I have never noticed any pictures in a German
kitchen, but there are nearly always *Sprüche* both
in the kitchen, and the dining-room and sometimes
in the hall : rhyming maxims that are done in poker
work or painted on wood and hung in conspicuous
positions—

> "Wie die Küche so das Haus,
> Reinlich drinnen, reinlich draus"

is a nice one ; and so is

> " Trautes Heim
> Glück allein."

There was one in the *Lette-Haus* or some other big
institution about an hour in the morning being worth
several hours later in the day, which would prick our
English consciences more sharply than it can most
German ones, for they are a nation of early risers.
Schools and offices all open so early that a household
must of necessity be up betimes to feed its menfolk
and children with bread and coffee before their day's
work.   In most German towns the tradespeople do
not call for orders, but they do in Hamburg ; and a
friend born there told me in a whisper, so that her
husband should not hear the awful confession, that she
would never be a good "provider" in consequence.
She went to market regularly, for many housewives
will not delegate this most important business to a
cook, but she had not the same eye for a tough goose
or a poor fish, perhaps not the same backbone for a
bargain, as a housewife used from childhood to these
sorties.   In some towns the butcher calls over night
for orders.   The baker's boy brings rolls before anyone is up, and hangs them outside the flat in one of
two bags every household possesses.   After the early

breakfast either the mistress or the cook fetches what is required for the day.

When the good German housewife is not in her kitchen, English tradition believes her to be at her linen cupboard.

" I am going to write a humble little gossiping book about German Home Life," I said to a learned but kindly professor last spring.

" German Home Life," he said, rather aghast at my daring, for we had only just made each other's acquaintance, and I believe he thought that this was my first visit to Germany and that I had been there a week. " It is a wide field," he went on. " However . . . if you want to understand our Home Life . . . just look at that. . . ."

We were having tea together in the dining-room in his wife's absence, and he suddenly got up from table and threw back both doors of an immense cupboard occupying the longest wall in the room. I gazed at the sight before me, and my thoughts were too deep for words. It was a small household, I knew. It comprised, in fact, the professor, his beautiful young wife, and one small maid-servant; and for their happiness they possessed all this linen : shelf upon shelf, pile upon pile of linen, exactly ordered, tied with lemon coloured ribbons, embroidered beyond doubt with the initials of the lady who brought it here as a bride. The lady, it may as well be said, is a celebrated musician who passes a great part of each winter fulfilling engagements away from home. " But what happens to the linen cupboard when you are away?" I asked her, later, for it was grievous to think of any servant, even a "pearl," making hay of those ordered shelves. " I come home for a few days in between and set things to rights again," she explained; and then, seeing that I was

interested, she admitted that she had put up and made
every blind and curtain, and had even carpentered and
upholstered an empire sofa in her drawing-room.   She
showed me each cupboard and corner of the flat, and I
saw everywhere the exquisite order and spotlessness
the notable German housewife knows how to maintain.   We even peeped into the professor's dressing-
room.

"He must be a very tidy man," I said, sighing and
reflecting that he could not be as other men are.   "Do
you never have to set things to rights here?"

"Every half hour," she said.

These enormous quantities of linen that are still the
housewife's pride used to be necessary when house and
table linen were only washed twice a year.   A German
friend who entertained a large party of children and
grandchildren every week, pointed out to me that she
used eighteen or twenty dinner napkins each time they
came, and that when washing day arrived at the end
of six months even her supply was nearly exhausted.
The soiled linen was stored meanwhile in an attic at
the top of the house.   The wash itself and the drying
and ironing all took place up there with the help of a
hired laundress.   In most German cities this custom of
washing at home still prevails, but in these days it is
usually done once a month.   The large attics that
serve as laundries are engaged for certain days by the
families living in the house, and one servant assisted
for one day by a laundry woman washes and irons all
the house and body linen used by her employers and
herself in four weeks.   It sounds impossible, but in
Germany nothing involving hard work is impossible.
All the differences of life between England and Germany,
in as far as expenses are concerned, seem to come to
this in the end: that over there both men and women

will work harder for less money. On the monthly washing day the ladies of the household do the cooking and housework, and on the following day they help to fold the clothes and iron them.

"I am very tired," confessed a little maid-servant who had been sent out at night to show me where to find a tram. "We got up at four o'clock this morning, and have been ironing all day. My mistress gets up as early, and works as hard as I do. She is very *tüchtig*, and where there are four children and only one servant there is a good deal to do."

Yet her mistress had asked me to supper, I reflected, and everything had been to time and well cooked and served. The rooms had looked as neat and orderly as usual. The *Hausfrau* had entertained me as pleasantly as if she had no reason to feel tired. We had talked of English novels, and of the invasion of England by Germany; for her husband was a soldier, and another guest present was a soldier too. The men had talked seriously, for they were as angry with certain English newspapers as we are over here with certain German ones. But the *Hausfrau* and I had laughed.

"When they come, I'm coming with them," she said.

"We will receive you with open arms," said I.

CHAPTER XIV

SERVANTS

THE first thing that English people notice about German servants is, that they are allowed to dress anyhow, and that the results are most unpleasing. In Hamburg, the city that gives you ox-tail soup for dinner and has sirloins of beef much like English sirloins, the maids used to wear clean crackling, light print gowns with elbow sleeves. This was their full dress in which they waited at table, and fresh looking country girls from Holstein and thereabouts looked very well in it. This costume is being superseded in Hamburg to-day by the English livery of a black frock with a white cap and apron. But in other German cities, in the ordinary middle-class household, the servants wear what they choose on all occasions. In most places they are as fond of plaids as their betters, and in a house where everything else is methodical and well arranged, you will find the dishes plumped on the table by a young woman wearing a tartan blouse decidedly decolletée, and ornamented with a large cheap lace collar. I have dined with people whose silver, glass, and food were all luxurious; while the girl who waited on us wore a red and white checked blouse, a plaid neck-tie with floating ends, and an enormous brooch of sham diamonds. In South Germany the servants wear a great deal of indigo blue: stuff skirts of plain blue woollen, with blouses and aprons of blue cotton that has a small white pattern on it. Some ladies keep smart white aprons to lend their servants on state occasions, but the laciest apron will not do much for a girl in a sloppy coloured blouse with a plaid neck-tie. But these same girls who look such slovens usually have stores of tidy well-made body linen and knitted stockings. In England a servant of the better class will not be seen out of doors in her working-dress. " In London," says the Idealist in her Memoirs, " no woman of the people, no servant-girl will stir a step from the house without a hat on her head, and this is one of the ugliest of English prejudices. While the clean white cap worn by a French maid looks pretty and suitable, the Englishwoman's hat which makes her " respectable" is odious, for it is usually dirty, out of shape, and trimmed with faded flowers and ribbons." It gives me pleasure to quote this criticism made by an observant German on our English servants, partly because it is true, and it is good for us to hear it, and partly because it encourages me to continue my criticism of German as compared with English servants. For it ought to be possible to criticise without giving offence. The Idealist has a very poor opinion of English lodging-house bedrooms and lodging-house keepers, and she states her opinion quite plainly, but I cannot imagine that anyone in this country would be hurt by what she says. On the contrary, it is amusing to find the ills from which most of us have suffered at times recognised by the stranger within our gates. None of us admire the battered tawdry finery we see in our streets every day, and I cannot believe that German ladies admire the shocking garments in which their servants will come to the door and wait at table. But though these clothes are sloppy looking and unsuitable, they are never ragged;

and the girl who puts on an impossible tie and blouse
will also wear an impeccable long white apron with an
embroidered monogram you can see across the room.
In most towns servants go shopping or to market with
a large basket and an umbrella.   They do not consider
a hat or a stuff gown necessary, for they are not in the
least ashamed of being servants.   Some years ago they
made no attempt to dress like ladies when they went
out for themselves, and even now what they do in this
way is a trifle compared to the extravagant get-up of
an English cook or parlour-maid on a Sunday afternoon.
A German girl in service is always saving with might
and main to buy her *Aussteuer*, and as she gets very
low wages it takes her a long time.   She needs about
£30, so husbands are not expensive in Germany in
that class.   German servants get less wages than ours,
and work longer hours.   Speaking out of my own
experience, I should say that they were indefatigable,
amiable, and inefficient.   They will do anything in the
world for you, but they will not do their own work in
a methodical way.   A lady whose uncle at one time
occupied an important diplomatic post in London, told
me that her aunt was immensely surprised to find that
every one of her English servants knew his or her work
and did it without supervision, but that none of them
would do anything else.   The German lady, not knowing English ways, used to make the mistake at first of
asking a servant to do what she wanted done instead
of what the servant had engaged to do; but she soon
found that the first housemaid would rather leave than
fill a matchbox it was the second housemaid's " place "
to fill; and what surprised her most was to find that
her English friends sympathised with the housemaids
and not with her.   " We believe in everyone minding
his own business," they said.

"We believe that it is the servant's business to do what his employer wants," says the German.

"You must tell him what you want when you engage him," you say. "Then he can take your place or leave it."

"But that is impossible . . . *Unsinn* . . . *Quatsch* . . ." says the German indignantly. "How can I tell what I shall want my servant to do three months hence on a Monday morning. *Das hat keinen Zweck.*"

"I know exactly what each one of my servants will do three months hence on a Monday morning," you say. "It is quite easy. You plan it all out. . . ."

But you will never agree. The German has his or rather her own methods, and you will always think her unmethodical but thrifty and knowledgable, and she will always think you extravagant and ignorant, but "chic," and on these terms you may be quite good friends. In most German households there is no such thing as the strict division of labour insisted on here. Your cook will be delighted to make a blouse for you, and your nurse will turn out the dining-room, and your chambermaid will take the child for an airing. They are more human in their relation to their employers. The English servant fixes a gulf between herself and the most democratic mistress. The German servant brings her intimate joys and sorrows to a good *Herrschaft*, and expects their sympathy. When a girl has bad luck and engages with a bad *Herrschaft* she is worse off than in England, partly because when German housekeeping is mean it sounds depths of meanness not unknown, but extremely rare here; and also because a German servant is more in the power of her employers and of the police than an English one. Anyone who has read Klara Viebig's remarkable novel, *Das Tägliche*

Brot (a story of servant life in Berlin) will remember the mistress who kept every bit of dainty food under lock and key, and fed the kitchen on soup-meat all the year round. The chambermaid gives way in a moment of hunger and temptation, manages to get the key, and is discovered by the worthless son of the house stealing cakes. He threatens her with exposure if she will not listen to his love-making. Even if there was no son and no love-making, a girl who once steals cakes in Germany may go from place to place branded as a thief. Because every servant has to have a *Dienstbuch*, which is under the control of the police, and has to be shown to them whenever she leaves her situation. There is no give and take of personal character in Germany. Ladies do not see the last lady with whom a girl has lived. They advertise or they go to a registry office where servants are waiting to be engaged. In Berlin every third house seems to be a registry office, and you hear as many complaints of the people who keep them as you hear here. So the government has set up a large Public Registry in Charlottenberg, where both sides can get what they want without paying fees. But servants are not as scarce in Germany yet as they are here and in America. German ladies tell you they are scarce, but it is only true in comparison with a former state of things. In comparison with London, servants are still plentiful in Germany. When a lady finds a likely looking girl at an office, she either engages her at once on the strength of the good character in her *Dienstbuch*, or, if she is very particular, she takes her home and discusses things with her there. The engagement is not completed until the lady has filled in several forms for police inspection; while the servant has to take her *Dienstbuch* to the police station both when she leaves and when she enters a situation. It is hardly necessary to say that when a girl does anything seriously bad, and her employers record it in the book, the book gets "lost." Then the police interfere and make things extremely disagreeable for the girl. A friend told me that in the confusion of a removal her own highly valued servant lost her *Dienstbuch*, or rather my friend lost it, for employers usually keep it while a girl is in their service; and though she took the blame on herself, and explained that the book was lost, the police were most offensive about it. In the end the book was found, so I am not in a position to say what penalties my friend and her maid would have incurred if they had never been able to produce it. But Germans have often told me that servants as a class have real good reason to complain of police insolence and brutality. Here is an entry from a German servant's *Dienstbuch*, with nothing altered but the names. On the first page you found the following particulars :—

GESINDE-DIENSTBUCH

Für	.	.	.	Anna Schmidt.
Aus	.	.	.	Rheinbeck.
Alt	.	.	.	Geb. 20 Juni 1885.
Statur	.	.	.	Schlank.
Augen	.	.	.	Grau.
Nase ⎫ Mund ⎭	.	.	.	Gewöhnlich.
Haare	.	.	.	Dunkelblond.
Besondere Merkmale	.	.		

Official stamp.

(Official signature of Amtsvorsteher.)

Then came the record of her previous situations :—

NR.	NAME, STAND, UND WOHNUNG DER DIENERSCHAFT	INHABER IST ANGE-NOMMEN ALS	TAG DES DIENST-ANTRITTS	TAG DES DIENST-AUSTRITTS	GRUND DES DIENST-AUSTRITTS UND DIENSTABSCHIEDS-ZEUGNISS	BEGLAUBIGUNG UND BEMERKUNG DER POLIZEI-BEHÖRDE
1	Wittwe Auguste Knoblauch	Dienstmagd	Den 20ten Oktober 1901	Den 2ten Januar 1902	Veränderung halber. Betragen gut	Gesehen (*Place and date, with official stamp and signature*)
2	Boretzky, Restaurant zur Post, Bärenstrasse 2	Dienst-mädchen	Den 2ten Februar 1902	Den 2ten Oktober 1904	Wird entlassen weil ihr Benehmen mir nicht mehr passt. Sonst fleissig und ehrlich	Gesehen (*Place and date, with official stamp and signature*)

It will be seen that the characters given tell nothing about a servant's qualities and knowledge ; while the vague complaint that Anna Schmidt's behaviour no longer suited her mistress might mean anything or nothing. In this case it meant that a son of the house had annoyed the girl with his attentions, and she had in consequence treated him with some brusquerie. But ten minutes' talk with a lady who knows the best and the worst of a servant is worth any *Dienstbuch* in Germany. And when English servants write to the *Times* and ask to have the same system here, I always wonder how they would like their failings sent with them from place to place in black and white ; every fresh start made difficult, and every bad trait recorded against them as long as they earn their daily bread.

Wages are much lower in Germany than here. Some years ago you could get a good cook for from £7 to £12, but those days are past. Now you hear of a general servant getting from £10 to £12, and a good plain cook from £15 upwards. These are servants who would get from £22 to £30 in England, and more in America. But the wages of German servants are supplemented at Christmas by a system of tips and presents that has in course of time become extortionate. Germans groan under it, but every nation knows how hard it is to depart from one of these traditional indefinite customs. The system is hateful, because it is neither one of free gift nor of business-like payment, but hovers somewhere between and gives rise to much friction and discontent. In a household account book that a friend allowed me to see I found the following entry. " Christmas present for the servant. 30 marks in money. Bed linen, 9.50. Pincushion, 1.5. Five small presents. In all 42 marks. *Was not contented*." This was a general servant in a family of two occupying a good social position, but living as so many Germans do on a small income. But then the servant's wages for doing the work of a large well-furnished, well-kept flat was £14, and these same friends told me that servants now expect to get a quarter of their wages in money and presents at Christmas. A German servant gets a great deal more help from her mistress, and is more directly under her superintendence, than she would be in a household of the same social standing in this country. I have heard an English lady say that when she had asked people to dinner she made it a rule to go out all day, because if she did not her servants worried her with questions about extra silver and other tiresome details. All the notable housewives in England will say that this lady was a "freak," and must not be held up to the world as an English type. But I think there is something of her spirit in many English-women. They engage their servants to do certain work, and hold them responsible. The German holds herself responsible for every event and every corner in her husband's house, and she never for a moment closes her eyes and lets go the reins. The servants are used to working hand in hand with the ladies of the household, and do not regard the kitchen as a department belonging exclusively to themselves after an early hour in the morning.

"Why did you leave your last place?" you say to an English cook applying for yours.

"Because the lady was always in the kitchen," she replies quite soberly and civilly. "I don't like to see ladies in my kitchen at all hours of the day. It is impossible to get on with the work."

But in Germany the kitchen is not the cook's kitchen. It belongs to the people who maintain it, and they enter it when they please. It is always so spick and span that you sigh as you see it, because you think of your own kitchen at home with its black pans and unpleasant looking sink. *There are no black pans in a German kitchen*; you never see any grease, and you never by any chance see a teacloth or a duster with a hole in it. An English kitchen in a small household is furnished with more regard to the comfort of the servants than a German one, and with less concern for the work to be done there. We supply comfortable chairs, a coloured table-cloth, oil-cloth, books, hearth-rug, pictures, cushions, inkstand, and a roaring fire. The German kitchen lacks all these things. It does not look as if the women who live in it ever expected to pursue their own business, or rest for an hour in an easy chair. But the shining brightness of it rejoices you,—every vessel is of wood, earthenware, enamel, or highly polished metal, and every one of them is scrupulously clean. The groceries and pudding stuffs are kept in fascinating jars and barrels, like those that come to children at Christmas in toy kitchens made in Germany. The stove is a clean, low hot table at which you can stand all day without getting black and greasy. In this sensible spotless workshop a German servant expects to be busy from morning till night. Neither for herself nor for her fellow-servants will she ever set a table for a tidy kitchen meal. She eats anywhere and anywhen, as the fancy takes her and the exigencies of the day permit. Her morning meal will consist of coffee and rye bread without butter. In the middle of the morning she will have a second breakfast, rye bread again with cheese or sausage. In a liberal household she will dine as the family dines; in a stingy one she will fare worse than they. In an old-fashioned household her portion will be carved for her in the dining-room, because the joint will not return to the kitchen when the family has done with it, but be placed straightway in the *Speiseschrank* under lock and key. In the afternoon she will have bread and coffee again, and for supper as a rule what the family has, sausage or ham or some dish made with eggs. One friend who goes out so much with her husband that they are rarely at home to supper, told me that she made her servant a monthly allowance to buy what she liked for supper. German servants are allowed coffee and either beer or wine, but they are never given tea. Except for the scarcity of butter in middle-class households, they live very well.

They go out on errands and to market a great deal, but they do not go out as much for themselves as our servants do. A few hours every other Sunday still contents them in most places. Their favourite amusement is the cheap public ball, and the careful German householder is actually in the habit of trusting the key of the flat to his maid-of-all-work, and allowing her to return at any hour of the night she pleases. This at any rate is the custom in Berlin and some other large German towns, and the evil results of such a system are manifold. Over and over again burglaries have been traced to it. One beguiling man engages your maid to dance and sup with him, while his confederate gets hold of her key and comfortably rifles your rooms. On the girls themselves these entertainments are said to have the worst possible influence, and most sensible Germans would put a stop to them if they could.

You must not expect in Germany to have hot water brought to you at regular intervals as you do in every orderly English household. The Germans have a curious notion that English life is quite uniform, and all English people exactly alike. One man, a notably wise man too, said to me that if he knew one English family he knew ten thousand. Another German told me that this account of German life would be impossible to write, because one part of Germany differed from the other part; but that a German could easily write the same kind of book about England, because from Land's End to John o' Groats we were so many peas in a pod. To us who live in England and know the differences between the Cornish and the Yorkshire people, for instance, or the Welsh and the East Anglians, this seems sheer nonsense. I have tried to understand how Germans arrive at it, and I believe it is by way of our cans of hot water brought at regular intervals every day in the year in every British household. I remember that their machine-like precision impressed M. Taine when he was in England, and certainly miss them sadly while we are abroad. Gretchen brings you no hot water unless you ask for it; but she will brush your clothes as a matter of course, though she does all the work of the household. She will, however, be hurt and surprised if you do not press a small coin into her hand at the end of each week, and one or two big ones at parting. One friend told me that when she stayed with her family at a German hotel her German relatives told her she should give the chambermaid a tip that was equal to 20 pf. for each pair of boots cleaned during their stay. It seems an odd way of reckoning, because the chambermaid does not clean boots. However, the tip came to £3, which seems a good deal and helps to explain the ease with which German servants save enough for their marriage outfit on small wages. It is usual also to tip the servant where you have supped or dined. Your opportunity probably comes when she precedes you down the unlighted stairs with a lantern or a candle to

the house door. But you need not be at all delicate
about your opportunity. You see the other guests
make little offerings, and you can only feel that the
money has been well earned when you have eaten the
elaborate meal she has helped to cook, and has after-
wards served to you.

Domestic servants come under the law in Germany
that obliges all persons below a certain income to
provide for their old age. The Post Office issues cards
and 20 pf. stamps, and one of these stamps must be
dated and affixed to the card every Monday. Sometimes the employers buy the cards and stamps, and
show them at the Post Office once a month ; sometimes
they expect the servant to pay half the money required.
Women who go out by the day to different families
get their stamps at the house they work in on Mondays.
If a girl marries she may cease to insure, and may
have a sum of money towards her outfit. In that case
she will receive no Old Age Pension. But if she goes
on with her insurance she will have from 15 to 20
marks a month from the State after the age of 70.
In cases of illness, employers are legally bound to
provide for their domestic servants during the term of
notice agreed on. At least this is so in Prussia, and
the term varies from a fortnight to three months. In
some parts of Germany servants are still engaged by
the quarter, but in Berlin it has become unusual of late
years. The obligation to provide for illness is often a
heavy tax on employers, especially in cases when the
illness has not been caused by the work or the circumstances of the situation, but by the servant's own
carelessness and folly. Most householders in Berlin
subscribe 7.50 a year to an insurance company, a
private undertaking that provides medical help, and
when necessary sends the invalided servant to a

hospital and maintains her there. It even pays for any special food or wine ordered by its own doctor.

One cause of ill health amongst German servants must often be the abominable sleeping accommodation provided for them in old-fashioned houses. It is said that rooms without windows opening to the air are no longer allowed in Germany, and there may be a police regulation against them. Even this cannot have been issued everywhere, for not long ago I had a large well furnished room of this kind offered me in a crowded hotel. It had windows, but they opened on to a narrow corridor. The proprietor was quite surprised when I said I would rather have a room at the top of the house with a window facing the street. I know a young lady acting as *Stütze der Hausfrau* who slept in a cupboard for years, the only light and air reaching her coming from a slit of glass over the door. I remember the consumptive looking daughter of a prosperous tradesman showing us some rooms her father wished to let, and suggesting that a cupboard off a sitting-room would make a pleasant study. She said she slept in one just like it on a higher floor. Of course she called it a *Kammer* and not a cupboard, but that did not make it more inviting. Over and over again I have known servants stowed away in holes that seemed fit for brooms and brushes, but not for creatures with lungs and easily poisoned blood. This is one of the facts of German life that makes comparison between England and Germany so difficult and bewildering. Everyone knowing both countries is struck by the amount of State and police surveillance and interference the Germans enjoy compared with us. I do not say "endure," because Germans would not like it. Most of them approve of the rule they are used to, and they tell us we live in a horrid go-as-you-please fashion with the worst results. I suppose we do. But I have never known an English servant put to sleep in a cupboard, though I have heard complaints of damp fireless rooms, especially in old historical palaces and houses. And I have never been offered a room in a good English inn that had no windows to the open air. These windowless rooms may be forbidden as bedrooms by the German police, but it would take a bigger earthquake than the empire is likely to sustain to do away with those still in use.

CHAPTER XV

FOOD

ALTHOUGH the Germans as a nation are large eaters, they begin their day with the usual light continental breakfast of coffee and rolls. In households where economy is practised it is still customary to do without butter, or at any rate to provide it only for the master of the house and for visitors. In addition to rolls and butter, you may, if you are a man or a guest, have two small boiled eggs; but eggs in a German town are apt to remind you of the Viennese waiter who assured a complaining customer that their eggs were all stamped with the day, month, and year. Home-made plum jam made with very little sugar is often eaten instead of butter by the women of the family; and the servants, where white rolls are regarded as a luxury, have rye bread. No one need pity them on this account, however, as German rye bread is as good as bread can be. Ordinary London household bread is poor stuff in comparison with it. The white rolls and butter are always excellent too, and I would even say a good word for the coffee. To be sure, Mark Twain makes fun of German coffee in the *Tramp Abroad*: says something about one chicory berry being used to a barrel of water; but the poorest German coffee is better than the tepid muddy mixture you get at all English railway stations, and at most English hotels and private houses. Milk is nearly always poor in Germany, but whipped cream is often added to either coffee or chocolate.

The precision that is so striking in the arrangement of German rooms is generally lacking altogether in the serving of meals. The family does not assemble in the morning at a table laid as in England with the same care for breakfast as it will be at night for dinner. It dribbles in as it pleases, arrayed as it pleases, drinks a cup of coffee, eats a roll and departs about its business. Formerly the women of the family always spent the morning in a loose gown, and wore a cap over their undressed hair. This fashion, Germans inform you, is falling into desuetude; but it falls slowly. Take an elderly German lady by surprise in the morning, and you will still find her in what fashion journals call a *negligé*, and what plain folk call a wrapper. When it is of shepherd's plaid or snuff-coloured wool it is not an attractive garment, and it is always what the last generation but one, with their blunt tongues, called "slummocking." Most German women are busy in the house all the morning, and when they are not going to market they like to get through their work in this form of dress and make themselves trim for the day later. The advantage claimed for the plan is one of economy. The tidy costume worn later in the day is saved considerable wear and tear. The obvious disadvantage is the encouragement it offers to the sloven. In England whatever you are by nature you must in an ordinary household be down to breakfast at a fixed hour, presentably dressed; at any rate, with your hair done for the day, and, it is to be supposed, with your bath accomplished. Directly you depart from this you open the door to anything in the dressing-gown and

slipper way, to lying abed like a sluggard, and to a
waste of your own and the servants' time that under-
mines the whole welfare of a home. At least, this
is how the question presents itself to English eyes.
Meanwhile the continent continues to drink its coffee
attired in dressing-gowns, and to survive quite comfortably. In every trousseau you still see some of these
confections, and on the stage the young wife who has
to cajole her husband in the coming scene usually
appears in a coquettish one. But then it will not be
made of shepherd's plaid or snuff-coloured wool.

The dinner hour varies so much in Germany that it
is impossible to fix an hour for it. In country places
you will find everyone sitting down at midday, in
towns one o'clock is usual, in Hamburg five is the
popular hour, in Berlin you may be invited anywhen.
But unless people dine at twelve they have some kind
of second breakfast, and this meal may correspond with
the French déjeûner, or it may be even more informal
than the morning coffee. It consists in many places
of a roll or slice of bread with or without a shaving of
meat or sausage. Servants have it, children take it to
school, charitable institutions supply the bread without
the meat to their inmates. In South Germany all the
men and many women drink beer or wine with this
light meal, but in Prussia most people are content with
a *belegtes Butterbrot*, a roll cut in two, buttered, and
spread with meat or sausage or smoked fish. This
carries people on till one or two o'clock, when the
chief meal of the day is served.

All over Germany dinner begins with soup, and in
most parts the soup is followed by the *Ochsenfleisch*
that made it. At least *Ochsenfleisch* should make it by
rights.

" I know what this is," said an old German friend,

prodding at a tough slice from a dish we all found uneatable. " This is not *Ochsenfleisch* at all. This is *cow*."

Good gravy or horseradish sauce is served with it, whether it is ox or cow, and for a time you take a slice day after day without complaining. It is the persistence of the thing that wears you out in the end. You must be born to *Ochsenfleisch* to eat it year in and year out as if it was bread or potatoes. It does not appear as regularly in North as in South Germany; and in Hamburg you may once in a way have dinner without soup. People who know Germany find this almost beyond belief, but Hamburg has many little ways of its own, and is a city with a strong individual character. It is extremely proud of its cooking and its food, and it has every right to be. I once travelled with two Germans who in a heated way discussed the comparative merits of various German cities. They could not agree, and they could not let the matter drop. At last one man got the best of it. " I tell you that Hamburg is the finest city in Germany," he said. " In a Hamburg hotel I once ate the best steak I ever ate in my life." The other man had nothing to say to that. Hamburg has a splendid fish supply, and Holstein brings her quantities of fruit and of farm produce. Your second breakfast there is like a French déjeûner, a meal served and prepared according to your means, but a regular meal and not a mere snack. You drink coffee after it, and so sustain life till five o'clock, when you dine. Then you drink coffee again, and as your dinner has probably been an uncommonly good one you only need a light supper at nine o'clock, when a tray will arrive with little sandwiches and slender bottles of beer. In North Germany, where wine is scarce and dear, it is hardly ever seen in many households, so that a young Englishman wanting to describe his German friends, divided them for convenience into wine people and beer people. The wine people were plutocrats, and had red or white Rhine wine every day for dinner. I probably need not tell my well-informed country people that Germans never speak of hock.

In households where the chief meal of the day is at one or two o'clock there is afternoon tea or coffee. It used invariably to be coffee, good hot coffee and fresh rusks and dainty little *Hörnchen* and *Radankuchen*, an excellent light cake baked in a twisty tin. German cakes want a whole chapter to themselves to do them justice, and they should have it if it were not for a dialogue that frequently takes place in a family well known to me. The wife is of German origin, but as she has an English husband and English servants she keeps house in the English way. Therefore mutton cold or hashed is her frequent portion.

" How I hate hashed mutton," she sometimes says.

" Why do you have it, then ? " says the husband, who has a genius for asking apparently innocent but really provoking questions.

" What else can I have ? " says the wife.

" Eel in jelly," says the husband. He once tasted it in Berlin, and it must have given him a mental shock ; for whenever his wife approaches him with a domestic difficulty, asks him, for instance, what he would like for breakfast, he suggests this inaccessible and uninviting dish.

" There is never anything to eat in England except mutton and apple-tart," says the wife. " Your plain cooks can't cook anything else. They can't cook those really. Think of a German apple-tart——"

" Why should I ? I don't want one."

" That's the hopeless part of it. You are all content

with what Daudet called your *abominable cuisine.* I thank him for the phrase. It is descriptive."

"Oh, well," says the husband, "we're not a greedy nation."

So if this is the English point of view the less said about cakes the better. And anyhow, it is in this country that afternoon tea is an engaging meal. Berlin offers you tea nowadays, but it is never good, and instead of freshly cut bread and butter they have horrid little chokey biscuits flavoured with vanilla. Old-fashioned Germans used to put a bit of vanilla in the tea-pot when they had guests they delighted to honour, but they all know better than that nowadays. The milk is often boiled milk, but even that scarcely explains why tea is so seldom fit to drink in Germany. Supper is a light meal in most houses. The English mutton bone is never seen, for when cold meat is eaten it is cut in neat slices and put on a long narrow dish. But there is nearly always something from the nearest *Delikatessen* shop with it,—slices of ham or tongue, or slices of one or two of the various sausages of Germany : *Blutwurst, Mettwurst, Schinkenwurst, Leberwurst,* all different and all good. When a hot dish is served it is usually a light one, often an omelette or some other preparation of eggs; and in spring eggs and bits of asparagus are a great deal cooked together in various ways : not asparagus heads so often as short lengths of the stalk sold separately in the market, and quite tender when cooked. There is nearly always a salad with the cold meat or a dish of the salted cucumbers that make such a good pickle. The big loaves of light brown rye bread appear at this meal instead of the little white rolls eaten at breakfast. Beer or wine is drunk, and very often of late years tea as well. Sweets are not usually served at supper, unless guests are present. They are eaten at the midday dinner, and each part of Germany has its own favourite dishes.

Soups are nearly always good in Germany, and some of the best are not known in England. The dried green corn so much used for soup in South Germany can, however, be bought in London from the German provision merchants, so at the end of this greedy chapter I will give a recipe for making it. *Nudel-suppe* of strong chicken stock and home-made *Nudeln* used to be what the Berliner called his roast goose— "*eine jute Jabe Jottes,*" but the degenerate Germans of to-day buy tasteless manufactured *Nudeln* instead of rolling out their own. *Nudeln* are the German form of macaroni, but when properly made they are better than any macaroni can be. If you have been brought up in an old-fashioned German ménage, and, as a child likes to do, peeped into the kitchen sometimes, you will remember seeing large sheets of something as thin and yellow as chamois leather hung on a clothes horse to dry. Then you knew that there would be *Nudeln* for your dinner, either narrow ones in soup, or wider ones boiled in water and sprinkled with others cut as fine as vermicelli and fried brown in butter. The paste is troublesome to make. It begins with a deceptive simplicity. Take four whole eggs and four tablespoonsful of milk if you want enough for ten people, says the cookery book, and make a light dough of it with a knife in a basin. Anyone can do that, you find. But then you must put your dough on the pastry board, and work in more flour as you knead it with your hands. "the longer you knead and the stiffer the dough is the better your *Nudeln* will be," continues the cookery book. But the next operation is to cut the dough into four, and roll out each portion *as thin as paper*, and no one who has not seen German *Nudeln* before they are cooked can believe that this is actually done. It is no use to give the rest of the recipe for drying them, rolling each piece loosely and cutting it into strips and boiling them with salt in water. If you told your English cook to make you *Nudeln* she would despise it for a foreign mess, and bring you something as thick as a pancake. If you want them you had better get them in a box from a provision merchant, as the *Hausfrau* herself does nowadays.

English people often say that there is no good meat to be had in Germany. I would say that there is no good mutton, and a great deal of poor coarse beef. But the *Filetbraten* that you can get from the best butchers is excellent. It is a long roll of undercut of beef, so long that it seems to be sold by the yard. If you cook it in the English way, says my German cookery book, you rub it well with salt and pepper and baste it with butter; while the gravy is made with flour, mushrooms, cream, and extract of beef. I should like to see the expression of the English plain cook if she was told to baste her beef with butter and make her gravy for it with mushrooms. I once came back from Germany with a new idea for gravy, and tried it on a cook who seemed to think that gravy was made by upsetting a kettle over a joint and then adding lumps of flour.

"My sister's cook always puts an onion in the tin with a joint," I said tentatively, for I was not very hopeful. I know that there is always some insuperable objection to anything not consecrated by tradition.

"It gives the gravy a flavour," I went on,—"not a strong flavour"—

I stopped. I waited for the objection.

"We couldn't do that HERE," said the cook.

"Why not?—We have tins and we have onions."

" It would spoil the dripping. What could I do with dripping as tasted of onion? "

I had never thought of that, and so I had never asked my sister what was done in her household with dripping as tasted with onion.

" I should think," I said slowly, " that it could be used to baste the next joint."

" Then that would taste of onion," said the cook, " and I should have no dripping when I wanted it."

I have always thought dripping a dull subject, and I know that it is an explosive one, so I said nothing more. I went on instead to describe a piece of beef stewed in its own juices on a bed of chopped vegetables. We actually tried that, and when it was cold it tasted agreeably of the vegetables, and was as tender to carve as butter.

" How did you like the German beef? " I said to an Englishwoman who had been with me a great many years.

" I didn't like it at all, M'm."

" But it was so tender."

" Yes, M'm, it made me creep," she said.

So this chapter is really of no use from one point of view. You may hear what queer things benighted people like the Germans eat and drink, but you will never persuade your British household to condescend to them.

Except in the coast towns, sea fish is scarce and dear all over Germany. Salt fish and fresh-water fish are what you get, and except the trout it is not interesting. A great deal of carp is eaten, cooked with vinegar to turn it blue, and served with horseradish or wine sauce. At a dinner party I have seen tench given, and they were extremely pretty, like fish in old Italian pictures, but they were not worth eating. At least a pound of fresh butter was put on each dish of them,

11

handed round, and you took some of it as well as a sort
of mustard sauce.   Perch, pike, and eel are all eaten
where nothing better is to be had; but the standing
fish-course of inland Germany is trout.   Most hotels
have a tank where they keep it alive till it is wanted,
and in the Black Forest the peasants catch it and
peddle it, walking miles to make good sales.   We went
into the garden of our hotel in the Wiesenthal one day,
and found the basin of the fountain there crammed
with live trout.   It was so full that you could take one
in your hand for a moment and look at its speckles, as
lovely as the speckles on a thrush's breast.   The man
who was carrying them on his back in a wooden water-
tight satchel was having a drink, and he had put out
his fish for a drink while he rested.   I have never been
within reach of fresh herrings in Germany, and have
never seen them there, but smoked ones are eaten
everywhere, often with salad, or together with smoked
ham and potatoes in their jackets.   Neither the ham
nor the herrings are ever cooked when they have been
smoked, and the ham is very tough in consequence.
The breast of a goose, too, is eaten smoked but not
cooked, and is considered a great delicacy.   Poultry
varies in quality a good deal.   Everyone knows the
little chickens that come round at hotel dinners, all
legs and bones.   A German family will sit down
contentedly to an old hen that the most economical of
us would only use for soup, and they will serve it
roasted though it is as tough as leather.   I think it
must be said that you get better fowls both in France
and England than in Germany.   The German national
bird is the goose.   In England, if you buy a goose
your cook roasts it and sends it up, and that is all you
ever know of it.   In Germany a goose is a carnival,
rather as a newly killed pig is in an English farmhouse.

You begin with a stew of the giblets, you perhaps continue with the bird itself roasted and stuffed with chestnuts, you may have a dozen different dishes made of its remains, while the fat that has basted it you hoard and use sparingly for weeks. For instance, you cook a cabbage with a little of it instead of with water. In South Germany, goose livers are prepared with it, and are just as much liked as *pâté de foie gras*.

Hares are eaten and most carefully prepared in Germany. They are skinned in a way that an English poulterer has been known to learn from his German customers and pronounce very troublesome, and the back is usually served separately, larded and basted with sour cream. Vegetables are cooked less simply than in England, and you will find the two countries disagree heatedly about them. The Englishman does not want his peas messed up with grease and vinegar, and though he will be too polite to say so, he will silently agree with his plain cook who says that peas served in the pod is a dish only fit for pigs and what she has never been accustomed to ; while the German will get quite dejected over the everlasting plain boiled cabbage and potatoes he is offered week after week in his English boarding-house. At home, he says, he is used to mountains of fat asparagus all the spring, and he thinks slightly of your skinny green ones or of the wooden stuff you import and pay less for because it is " foreign." He likes potatoes cooked in twenty various ways, and when mashed he is of opinion that they should not be black or lumpy. He wants a dozen different vegetables dished up round one joint of beef, and in summer salads of various kinds on various occasions, and not your savage mixed salad with a horrible sauce poured out of a bottle ; furniture polish he believes it to be from its colour. In the autumn he expects chestnuts cooked with gravy and vegetables, or made into light puddings; and apple sauce, he assures you, should be a creamy white, and as smooth as a well made purée.   If he is of the South he would like a *Mehlspeise* after his meat, *Spetzerle* if he comes from Würtemberg; one of a hundred different dishes if he is a Bavarian.   He will not allow that your national milk puddings take their place.   If he is a North German his *Leibgericht* may be *Rote Grütze*.   This is eaten enormously all over Denmark and North Germany in summer, and is nothing in the world but a ground rice or sago mould made with fruit juice instead of milk. The old-fashioned way was to squeeze raspberries and currants through a cloth till you had a quart of pure juice, which you then boiled with 4 oz. ground rice and sugar to taste, stirring carefully lest it should burn, and stirring patiently so that the rice should be well cooked. But where fruit is dear you can make excellent *Rothe Grütze* by stewing the fruit first with a little water and straining off the juice.   A quart of currants and a pound of raspberries should give you a good quart mould.   The Danes make it of rhubarb and plum juice in the same way; and my German cookery book gives a recipe for *Grüne Grütze* made with green gooseberries, but I tried that once and found it quite inferior to our own gooseberry fool.

Food is so much a matter of taste and custom, that it seems absurd to make dogmatic remarks about the superiority of one kitchen to another.   If you like cold mutton, boiled potatoes and rice pudding, most days in the week, you like them and there is an end of it. The one thing you can say for certain is that to cook for you requires neither skill nor pains, while to cook for a German family, even if it lives plainly and poorly, takes time and trouble.   In trying to compare the methods of two nations, one must naturally be careful to compare households on the same social plane; and an English household that lives on cold mutton and rice pudding is certainly a plain and probably a poor one. In well-to-do English households you get the best food in the world as far as raw material goes, but it must be said that you often get poor cooking. It passes quite unnoticed too. No one seems to mind thick soups that are too thick and gravies that are tasteless, and melted butter like Stickphast paste, and savouries quite acrid with over much vinegar and anchovy. I once saw a whole company of English people contentedly eat a dish of hot scones that had gone wrong. They tasted of strong yellow soap. But I once saw a company of Germans eat bad fish and apparently like it. They were sea soles handed round in a Swiss hotel, and they should by rights have been buried the day before. I thought of Ottilie von Schlippenschlopp and the oysters. But the soles were carefully cooked, and served with an elaborate sauce.

GREEN CORN SOUP.—For six people take 7 oz. of green corn: wash it well in hot water, and cook it until it is quite soft in stock or salt water. Put it through a sieve, add boiling stock, and serve with fried slice of bread or with small semolina dumplings.

GREEN CORN SOUP.—Another way. For six people take $5\frac{1}{2}$ oz. of green corn, wash it well in hot water, and let it simmer for a few minutes with a little stock and $1\frac{1}{2}$ oz. butter. Then add strong stock, and let it simmer slowly with the lid on till the corn is soft. Then stir a tablespoonful of fine flour with half a cupful of milk, and add it to the soup, stirring all the time. This must then cook an hour longer. When ready to serve, mix the yolks of two eggs with a little sour cream, and add the soup carefully so that it is not curdled. The soup is not strained through a sieve when it is served without dumplings.

The little dumplings are first cooked as a panada of semolina, butter, milk and egg, and then dropped into the soup and cooked in it for ten minutes.

CHAPTER XVI

SHOPS AND MARKETS

BERLIN people compare their Wertheim with the Bon Marché at Paris, or with Whiteley's in London ; only always adding that Wertheim is superior to any emporium in France or England. So it really is in one way. A great artist designed it, and the outside of the building is plain and stately, a most refreshing contrast to most Berlin architecture. On the ground floor there is a high spacious hall that is splendid when it is lighted up at night, and a staircase leads up and down from here to the various departments, all decorated soberly and pleasantly, mostly with wood. You can buy almost anything you want at Wertheim's, from the furniture of your house to a threepenny pair of cotton mittens with a thumb and no fingers. You can see tons of the most hideous rubbish there, and you can find a corner reserved for original work, done by two or three artists whose names are well known in Germany. For instance, Wertheim exhibits the very clever curious "applications" done by Frau Katy Münchhausen, groups of monkeys, storks, cocks and hens, and other animals, drawn with immense spirit and life on cloth, cut out and then *machined* on a background of another colour. The machining has a bad sound, I admit, but for all that the " applications " are enchanting. Wertheim, too, shows some good furniture; he sells theatre tickets, books, fruit, groceries, Liberty cushions, embroideries, soaps, perfumes, toys, ironmongery, china, glass, as well as everything that can be called drapery.   He has a tea-room as well as a large general refreshment-room, where you can get ices, iced coffee, beer, all kinds of sandwiches, and the various *Torten* Germans make so very much better than other people.   In this room no money is wasted on waiters or waitresses, and no one expects to be tipped.   You fetch what you want from a long bar running along two sides of the room, and divided into short stretches, each selling its own stuff; you pay at the counter, and you carry your ice or your cake to any little marble-topped table you choose. The advantage of the plan is that you do not have to wait till you catch the eye of a waitress determined not to look your way : the disadvantage is that you have to perform the difficult feat of carrying a full cup or a full glass through a crowd.   Whatever you buy at the counter is sure to be good, but if all you could get was a Mugby Junction bun you would have to eat it after the exhausting process of buying a yard of ribbon or a few picture postcards at Wertheim's.

To begin with, there are no chairs.   You cannot sit down.   On a hot summer morning, when you have perhaps been to the market already, you go to the Leipziger Strasse for theatre tickets, a pair of gloves, and two or three small odds and ends.   On the ground floor you see gloves, innumerable boxes of them besieged by a pushing, determined crowd of women.   The shop ladies in any coloured blouses look hot and weary, but try to serve six customers at once.   When you have chosen what you want, and know exactly how sharp the elbows to left and right of you are, you see your lady walk off with your most pushful neighbour and the pair of three-

penny gloves she has after much argument agreed
to buy ; for at Wertheim's you cannot depart with so
much as a halfpenny postcard till it has passed through
three pairs of hands besides your own. First the
shop lady must deposit it with a bill at the cashier's
desk. Then, when the cashier can attend to you, you
pay for it. Then you may wait any time until the
third person concerned will do it up in paper and string.
This last proceeding is often so interminably delayed
that if you were not in Germany you would snatch at
what you have paid for and make off. But the *Polizei*
alone knows what would happen if you ran your head
against the established pedantry of things in the city
of the Spree. You would probably find yourself in
prison for *Beamtenbeleidigung* or *lèse majesté.* "The
Emperor is a fool," said some disloyal subject in a
public place. "To prison with him," screamed every
horror-struck official. "Off with his head!" "But I
meant the Emperor of China," protested the sinner.
"That's impossible," said the officials in chorus. "Anyone who says the Emperor is a fool means our Emperor."
And an official spirit seems to encroach on the business
one, and drill its very customers while it anxiously
serves them. For instance, the arrangements for sending what you buy are most tiresome and difficult to
understand at Wertheim's. His carts patrol the streets,
and your German friends assure you that he sends
anything. You find that if you shop with a country
card the things entered on it will arrive ; but if you
buy a bulky toy or some heavy books and pay for them
in their departments, you meet with fuss and refusal
when you ask as a matter of course to have them sent.
It can be done if your goods have cost enough, but not
if you have only spent two or three shillings. It is
the fashion in England just now for every man who

writes about Germans to say that they are immensely ahead of us in business matters. I cannot judge of them in their factories and warehouses, but I am sure they are behind us in their shops. A woman cannot live three hundred miles from Berlin and get everything she wants from Wertheim delivered by return and carriage free. Nor will he supply her with an immense illustrated catalogue and a book of order forms addressed to his firm, so that the trouble of shopping from a distance is reduced to a minimum. In England you can do your London shopping as easily, promptly, and cheaply from a Scotch or a Cornish village as you can from a Surrey suburb.

In most German towns you still find the shops classified on the old lines. You go to one for drapery, and to another for linen, and to another for small wares, and to yet another for ribbons. There are sausage shops and chocolate shops, and in Berlin there are shops for the celebrated Berlin *Baumkuchen*. There are a great many cellar shops all over Germany, and these are mostly restaurants, laundries, and greengrocers. The drinking scene in *Faust* when Mephisto made wine flow from the table takes place in Auerbach's Keller, a cellar restaurant still in existence in Leipzig. The lower class of cellar takes the place in Germany of our slums, and the worst of them are regular thieves' kitchens known to the police. There is an admirable description of life in a cellar shop in Klara Viebig's *Das Tägliche Brot*. The woman who keeps it has a greengrocery business and a registry office for servants, and as such people go is respectable; but I recommend the book to my countrymen who go to Berlin as officials or journalists for ten days, are taken over various highly polished public institutions, and come back to tell us that the Germans are every man jack of them clean, prosperous, well mannered, and healthy. It is true that German municipal government is striving rather splendidly to bring this state of things about, but they have plenty of work before them still. These cellar shops, for instance, are more fit for mushroom growing than for human nurseries, and yet the picture in the novel of the family struggling with darkness and disease there can still be verified in most of the old streets of Germany.

When our English journalists write column after column about the dangerous explosive energy and restlessness of modern Germany, I feel sure that they must be right, and yet I wish they could have come shopping with me a year or two ago in a small Black Forest town. One of us wanted a watch key and the other a piece of tape, and we set off light-heartedly to buy them, for we knew that there was a draper and a watchmaker in the main street. We knew, too, that in South Germany everyone is first dining and then asleep between twelve and two, so we waited till after two and then went to the watchmaker's. There was no shop window, and when, after ringing two or three times, we were let in we found there was no shop. We sat down in a big cool sitting-room, beautifully clean and tidy. The watchmaker's wife appeared in due course, looked at us with friendly interest, asked us where we came from, and how long we meant to stay, wondered if we knew her cousin Johannes Müller, a hairdresser in Islington, discussed the relative merits of emigration to England and America, offered us some cherries from a basketful on the table, and at last admitted unwillingly that her husband was not at home, and that she herself knew not whether he had watch keys. So we set off to buy our tape, and again found a private room, an amiable family, but no one who felt able to sell anything. It seemed an odd way of doing business we said to our landlord, but he saw nothing odd in it. Most people were busy with their hay, he explained. Towards the end of a week we caught our watchmaker, and obtained a key, but he would not let us pay for it. He said it was one of an old collection, and of no use to him. The etiquette of shopping in Germany seems to us rather topsy-turvy at first. In a small shop the proprietor is as likely as not to conduct business with a cigar in his mouth, even if you are a lady, but if you are a man he will think you a boor if you omit to remove your hat as you cross his threshold. Whether you are a man, woman, or child, you will wish him good-morning or good-evening before you ask for what you want, and he will answer you before he asks what your commands are. If you are a woman, about as ignorant as most women, and with a humble mind, you will probably have no fixed opinion about the question of free or fair trade. You may even, if you are very humble, recognise that it is not quite the simple question Dick, Tom, and Harry think it is. But you will know for certain that when you want ribbons for a hat you had better buy them in Kensington and not in Frankfurt, and that though there are plenty of cheap materials in Germany, the same quality would be cheaper still in London. Everything to do with women's clothing is dearer there than here. So is stationery, so are groceries, so are the better class of fancy goods. But the Germans, say the Fair Traders, are a prosperous nation, and it is because their manufactures are protected. This may be so. I can only look at various quite small unimportant trifles, such as ribbons, for instance, or pewter vases or blotting-paper or peppermint drops. I know that a German woman either wears a common ribbon on her hat, or pays twice as much as I do for a good one; she is content with one pewter vase where your English suburban drawing-room packs twenty into one corner, with twenty silver frames and vases near them. A few years ago the one thing German blotting-paper refused to do was to absorb ink, and it was so dear that in all small country inns and in old-fashioned offices you were expected to use sand instead. The sand was kept beside the ink in a vessel that had a top like a pepper pot; and it was more amusing than blotting-paper, but not as efficacious. As for the peppermint drops, they used to be a regular export from families living in London to families living in Germany. They were probably needed after having goose and chestnuts for dinner, and ours were twice as large as the German ones and about six times as strong, so no doubt they were like our blotting-paper, and performed what they engaged to perform more thoroughly.

But shops of any kind are dull compared with an open market held in one of the many ancient market places of Germany. The photograph of Freiburg gives a bird's-eye view of the town with the minster rising from the midst of its red roofs; but there is just a peep at the market which is being held at the foot of the minster. On the side hidden from us in the photograph there are some of the oldest houses in Freiburg. It is a large crowded market on certain days of the week, and full of colour and movement. The peasants who come to it from the neighbouring valleys wear bright-coloured skirts and headgear, and in that part of Germany fruit is plentiful, so that all through the summer and autumn the market carts and barrows are heaped with cherries, wild strawberries, plums, apricots, peaches, and grapes in their season

The market place itself, and even the steps of the
minster and of the surrounding houses, are crowded
with the peasants and their produce, and with the
leisurely servants and housewives bargaining for the
day's supplies. The other photograph of the market
place at Cottbus in Brandenburg gives more idea of
the people at a German market; the servants with
their umbrellas, their big baskets, their baggy blouses
and no hats, the middle class housewife with a hat or
a bonnet, and a huge basket on her arm, a nursemaid
in peasant costume stooping over her perambulator, other
peasants in costume at the stalls, and two of the farm
carts that are in some districts yoked oftener with oxen
than with horses. There is naturally great variety in
the size and character of markets, according to the needs
they supply. In Hamburg the old names show you
that there were separate markets for separate trades,
so that you went to the Schweinemarkt when
you wanted pigs, and to some other part of the
city when you wanted flowers and fruit. In Berlin
there are twelve covered markets besides the open
ones, and they are all as admirably clean, tidy,
and unpoetical as everything else is in that spick
and span, swept and garnished Philistine city. The
green gooseberries there are marked " unripe fruit "
by order of the police, so that no one should think
they were ripe and eat them uncooked; and you can
buy rhubarb nowadays, a vegetable the modern Berliner
eats without shuddering. But in a Berlin market
you buy what you need as quickly as you can and
come away. There is nothing to tempt you, nothing
picturesque, nothing German, if German brings to your
mind a queer mixture of poetry and music, gabled,
tumbledown houses, storks' nests, toys, marvellous
cakes and sweets and the kindliest of people. If you

are so modern that German means nothing to you but drill and hustle, the roar of factories and the pride of monster municipal ventures, then you may see the markets of Berlin and rest content with them. They will show you what you already know of this day's Germany. But my household treasures gathered here and there in German markets did not have one added to their number in Berlin.

"That!" said a German friend when I showed her a yellow pitcher dabbed with colour, and having a spout, a handle, and a lid,—"that! I would not have it in my kitchen."

It certainly only cost the third of a penny, but it lived with honour in my drawing-room till it shared the fate of all clay, and came in two in somebody's hands. The blue and grey bellied bottle, one of those in which the Thuringian peasants carry beer to the field, cost three halfpence, but the butter-dish with a lid of the same ware only cost a halfpenny. There is always an immense heap of this rough grey and blue pottery in a South German market, and it is much prettier than the more ornate Coblenz ware we import and sell at high prices. So is the deep red earthen-ware glazed inside and rough outside and splashed with colours. You find plenty of it at the Leipziger Messe, that historical fair that used to be as important to Western Europe as Nijni Novgorod is to Russia and the East. To judge from modern German trade circulars, it is still of considerable importance, and the buildings in which merchants of all countries display their wares have recently been renovated and enlarged. Out of doors the various market-places are covered with little stalls selling cheap clothing, cheap toys, jewellery, sweets, and gingerbread; all the hetero-geneous rubbish you have seen a thousand times at

German fairs, and never tire of seeing if a fair delights you.

But better than the Leipziger Messe, better even than a summer market at Freiburg or at Heidelburg, is a Christmas market in any one of the old German cities in the hill country, when the streets and the open places are covered with crisp clean snow, and the mountains are white with it, and the moon shines on the ancient houses, and the tinkle of sledge bells reaches you when you escape from the din of the market, and look down at the bustle of it from some silent place, a high window perhaps, or the high empty steps leading into the cathedral. The air is cold and still, and heavy with the scent of the Christmas trees brought from the forest for the pleasure of the children. Day by day you see the rows of them growing thinner, and if you go to the market on Christmas Eve itself you will find only a few trees left out in the cold. The market is empty, the peasants are harnessing their horses or their oxen, the women are packing up their unsold goods. In every home in the city one of the trees that scented the open air a week ago is shining now with lights and little gilded nuts and apples, and is helping to make that Christmas smell, all compact of the pine forest, wax candles, cakes, and painted toys, you must associate so long as you live with Christmas in Germany.

CHAPTER XVII

EXPENSES OF LIFE

A FEW years ago a German economist reckoned that
there were only 250,000 families in the empire
whose incomes exceeded £450, a year. There were
nearly three million households living on incomes
ranging from £135 to £450, and nearly four millions
with more than £90 but less than £135. But there
were upwards of five millions whose incomes fell below
£45. Since that estimate was made, Germany has
grown in wealth and prosperity; and in the big cities
there is great expenditure and luxury amongst some
classes, especially amongst the Jews who can afford it,
and amongst the officers of the army who as a rule
cannot. But the bulk of the nation is poor, and class
for class lives on less than people do in England.
For instance, the headmaster of a school gets about
£100 a year in a small town, and from £200 to £300
in a big one. A lieutenant gets about £65 a year,
and an additional £12 if he has no private means. His
uniform and mess expenses are deducted from this.
He is not allowed to marry on his official income,
unless he or his wife has an income of £125 in
addition to his pay, as even in Germany an army man
can hardly keep up appearances and support a wife
and family on less than £190 a year. It is quite
common to hear of a clerk living on £40 or £50, or of

a doctor who knows his work and yet can only make £150. The official posts so eagerly sought after are poorly paid; so are servants, agricultural labourers, and artisans. When you are in Germany, if you are interested in questions of income and expenditure, you are always trying to make up your mind why a German family can live as successfully on £400 as an English family on £700, for you know that rent and taxes are high and food and clothing dear. If you are a woman and think about it a great deal, and look at family life in as many places and classes as you can, you finally decide that there are three chief reasons for the great difference between the cost of life in England and Germany. In the first place, labour is cheaper there; in the second place, the standard of luxury and even of comfort is lower; in the third place, the women are thriftier and more industrious than Englishwomen. This, too, leaves out of account the most important fact, that the State educates a man's children for next to nothing; and drills the male ones into shape when they serve in the army.

Servants, we have seen, get lower wages than they do here, but the real economy is in the smaller number kept. Where we pay and maintain half a dozen a German family will be content with two, and the typical small English household that cannot face life without its plain cook in the kitchen and its parlour-maid in her black gown at the front door, will throughout the German Empire get along quite serenely with one young woman to cook and clean and do everything else required. If she is a "pearl" she probably makes the young ladies' frocks and irons the master's shirts to fill in her time. Germans do not trouble about the black frock and the white apron at the front door. They will even open the door to you themselves if the "girl" is washing or cooking. A female servant is always a "girl" in Germany. I once heard a young Englishwoman who had not been long in Germany ask an elderly acquaintance to recommend a dressmaker.

"The best one in —— is Fräulein Müller," said the elderly acquaintance.

"But she is too expensive," said the Englishwoman, and she glanced across the room at the lady's nieces, who were neatly and plainly dressed. "Do girls go to Fräulein Müller?"

"Girls! Certainly not," said the lady, with the expression Germans keep for the insane English it is their fate to encounter occasionally.

"But that is what I want to know, . . . a dressmaker girls go to . . . girls with a small allowance."

"I am afraid I cannot help you," said the lady stiffly. "I know nothing about the dressmakers girls employ."

"Perhaps Miss Brown means 'young girls,'" said one of the nieces, who was not as slow in the uptake as her aunt, and it turned out that this was what Miss Brown did mean; but she had not known that in everyday life *Mädchen* without an adjective usually means a servant. She had heard of *Das Mädchen aus der Fremde* and *Der Tod und das Mädchen*, and blundered.

I once made a German exceedingly angry by saying that the standard of comfort was higher in England than in Germany. She said it was lower. When you have lived in both countries and with both peoples you arrive in the end at having your opinions, and knowing that each one you hold will be disputed on one side or the other. "Find out what means

Gemütlichkeit, and do it without fail," says Hans Breitmann, but *Gemütlichkeit* and comfort are not quite interchangeable words. Our word is more material. When we talk of English comfort we are thinking of our open fires, our solid food, our thick carpets, and our well-drilled smart-looking servants. The German is thinking of the spiritual atmosphere in his own house, the absence, as he says, of ceremony and the freedom of ideas. He talks of a man being *gemütlich* in his disposition, kindly, that is, and easy going. We talk of a house being comfortable, and when we do use the word for a person usually mean that she is rather stout. When both you and the German have decided that " comfort " for the moment shall mean material comfort, you will disagree about what is necessary to yours. You must have your bathroom, your bacon for breakfast, your table laid precisely, your meals served to the moment, your young women in black or your staid men to give them to you, and your glowing fires in as many rooms as possible. The German cares for none of these things. He would rather have his half-pound of odds and ends from the provision shop than your boiled cod, roast mutton, and apple-tart; he wants his stove, his double windows, his good coffee, his *kräftige Kost*, and freedom to smoke in every corner of his house. He is never tired of telling you that, though you have more political freedom in England, you are groaning under a degree of social tyranny that he could not endure for a day. The Idealist, quoted in a former chapter, is for ever talking of the " hypocrisy " of English life, and her burning anxiety is to save the children of certain Russian and German exiles from contact with it. Another German tells you that our system of collegiate life for women would not suit her countryfolk, because

they are more "individual." Each one likes to choose
her own rooms, and live as she pleases. The next
German has suffered torments in London because he
had to sit down to certain meals at certain hours
instead of eating anything he fancied at any time he
felt hungry, and I suppose it is only your British
Heuchelei that leads you to smile politely instead of
adding, "As the beasts of the field do." But I am
always mazed, as the Cornish say, when Germans talk
of their freedom from convention. In Hamburg I was
once seriously rebuked by an old friend for carrying a
book through the streets that was not wrapped up in
paper. In Hamburg that is one of the things people
don't do. In Mainz and in many other German towns
there are certain streets where one side, for reasons no
one can explain, is taboo at certain hours of the day;
not of the night, but of the day. You may go to a
music shop at midday to buy a sonata, and find,
if you are a girl, that you have committed a crime.
The intercourse between young people outside their
homes is hedged round with convention. German
titles of address are so absurdly formal that Germans
laugh at them themselves. Their ceremonies in connection with anniversaries and family events bristle
with convention, and offer pitfalls at every step to the
stranger or the blunderer. It is true that men do
not dress for dinner every day, and wax indignant over
the necessity of doing so for the theatre in England;
but there are various occasions when they wear evening
dress in broad daylight, and an Englishman considers
that an uncomfortable convention. The truth is, that
these questions of comfort and ceremonial are not
questions that should be discussed in the hostile
dogmatic tone adopted in both countries by those who
only know their own. The ceremonies that are

foreign to you impress you, while those you have been used to all your life have become a second nature. An Englishwoman feels downright uncomfortable in her high stuff gown at night, and a German lady brought up at one of the great German Courts told me that when she stayed in an English country house and put on what she called a ball dress for dinner every night, she felt like a fool.

To come back to questions of expenditure so intimately related to questions of comfort, it must be remembered that in an English household there are two dinners a day : one early for the servants and children, and one late for the grown-ups ; and solid dinners cost money even in England, where at present there is no meat famine. When Germans dine late they don't also dine early, even where there are children ; while the kitchen dinner, that meal of supreme importance here, is eaten when the family has finished theirs, and is as informal as the meal a bird makes of berries. In a German household, living on a small income, nothing is wasted,—not fuel, not food, not cleaning materials, as far as possible not time. The *tüchtige Hausfrau* would be made miserable by having to pay and feed a woman who put on gala clothes at midday, and did no work to soil them after that.

" Two girls," I once heard a German say to an Englishwoman who had just described her own modest household which she ran, she said, with two maids. " Two girls . . . for you and your husband. But what, I ask you, does the second one do ? "

" She cleans the rooms and waits at table and opens the door," said the Englishwoman.

" All that can one girl do just as well. I assure you it is so. There cannot possibly be work in your household for two girls. You have told me how quietly you live, and I know what English cooking is, if you can call it cooking."

" You see, there must be someone to open the door."

" Why could one girl not answer the door, . . . unless she was washing. Then you would naturally go yourself."

" But it wouldn't be natural in England," said the Englishwoman. " It would be odd. Besides, if you only have one servant, she can't dress for lunch."

" Why should she dress for lunch ? " asked the German. " My Auguste is a pearl, but she only dresses when we have *Gesellschaft*. Then she wears a plaid blouse and a garnet brooch that I gave her last Christmas, and she looks very well in them. But every day . . . and for lunch, when half the work of the day is still to be done. . . . What, then, does your second girl do in the afternoons ? "

" She brings tea and answers the door."

" Always the door. But your husband is not a doctor or a dentist. Why do so many people come to your door that you need a whole girl to attend to them ? "

" Oh ! They don't," said the Englishwoman, getting rather worn. " There are very few, really. It's the custom."

" Ah ! " said the German, with a long deep breath of satisfaction. " So are you English . . . such slaves to custom. *Gott sei Dank* that I do not live in a country where I should have to keep a girl in idleness for the sake of the door. With us a door is a door. Anyone who happens to be near opens it."

" I know they do," said the Englishwoman, " and when a servant comes she expects you to say *Guten Tag* before you ask whether her mistress is at home ? "

"Certainly. It is a politeness. We are a polite nation."

"And once, when I had just come back from Germany, I said Good-morning to an English butler before I asked if his mistress was at home, and he thought I was mad. We each have our own conventions. That's the truth of the matter."

"Not at all," said the German. "The truth of the matter is, that the English are extremly conventional, and follow each other as sheep do; but the German does what pleases him, without asking first whether his neighbour does likewise."

This is what the German really believes, and you agree or disagree with him according to the phase of life you look at when he is speaking. You find that when he comes to England he honestly feels checked at every turn by our unwritten laws, while when you go to Germany you wonder how he can submit so patiently to the pettiness and multiplicity of his written ones. He vaguely feels the pressure and criticism of your indefinite code of manners; you think his elaborate system of titles, introductions, and celebrations rather childish and extremely troublesome. If you have what the English call manners you will take the greatest care not to let him find this out, and in course of time, however much you like him on the whole, you will lose your patience a little with the individual you are bound to meet, the individual who has England on his nerves, and exhausts his energy and eloquence in informing you of your country's shortcomings. They are legion, and indeed leave no room for the smallest virtue, so that in the end you can only wonder solemnly why such a nation ever came to be a nation at all.

"That is easily answered," says your Anglophobe. "England has arrived where she is by seizing everything she can lay hands on. Now it is going to be our turn."

You express your interest in the future of Germany as seen by your friend, and he shows you a map of Europe which he has himself marked with red ink all round the empire as it will be a few years hence. There is not much Europe outside the red line.

" But you haven't taken Great Britain," you say, rather hurt at being left out in this way.

" We don't want it . . . otherwise, . . . but India . . . possibly Australia." He waves his hands.

You look at him pensively, and suddenly see one of the great everyday distances between your countryfolk and his. You think of a French novel that has amused you lately, because the parents of the heroine objected to her marriage with the hero on grounds you were quite incapable of understanding. The young man's work was in Cochin-China, and the young lady's father and mother did not wish her to go so far. Never in your life have you heard anyone raise such a trivial difficulty. You live in a dull sober street mostly inhabited by dull sober people, but there is not one house in it that is not linked by interest or affection, often doubly linked, with some uttermost end of the earth. You can hardly find an English family that has not one member or more in far countries, and so the common talk of English people in all classes travels the width of the world in the wake of those dear to them. But in 1900 only 22,309 Germans out of a population of 60,400,000 emigrated from Germany, and these, says Mr. Eltzbacher, whose figures I am quoting, were more than counterbalanced by immigration into Germany from Austria, Russia, and Italy. It is true that the population of Germany is increasing with immense rapidity, and that the question of expansion is becoming a burning one; but it is a question quite outside the strictly home politics of this unpretending chronicle. We are only concerned with the obvious fact that Germans settle in far countries in much smaller numbers than we do, and that those who go abroad mostly choose the British flag and avoid their own. It does not occur as easily to a German as to an Englishman that he may better his fortunes in another part of the world, or if he is an official that he will apply for a post in Asia or Africa. He wants to stay near the Rhine or the Spree where he was born, and to bring up his children there; and with the help of the State and his wife he contrives to do this on an extraordinary small income. The State, as we have seen, almost takes his children off his hands from the time they are six years old. It brings them up for nothing, or next to nothing; in cases of need it partially feeds and clothes them, it even washes them. Some English humorist has said that a German need only give himself the trouble to be born; his government does the rest. But first his mother and then his wife do a good deal. They are like the woman in Proverbs who worked willingly with her hands, rose while it was night, saw well to the ways of her household, and ate not the bread of idleness.

I have before me the household accounts of several German families living on what we should call small incomes; and they show more exactly than any vague praise can do the prodigies of thrift accomplished by people obliged to economise, and at the same time to present a respectable appearance. The first one is the budget of a small official living with a wife and two children in a little town where a flat on the fourth or fifth floor can be had at a low rent :—

	£	s.	d.
Rent	20	0	0
Fuel	3	10	0
Light	1	10	0
Clothes for the man	3	0	0
Clothes for the wife	2	0	0
Clothes for the children	1	0	0
Boots for the man	1	0	0
Boots for the wife and children	1	5	0
Repairs to boots	0	17	6
Washing and house repairs	3	0	0
Doctor	2	0	0
Newspaper	0	12	0
Charwoman	3	0	0
Taxes	2	10	0
Postage	1	4	0
Insurances	2	10	0
Amusements	3	0	0
Housekeeping	45	0	0
Sundries	3	1	6
	£100	0	0

The fuel allowed in this budget consists of 30 cwt. of *Steinkohlen* at 1 mark 15 pf. the cwt., 30 cwt. of *Braunkohlen* at 70 pf. the cwt., and 4 cwt. of kindling at 1 mark 10 pf. the cwt. This quantity, 3 tons without the kindling, would have to be used most sparingly to last through a long rigorous German winter, as well as for cooking and washing in summer. The amount set apart for lights allows for one lamp in the living room and two small ones in the passage and kitchen. The man may have a new suit every year, one year in winter and the next year in summer, and his suit may cost £2, 10s. His great-coat also is to cost £2, 10s., but he can't have a new suit the year he buys one, and it should last him at least four years. The ten shillings left is for all his other clothes except boots, and presumably for all his personal expenses, including tobacco, so he had better not spend it all at once. His wife

performs greater miracles still, for she has to buy a
winter gown and a summer gown, a hat and gloves, for
her £2. These are not fancy figures. The miracle is
performed by tens of thousands of German women every
year. They buy a few yards of cheap stuff and get in
a sewing-woman to make it up, for as a rule they are
not nearly as clever and capable as Englishwomen
about making things for themselves. Your English
maid-servant will buy a blouse length at a sale for a
few pence, make it up smartly, and wear it out in a
month of Sundays. Your German she-official will have
a blouse made for her, and it will probably be hideous ;
but she will wear it so carefully that it lasts her two
years. Under-raiment she will never want to buy, as
she will have brought a life-long supply to her home
at marriage. You easily figure the children who are
dressed on twenty marks a year, the girl in a shoddy
tartan made in a fashion of fifty years ago with the
" waist " hooked behind, and the boy in some snuff-
coloured mixture floridly braided. But the interesting
revelation of this small official budget is in its carefully
planned fare made out for a fortnight in summer and
a fortnight in winter. In winter the *Hausfrau* may
spend about 17s. a week on her food and in summer 19s.
That leaves only 2s. a month for the extra days of the
month, and for small expenses, such as soda, matches,
blacking, and condiments. Breakfast may cost sixpence
a day, and for this there is to be $\frac{3}{4}$ litre of milk, 4 small
white rolls, $\frac{1}{2}$ lb. rye bread, 2 oz. of butter, 1 oz. of
coffee. Nothing is set down for sugar, and I think that
most German families of this class would not use sugar,
and would eat their bread without butter. On Sunday
they have a goose for dinner, and pay 4s. 6d. for it, and
though 4s. 6d. is not much to pay for a goose, it seems
an extravagant dish for this family, until you discover

that they are still dining on it on Wednesday. Not only has the *Hausfrau* brought home this costly bird, but she has laid in a whole pound of lard to roast with it, white bread for stuffing, and cabbage for a vegetable. Pudding is not considered necessary after goose, and for supper there is bread and milk for the children, and bread, butter, cheese, and beer for the parents. On Monday they have a rest from goose, and dine on *gehacktes Schweinefleisch*. German butchers sell raw minced meat very cheaply, and the *Hausfrau* would probably get as much as she wanted for three-halfpence. On Tuesday they get back to the goose, and have a hash of the wings, neck, and liver with potatoes. For supper, rice cooked with milk and cinnamon. Germans use cinnamon rather as the Spaniards use garlic. They seem to think it improves everything, and they eat quantities of milky rice strewn with it. On Wednesday my family has soup for dinner, a solid soup made of goose, rice, and a pennyworth of carrots. For supper there is sausage, bread, and beer. By the way, this official is not really representative, for he spends nothing on tobacco, and only a penny every other day on beer He cannot have been a Bavarian. His wife gives him cod with mustard sauce on Thursday, Sauerkraut and shin of beef on Friday, and on Saturday lentil soup with sausages, an excellent dish when properly cooked for those who want solid nourishing food. On the following Sunday 3 pounds of beef appears, and potato dumplings with stewed fruit, another good German mixture if the dumplings are as light as they should be The husband has them warmed up for supper next day One day he has bacon and vegetables for dinner, and another day only apple sauce and pancakes, but at every midday meal throughout the fortnight he has carefully planned food on which his wife spends con-

siderable time and trouble. He never comes home
from his work on a winter's day to have a mutton bone
and watery potatoes set before him. In summer the
bill of fare provides soups made with wine, milk, or cider;
sometimes there are curds for supper, and if they have
a chicken, rice and stewed fruit are eaten with it. But
a chicken only costs this *Hausfrau* 1 mark 20 pf., so it
must have been a small one. I have often bought
pigeons for 25 pf. apiece in Germany, and stuffed in the
Bavarian way with egg and bread crumbs they are
good eating. Fruit is extremely cheap and plentiful
in many parts of Germany, but not everywhere. We
have Heine's word for it that the plums grown by the
wayside between Jena and Weimar are good, for most
of us know his story of his first interview with Goethe;
how he had looked forward to the meeting with ecstasy
and reflection, and how when he was face to face with
the great man all he found to say was a word in praise
of the plums he had eaten as he walked. In the fruit-
growing districts most of the roads are set with an
avenue of fruit trees, and so law-abiding are the boys
of Germany, and so plentiful is fruit in its season, that
no one seems to steal from them. I have talked with
elderly Germans, who remembered buying 3 pounds
of cherries for 6 kreuzers, a little more than a penny,
when they were boys. But those days are over. The
small sweet-water grapes from the vineyards of South
Germany are to be had for the asking where they are
grown, and apricots are plentiful in some districts, and
the little golden plums called *Mirabellen* that are dried
in quantities and make the best winter compote there
is. When I see English grocers' shops loaded up with
dried American apples and apricots that are not worth
eating, however carefully they are cooked, I always
wonder why we do not import *Mirabellen* instead.

Sweetbreads in the Berlin markets were about 1 mark 10 pf. each last year, small tongues were 1 mark 10 pf. *Morscheln*, a poor kind of fungus much used in Germany, were 65 pf. a pound, real mushrooms were 1 mark 50 pf., and the dried ones used for flavouring sauces were the same price. Butter and milk are usually about the same price as with us, but eggs are cheaper. You get twenty for a mark still in spring, and I remember making an English plumcake once in a Bavarian village and being charged 6 pf. for the three eggs I used. A rye loaf weighing 4 pounds costs 50 pf., the little white rolls cost 3 pf. each. In Berlin last year vegetables were nearly as dear as in London, but in many parts of Germany they are much cheaper. I know of one housewife who fed her family largely on vegetables, and would not spend more than 10 pf. a day on them, but she lived in a small country town where green stuff was a drug in the market. Asparagus is cheaper than here, for it costs 35 pf. to 40 pf. a pound, and is eaten in such quantities that even an asparagus lover gets tired of it. Meat has risen terribly in price of late years. In the open market you can get fillet of beef for 1 mark 60 pf., sirloin for 90 pf., good cuts of mutton for 90 pf. to 1 mark, and veal for 1 mark, but all these prices are higher at a butcher's shop. Fillet of beef, for instance, is 2 marks 40 pf. a pound there.

The budget of a family living on £250 a year does not call for so much comment as the smaller one, because £250 is a fairly comfortably income in Germany. Either a schoolmaster or a soldier must have risen in his profession before he gets it; but the following estimate is made out for a business man who does not get a house free or any other aid from outside :—

					£	s.	d.
Rent .	.	.	.	.	50	0	0
Fuel .	.	.	.	.	7	10	0
Light .	.	.	.	.	5	0	0
Clothes—husband	.	.	.	.	6	0	0
„ wife .	.	.	.	.	4	0	0
„ children	.	.	.	.	2	10	0
Shoes .	.	.	.	.	4	0	0
School fees	.	.	.	.	5	0	0
Washing	.	.	.	.	5	0	0
Repairs to linen	.	.	.	.	2	10	0
Doctor and dentist	.	.	.	.	5	0	0
Newspapers and magazines	.	.	.	.	2	0	0
Servant's wages	.	.	.	.	9	0	0
Servant's insurance and Christmas present			.	.	2	0	0
Taxes .	.	.	.	.	6	0	0
Postage .	.	.	.	.	1	10	0
Insurances	.	.	.	.	5	0	0
Housekeeping .	.	.	.	.	90	0	0
Amusements and travelling	.	.	.	.	25	0	0
Christmas and presents .	.	.	.	.	10	0	0
Sundries	.	.	.	.	3	0	0
					£250	0	0

On examining this budget it will occur to most
people that the poor *Hausfrau* might spend a little
more on her clothes and a little less on her presents,
and as a matter of fact even in Germany, where
Christmas is a burden as well as a pleasure, this would
be done. The next budget is the most interesting,
because it is not an ideal one drawn up for anyone's
guidance, but is taken without the alteration of one
penny from the beautifully kept account book of a
friend. There were no children in the family, so
nothing appears for school fees or children's clothes.
The household consisted of husband and wife and one
maid. They lived in one of the largest and dearest of
German cities, and the husband's work as well as their
social position forced certain expenses on them. For

instance, they had to live in a good street and on the
ground floor; and they had to entertain a good deal.

	M.	Pf.
Bread	180	—
Meat	310	95
Fish and poultry	98	55
Aufschnitt	67	25
Potatoes	19	10
Vegetables	110	50
Fruit	87	95
Eggs	83	90
Milk	121	85
Butter	195	—
Lard	36	55
Flour, Gries, etc.	25	60
Sugar and treacle	66	20
Groceries	22	50
Coffee	67	—
Tea and chocolate	17	95
Drinks	159	10
Lights	30	55
Washing	126	80
Laundress	32	25
Ice	10	20
Coal and wood	170	10
Turf and other fuel	159	25
Matches	3	—
Cleaning	60	—
Furniture	4	55
Repairs	19	50
Crockery and kitchenware	38	—
Repairs	49	—
China and glass	30	5
Clothes—husband	181	20
,, wife	452	85
Boots—husband	24	10
,, wife	60	35
Linen	17	5
Charities	232	20
Rent	2150	—
Rent of husband's share of professional rooms	318	70
Carry forward	5839	45

	M.	Pf.
Brought forward	5839	45
Fares	46	10
Books	64	25
Writing materials	30	50
Charwoman and tips . . .	85	95
Wages and servants' presents . .	335	50
Papers	35	25
Carpenter	125	—
Tobacco and cigars	165	90
Sundries	39	35
Photography and fishing tackle . .	141	10
Music lessons	15	10
Medicine	13	80
Hairdresser	2	40
Presents—family	291	75
,, friends	119	—
Amusements	137	25
Travelling	736	40
Stamps	99	65
Entertaining (at Home) . . .	232	—
Charities [1]	24	—
Subscriptions	119	80
Fire insurance	12	30
Old age insurance . . .	10	40
	8722	20

There are some interesting points about this budget as compared with an English one of £436. It will be seen that although meat is so dear in Germany the weekly butcher's bill for three people was only 6s., fish and poultry together only 2s., and the ham sausage, etc. from the provision shop under 1s. 6d. a week. The washing bill for the year is low, because nearly everything was washed at home, and dear as fuel is in Germany this household spent about £16, where an English one presenting the same front would spend £20 to £25. Observe, too, the amount spent on servants' wages by people who lived in a large charm-

[1] Probably private charities.

ingly furnished flat, and had a long visiting list. The wife, too, a very pretty woman and always well dressed, spent much less on her toilet than anyone would have guessed from its finish and variety, for she came from one of the German cities where women do dress well. There is nearly as much difference amongst German cities in this respect as there is amongst nations. Berlin is far behind either Hamburg or Frankfurt, for instance. The middle-class women of Berlin have an extraordinary affection all through the summer season for collarless blouses, bastard tartans, and white cotton gloves with thumbs but no fingers. In England the force of custom drives women to uncover their necks in the evening, whether it becomes them or not, and it is not a custom for which sensible elderly women can have much to say. But pneumonia blouses have never been universal wear in any country, and it is impossible to explain their apparently irresistible attraction for all ages and sizes of women in the Berlin electric cars. Those who were not wearing pneumonia blouses a year ago were wearing *Reform-Kleider*, shapeless ill-cut garments usually of grey tweed. The oddest combination, and quite a common one, was a sack-like *Reform-Kleid*, with a saucy little coloured bolero worn over it, fingerless gloves, and a madly tilted beflowered hat perched on a dowdy coiffure. These are rude remarks to make about the looks of foreign ladies, but the *Reform-Kleid* is just as hideous and absurd in Germany now as our bilious green draperies were on the wrong people twenty-five years ago, and I am sure every foreigner who came to England must have laughed at them. On the whole, I would say of German women in general what a Frenchwoman once said to me in the most matter-of-fact tone of Englishwomen, *Elles s'habillent si mal.*

CHAPTER XVIII

HOSPITALITY

IF a German cannot afford to ask you to dinner he asks you to supper, and makes his supper inviting. At least, he does if he is sensible, and if he lives where an inexpensive form of entertainment is in vogue. But even in Germany people are not sensible everywhere. The headmaster of a school in a small East Prussian town told me that his colleagues, the higher officials and other persons of local importance, felt bound to entertain their friends at least once a year, and that their way was to invite everyone together to a dinner given at the chief hotel in the town; and that to do this a family would stint itself for months beforehand. He spoke with knowledge, so I record what he said; but I have never been amongst Germans who were hospitable in this painful way. Hotels are used for large entertainments, just as they are in England, but most people receive their friends in their homes, and only hire servants for some special function, like a wedding or a public dinner.

The form of hospitality most popular in England now, the visit of two or three days' duration, is hardly known in Germany, and I believe that they have not begun yet to supply their guests with small cakes of soap labelled "Visitors," and meant to last for a week-end but not longer. In towns no one dreams of having a constant succession of staying guests, and either in town or country when a German family expects a guest at all it is more often than not for the whole summer or winter. You do not find a German girl arranging, as her English cousin will, for a round of visits, fitting in dates, writing here and there to know if people can take her in, and by the same post answering those who are planning a pilgrimage for themselves and wish to be taken. A visit in Germany is not the flighty affair it is with us.

"This winter," says your friend, "my niece from Posen will be with us," and presently the niece arrives and stays about three months. There is rarely more than one spare room on a flat, and that is often a room not easily spared. In country houses there are rows of rooms, but they are not filled by an everlasting procession of guests in the English way. When you stay in a country house at home you wonder how your hosts ever get anything done, and whether they don't sometimes wish they had a few days to themselves. To be sure, English hosts go about their business and leave you to yours, more than Germans think polite. I once spent six weeks, quite an ordinary visit as to length, with some friends who had several grown-up children. It was a most cheerful friendly household, but one day I got into a corner near the stove, rather glad for a change to be myself for a while with a novel for company. When I had been there a little time the second daughter looked in and at once apologised.

"Mamma sent me to see," she explained,—"she feared you were by yourself."

It is not easy to tell your German hosts that you like and wish to be by yourself sometimes ; and if you say that you are used to it in England you won't impress them. The English are so inhospitable and unfriendly, they will say, for that is one of the many popular myths that are believed about us. I have been told of a German lady who has lived here most of her life, and complains to her German friends that she has never spent a night under an English roof; but then, she chooses to associate exclusively with Germans, whose roofs she refuses to regard as English ones, even when they are in Kensington; and she cherishes such an invincible prejudice against the born English that she lives amongst them year after year without making a friend. It would be quite simple to perform the same feat in Paris, or even in Berlin, although there you would not have such a large foreign colony to stand between you and the detestable natives.

The real difficulty in writing about German hospitality is to find and express the ways in which it differs from our own; and certainly these lie little in qualities of kindness and generosity. Amongst both nations, if you have a friendly disposition you will find friends easily, and receive kindness on all sides. Perhaps, as one concrete instance is worth many assertions, I may describe a visit I paid many years ago to a family who invited me because a marriage had recently connected us. I had seen some of the family at the wedding, and had been surprised to receive a warm invitation, not for a week-end and a cake of visitors' soap, but for the rest of the winter; six weeks or two months at least. The family living at home consisted of the parents, a grown-up son and two grown-up daughters. Some of them met me at the station, for the German does not breathe who would let a guest arrive or depart alone. Your friends often give you flowers when you arrive, and invariably when you go away. I cannot remember about the flowers on this occasion, but I remember vividly that the day after my arrival the two married

daughters living in the same town both called on me
and brought me flowers. Week after week, too, they
made it their pleasure to entertain me just as kindly as
my immediate hosts, taking me to concerts or the opera,
asking me to dinner or supper, including me on every
occasion in the family festivities, which were numerous
and lively. In some ways my hosts found me a disappointing guest, and said so. The trouble was that I
liked plain rolls and butter for breakfast, while the
daughters for days before I came had baked every size
and variety of rich cake for me to eat first thing in the
morning with my coffee. I never could eat enough to
please anyone either. You never can in Germany, try
as you may. Yet it was hungry weather, for the Rhine
was frozen hard all the time I was there, and we used
to skate every day in the harbour when the daughters
of the house had finished their morning's work. Two
maids were kept on the flat, but, like most German
servants, they were supposed to require constant supervision, and when a room was turned out the young
ladies in their morning wrappers helped to do it. They
helped with the ironing too and the cooking, and
did all the mending of linen and clothes. " A child's
time belongs to her parents," said the father one day
when the elder daughter wanted to skate, but was told
that she could not be spared. " I've had a heavenly
time," said a girl friend who had been laid up for some
weeks with a sprained ankle ; " I've had nothing to do
but read and amuse myself." The household work,
however, was usually done before the one o'clock dinner,
and the afternoon was given up to skating, walks, and
visits. There were not so many formal calls paid as
in England, but there was a constant interchange of
hospitality amongst the members of the family, the
kind of intimate unceremonious entertaining described

in Miss Austen's novels. Every time one of the
many small children had a birthday there was a
feast of chocolate and cakes, a gathering of the whole
clan. The birthday cake had a sugared *Spruch* on
it, and a little lighted candle for each year of the
child's age, and the birthday table had a present on it
from everyone who came to the party, and many who
did not. Once a week the married daughters and
their husbands came to supper with my hosts, and
every day when they were not coming to supper they
called on their mother, and if she could coax them to
stay drank their afternoon coffee with her. Sometimes
one or two strangers were asked to coffee, for this
household was an old-fashioned one, and gave you
good coffee rather than wishy-washy tea. It made a
point of honour of a *Meringuetorte* when strangers
came, and of the little chocolate cream cakes Germans
call Othellos. But it must not be supposed that one
or two strangers constitute a *Kaffee-Klatsch*, that
celebrated form of entertainment where at every sip
a reputation dies. A genuine *Klatsch* was, however,
given during my stay by a young married woman
who wished to entertain her friends and display her
furniture. About twenty ladies were invited, and when
they had assembled they were solemnly conducted
through every room of the flat from the drawing-room
to the spick-and-span kitchen, where every pan was of
shining copper and every cloth embroidered with the
bride's monogram. The procession as it filed through
the rooms chattered like magpies, for except myself
every member of it had been to school with the bride,
and had helped to adorn her home with embroidered
chair backs, cushions, cloths, newspaper stands, foot-
stools, duster bags, and suchlike, all of which they now
had the pleasure of seeing in the places suitable to

them. By the time we sat down in the dining-room to a table loaded with cakes, the slight frost of arrival had melted away. The strange Englishwoman no longer acted as a wet blanket, and when she tried to converse with her neighbours she found, as she still finds at German entertainments, that she could only do so by screaming at the top of her voice as you do in England in a high wind or in the sound of loud machinery. Everyone was in the highest spirits, and the collective noise they made was amazing. In Germany, when actors play English parts or when people in private life put on English manners, the first thing they do is to lower their voices as if they had met to bury a friend. This is the way our natural manner strikes them, while their natural manner strikes us as easy and jolly, but tiring to the voice and after a time to the spirit. There are quiet Germans, but when they sit at a good man's table they must certainly either shout or be left out of all that goes on. At a *Kaffee-Klatsch* you either shout or whisper, you eat every sort of rich cake presented to you if you can, you drink chocolate or coffee with whipped cream. Nowadays you would often find tea provided instead. When the hostess finds she cannot persuade anyone to eat another cake, she leads her guests back to the drawing-room, and the *Klatsch* goes on. There is often music as well as gossip, and before you are allowed to depart there are more refreshments, ices, sweetmeats, fruit, little glasses of lemonade or *Bowle*. When you get home you do not want any supper, and you are quite hoarse, though you have only been to a simple *Kaffee-Klatsch* without *Schleppe*. Your friends tell you that when they were young a *Kaffee-Klatsch mit Schleppe* was the favourite form of entertaining, and lasted the whole afternoon and evening. Men were asked to

come in when the *Klatsch* was over and a supper was
provided.   Those must have been proud and bustling
days for a *Hausfrau* with one " girl."

To be asked to dinner or supper in Germany may
mean anything.   Either form of invitation varies both
in hour and kind more than it does in England; but
unless you are asked to a dinner that precedes a dance
you hardly ever need evening dress.   Some years ago
you would have written that people never dressed for
dinner in Germany except when the dinner celebrated
a betrothal, a wedding, or some equally important and
unusual event.   But it has become the fashion in
Berlin lately to dress for large dinners and evening
entertainments.   No rule can be laid down for the
guidance of English visitors to Germany, because what
you wear must depend partly on the dinner hour and
partly on the ways of your hosts and their friends.
Last year when I was in Berlin I accepted a formal
invitation sent a fortnight beforehand to a dinner
given on a Sunday at five o'clock.   As the host was
a distinguished scientific man who had just returned
from a journey round the world, it promised to be an
interesting entertainment; and there were, in fact, some
of the most celebrated members of the University
present.   They were all in morning dress, and their
womenfolk wore what we should call Sunday frocks.
The dinner was beautifully cooked and served, and
was not oppressively long.   Soup began it of course,
roast veal with various vegetables followed, fish came
next, lovely little grey-blue fish better to look at than
to eat, then chicken, ice pudding, and dessert.   There
were flowers on the table, but not as many as we should
have with the same opportunities, for the house was
set in an immense garden; and all down the long
narrow table there were bottles of wine and mineral

water. When the champagne came, and that is served at a later stage in Germany than it is with us, speeches of congratulation were made to the host on his safe return, and every guest in reach clinked their glasses with his. After dinner men and women rose together in the German way, and drank coffee in the drawing-room. The men lighted cigars. A little later in the evening slender glasses of beer and lemonade were brought round, and just before everyone left at nine o'clock there was tea and a variety of little cakes and sandwiches, not our double sandwiches, but tiny single slices of buttered roll, each with its scrap of caviare or smoked salmon.

A ball supper or a Christmas supper in Germany consists of three or four courses served separately, and all hot except the sweet, which is usually *Gefrorenes*. Salmon, roast beef or veal, venison or chicken, and then ice would be an ordinary menu, and every course would be divided into portions and handed round on long narrow dishes. In most German towns you are often asked to supper, and very seldom to dinner. You never know beforehand what sort of meal to expect unless you have been to the house before. In some houses it will be hot, in others cold. In Berlin, supper usually offers you a dish made with eggs and mushrooms, eggs and asparagus, or some combination of the kind, and after this the usual variety of ham and sausages fetched from the provision shop. Tea and beer are drunk at this meal in most houses. Sometimes Rhine wine is on the table too. The sweets are often small fruit tartlets served with whipped cream. One menu I remember distinctly, because it was so quaint and full of surprises. We began with huge quantities of asparagus and poached eggs eaten together. Then we had *Pumpernickel*,

Gruyère cheese and radishes, and for a third course
vanilla ice. That was the end of the supper, but later
in the evening, just before we left, in came an enormous
dish covered with gooseberry tartlets, and we had to
eat them, for somehow in Germany it seems ungrateful
and unfriendly not to eat and drink what is provided.

After dinner or supper everyone wishes everyone
else *Mahlzeit*, which is to say, " I wish you a good
digestion." Sometimes people only bow as they say
it, but more often they shake hands. I know an
Englishman who was much puzzled by this ceremony
at his first German dinner-party. He saw everyone
shaking hands as if they were about to disperse the
instant the feast was over, and when his host came
to him with a smiling face, took his hand and mur-
mured *Mahlzeit*, he summoned what German he had
at his command and answered *Gute Nacht.*

CHAPTER XIX

GERMAN SUNDAYS

THERE was to be singing in the forest on Sunday afternoon, we were told, when we arrived at our little Black Forest town; and we were on no account to miss it. We did not want to miss anything, for whenever we looked out of our windows or strolled through the streets we were entertained and enchanted. From the hotel we could see women and girls pass to and fro all day with the great wooden buckets they carried on their backs and filled at the well close by. As dusk fell the oldest woman in the community hobbled out, let down the iron chains slung across the street, and lighted the oil lamps swinging from them. All the gossips of the place gathered at the well of evenings, and throughout the day barefooted children played there. Behind the main street there were gabled houses with ancient wooden balconies and gardens crammed with pinks. The population mostly sat out of doors after dark, and as it was hot weather no one went to bed early. Even in the dead of night the timber waggons drawn by oxen passed through the town, and the driver did his best to wake us by cracking his long whip. For though a Black Forest town is mediæval in its ways, it is not restful. It may soothe you by suggestion, the people seem so leisurely and the life so easy going; but there is not an hour in the twenty-four when you are secure from noise. The Sunday in question began with the bustle occasioned in a country inn by an unusual strain on its resources. There must be an extra good dinner for the expected influx of guests, said the landlord's niece, who kept house for him, while the wife and daughters ran a second hotel higher up the valley. We escaped to the forest, where the morning hours of a hot June day were fresh and scented, and we were sorry we had to return to the hotel for a long hot midday dinner. When it was over, we sat in the garden and wondered why people held a festival on the top of a hill on such a sleepy afternoon. However, when the time came we joined the leisurely procession making the ascent. An hour's stroll took us to the concert hall, a forest glade where people sat about in groups waiting for the music to begin. Barrels of beer had been rolled up here, and children were selling *Kringel*, crisp twists of bread sprinkled with salt. There were more children present than adults, and we observed, as you nearly always will in Germany, that though they belonged to the poorer classes they wore neat clothes and had quiet, modest manners. The older people often let them drink out of their glasses, for it was a thirsty afternoon, and when the singing began the children joined in some of the songs. The occasion of the festival was the friendly meeting of several choirs, and they sang fine anthems as well as *Volkslieder*. The effect of the music in the heart of the forest was enchanting, and we stayed till the end. These choral competitions or reunions often take place on a Sunday in Germany, and in summer are often held in an inn garden. They bring some custom to the innkeeper, but drunkenness and disorder are almost unknown. In fact, all the cases of drunkenness I have seen in Germany have been

in the Munich comic papers. You never by any
chance hear of it as you do in England amongst
people you know, and you may spend hours at the
Berlin Zoo on a Whit-Monday and see no one who is
not sober. University students get drunk and have
fights with innkeepers and policemen, but that is
etiquette rather than vice. Next day they suffer from
Katzenjammer, but feel that they are upholding ancient
tradition. Real intemperance is found almost entirely
amongst the dregs of the big cities and the lowest
class of peasants.

In Berlin the better class of artisans and small
tradespeople escape from their flats on Sundays to their
allotment gardens. You see whole tracts of these
gardens on the outskirts of the city, and many of them
have some kind of summer house or rough shelter.
Here the family spends the whole day in fresher air,
and presumably finds out how to grow the simpler
kinds of flowers and vegetables. Those who have no
garden and can afford a few pence for fares go farther
afield. They carry food for the day in tin satchels, or
rolls that look as if they ought to accompany butterfly
nets and contain entomological specimens. But they
are usually in the hands of a stout alpaca-clad
middle-class mater-familias, who looks rather anxious
and flustered while she herds her flock and hunts for a
garden with the announcement, " Hier können Familien
Kaffee kochen." There for a trifling indemnity she
can be accommodated with seats, cups and saucers,
and hot water; just as people can in an English tea-
garden. Provisions she has with her in her *Pickenick
Rolle*. If fate takes you to Potsdam on a fine
summer Sunday, you will think that the whole
bourgeoisie of Berlin has elected to come by the same
train and steamer, and that everyone but you has

brought food for the day in a green tin. You need not expect to find a seat either in the train or the steamer at certain hours of the day, and as you stand wedged in the crowd on the dangerously overladen boat, and look about you as best you can at the chain of wooded lakes, you wonder how it is that such overcrowding is permitted in a police-governed land. At home we take such things for granted as part of our system or want of system. But in Germany the moment you cross the frontier a thousand trifles make you feel that you are a unit in an army, drilled and kept under by the bureaucracy and the police. It surprises you to see an unmanageable crowd in a train or on a steamer, much as it would surprise you to see soldiers swarm at will into a troopship. You expect them to march precisely, each man to his place. And in Germany this nearly always happens in civil life; while even on a Sunday or a public holiday the mob behaves itself. At the Berlin Zoo, for instance, there are such masses of people every Sunday that you see nothing but people. It is impossible, or rather would not be agreeable, to force your way through the crowd surrounding the cages. But the people are interesting, and it is to see them that you have ventured here. You soon find, however, that it is not a venture at all. No one will offend you, no one is drunken or riotous. The gardens are packed with decent folk, mostly of the lower middle classes, and the only unseemly thing you see them do is to eat small hot sausages with their fingers in the open-air restaurants.

Sunday is the great day of the week at German theatres. In all the large towns there are afternoon performances at popular prices, and this means that people who can pay a few pence for a seat can see all the great classical plays and most of the successful modern ones; and they can hear many of the great operas as well as a variety of charming light ones never heard in this country. On one Sunday afternoon in Berlin, Hoffmann's *Erzählungen* was played at one theatre, and at others Gorky's *Nachtasyl*, Tolstoy's *Power of Darkness*, Hauptmann's *Versunkene Glocke*, the well known military play *Zapfenstreich*, and Lortzing's light opera *Der Waffenschmied*. The star players and singers do not usually appear at these popular performances, and the Wagnerian *Ring* has, as far as I know, never yet been given. But on Sunday afternoons all through the winter the playhouses are crowded with people who cannot pay week-day prices, and yet are intelligent enough to enjoy a fairly good performance of *Hamlet* or *Egmont*; who are musical and choose a Mozart opera; or who are interested in the problems of life presented by Ibsen, Gorky, Tolstoy, or their own great fellow-countryman Gerhardt Hauptmann. When summer comes, as long as the theatres are open the whole audience streams out between the acts to have coffee or beer in the garden, or when there is no garden, in the nearest restaurant; and then comes your chance of appraising the people who take their pleasure in this way. They look for the most part as if they belonged to the small official and shop-keeper class. If the play is a suitable one, there are sure to be a great many young people present, and at the State-supported theatres these Sunday performances are such as young people are allowed to see.

In the evening the Sunday play or opera is always one of the most important of the week; the play everyone wishes to see or the opera that is most attractive. A Wagner opera is often played on a Sunday evening in the theatre that undertakes Wagner. The smaller stages will give some old favourite, *Der*

14

Freischütz, Don Juan, Oberon, or *Die Zauberflöte.* In
fact, all through the winter the upper and middle classes
make the play and the opera their favourite Sunday
pastime. The lower classes depend a good deal on
the public dancing saloons, which seem to do as much
harm as our public-houses, and to be disliked and discouraged by all sensible Germans.

So far this account of a German Sunday suggests
that Germans always go from home for their weekly
holiday, and it is true that when Sunday comes the
German likes to amuse himself. But he is not
invariably at the play or in inn gardens. It is the
day when scattered members of a family will meet
most easily, and when the branch of the family that
can best do so will entertain the others. Some years
ago in a North German city I was often with friends
who had a dining-room and narrow dinner table long
enough for a hotel. The host and hostess, when they
were by themselves, dined in a smaller room, sitting
next to each other on the sofa ; but on Sundays their
children and grandchildren, some spinster cousins, some
Stammgäste (old friends who came every week) all met
in the drawing-room at five o'clock, and sat down soon
after to a dinner of four or five courses in a long dining-
room. It was a company of all ages and some variety
of station, and the patriarchal arrangement placed the
venerable and beloved host and hostess side by side at
the top of the room, with their friends in order of importance to right and left of them, until you came,
below the salt as it were, to the Mamsells and the little
children at the foot of the table. But the Mamsells did
not leave the room when the sweets arrived. Everyone
ate everything, including the preserved fruits that came
round with the roast meat, and the pudding that
arrived after the cheese. In those days it was not

considered proper in Germany for ladies to eat cheese, and no young lady would dream of taking one of the little glasses of Madeira offered on a tray. They were exclusively for *die Herren*, and always gave a fillip to the conversation, which was also more or less a masculine monopoly. Just before the end of the dinner it was the business of the Mamsell belonging to the house to light a little army of Vienna coffee machines standing ready on the sideboard, so that coffee could be served when everyone went back to the drawing-room. The men smoked their cigars there too, and someone would play the piano, and when no music was going on there was harmless, rather dull, family conversation. The spinster cousins got out their embroidery, the Mamsells disappeared with the children, *die Herren* either talked to each other or had a quiet game of *Skat*. The women and some of the men had been to church in the morning, but this did not prevent them from spending the rest of the day as it pleased them.

It will be seen that from the English point of view Sunday is not observed at all in Germany; yet this does not mean, as is often announced from English pulpits, that the whole nation is without religion. Unbelief is more widely professed than here, and many people who call themselves Christians openly reject certain vital doctrines of Evangelical faith,—are Unitarians, in fact, but will not say so. But the whole question of religious belief in Germany is a difficult and contentious one, for according to the people you meet you will be told that the nation lacks faith or possesses it. If you use your own judgment you must conclude that there is immensely more scepticism there than here, and that there is also a good deal of vague belief, a belief, that is, in a personal God and a life after death. But you must admit that except in an "evangelical" set belief sits lightly on both men and women. Certainly it has nothing to do with the way they spend Sunday, and if they go to church in the morning they are as likely as not to go to the theatre in the afternoon. They sew, they dance, they fiddle, they act, they travel on the day of rest, more on that day than on any other, and when they come to England there is nothing in our national life they find so tedious and unprofitable as our Sundays. They cannot understand why a people with so strong a tendency to drink should make the public-house the only counter attraction to the church on the working man's day of leisure; and when they are in a country place, and see our groups of idle, aimless young louts standing about not knowing what to do, they ask why in the name of common sense they should not play an outdoor game. The Idealist expresses the German point of view very well in her Memoirs, and in so far as she misunderstands our English point of view she is only on a line with those amongst us who denounce the continental Sunday as an orgy of noisy and godless pleasures. She says: " I had a thousand opportunities of noticing that the religious life did not mean a deep life-sanctifying belief, but simply one of those formulas that are a part of 'respectability,' as they understand it both in the family and in society. Nothing proves this better than their truly shocking way of keeping holy the Sabbath day, which is the very reverse of holy, inasmuch as it paves the way to the heaviest boredom and slackness of spirit. I have been in English houses on Sundays where the gentlemen threw themselves from one easy chair to the other, and proclaimed their empty state of mind by their awful yawns; where the children wandered about hopelessly depressed, because they might neither play nor read an amusing book, not even Grimm's *Fairy Tales*; where all the mental enjoyment of the household consisted of so-called 'sacred music,' which some young miss strummed on the piano or, worse still, sang. A young girl once spoke to me in severe terms about the Germans who visit theatres and concerts on Sundays. I asked her whether, if she put it to her conscience, she could honestly say that she had holier feelings and higher thoughts, whether, in fact, she felt herself a better human being on her quiet Sunday, than when she heard a Beethoven Symphony, saw a Shakespeare play, or any other noble work of art. She confessed with embarrassment that she could not say so, but nevertheless arrived at the logical conclusion that, for all that, it was very wicked of the Germans not to keep Sunday more holy. Another lady, a cultured liberal-minded person, invited me once to go with her to the Temple Church, one of the oldest and most beautiful London churches in the city, belonging to the great labyrinth of Temple Bar where English justice has its seat. The music of the Temple Church is famous, and I had expressed a wish to hear it. So I went with my house-mate and the lady in question, and sat between them. During the sermon I had great trouble not to fall asleep, but fought against it for the sake of decorum. To my surprise, when I glanced at my right-hand neighbour I saw that she was fast asleep, and when I glanced at the one on my left I saw that she was asleep too. I looked about at other people, and saw more than one sunk in a pious Nirvana. As we left the church I asked the Englishwoman, who had a strong sense of humour, whether she had slept well. 'Yes,' she said, laughing, 'it did me a lot of good.' 'But why do you go?' I said. 'Oh, my dear,' said she, 'what can one do? It has to be on Sundays.'

" But this narrow Sunday observance is worse for the lower than for the upper classes. At that time the great dispute was just beginning as to whether the people should be admitted to the Crystal Palace, to museums, and suchlike institutions. The question was discussed in Parliament, and decided in the negative. It was feared that the churches would remain empty, and that morals would suffer if the people began to like heathen gods, works of art and natural curiosities, better than going to church. At least, this is the only explanation one can give of such a decision. The churches and the public-houses remained the only public places open on Sundays. The churches were all very well for a few hours in the morning, but what about the afternoon and evening? Then the beer-house was the only refuge for the artisan or proletarian bowed down by the weight of hard work, unused and untaught to wile away the idle hours of Sunday in any intellectual occupation, and having no friendly attractive home to make the peace of his own hearth the best refreshment after the exhausting week. And so it turned out : the public-houses were full to overflowing, and the holiness of Sunday was only too often dese-crated by the unholy sight of drunken men and, more horrible still, drunken women ; but this was not all, for so strong was the temptation thrust upon them, that the workman's hardly earned week's wages went in drink, and the children were left without bread and not a penny was saved to lighten future distress. The coarse animal natures of the only half-human beings became coarser and more animal through the degrading passion for drink that only too often has murder in its train, and murder in its most terrible and brutal guise ! "

There is not one idea or argument in this passage

that I have not heard over and over again from the lips of every German who has anything to say about our English Sunday, and every German who has been in England or heard much of English life invariably attacks what he considers this weak joint in our armour.

"What is the use?" he asks, "of going to church in the morning if you get drunk and beat your wife at night?"

"But the same man does not usually do both things in one day," you represent to him. "One set of people goes to church and keeps Sunday strictly, and another set goes to public-houses and is drunk and disorderly. You should try to get out of your head your idea that we are all exactly alike."

"But you are—exactly alike. Everyone of you goes to church with a solemn face, sings psalms, and comes back to his roast beef and apple-pie. All the afternoon you are asleep; and at night the streets and parks are not fit for respectable people."

"At night," you explain, "all the respectable people are at home eating cold beef and cold pie. The others . . ."

"The others you drive to drink and fight and kill by your pharisaical methods. You shut the doors of your theatres and your art galleries, and you set wide the doors of your drinking hells. How you can call yourself a religious people—it is Satanic . . ."

"But, my dear man," you say, taking a long breath, "the people who go to public-houses don't want theatres and art galleries. They are on too low a level."

"It is the business of the State to raise them—not to push them down. Besides, there is drinking—much drinking—in England on the higher levels too, as you well know . . ."

" Of course I know," you say impatiently. " All I am saying is that we do not bring it about by shutting the British Museum on Sundays."

But next time the subject comes up for discussion your German will say again, as he has said ever since he could speak, that the English Sunday is anathema, and a standing witness to British *Heuchelei*, because people sing psalms in the morning and get drunk and beat their wives at night. You can easily imagine the Hypocrite's Progress painted by a German Hogarth, and it would begin with a gentleman in a black coat and tall hat on his way to church, and would end with the same gentleman in the last stage of delirium tremens surrounded by his slaughtered family. For in Germany one of the curious deep rooted notions about us, who as people go are surely indifferent honest, is that we are *ein falsches Volk*. With the want of logic that makes human nature everywhere so entertaining, a German will nearly always cash a cheque offered by an English stranger when he would refuse to do so for a country-man. As far as one can get at it, what Germans really mean by our *Heuchelei* when they speak without malice is our regard for the unwritten social law. This is so strong in us from old habit and tradition that most of us do not feel the shackles ; but the stranger within our gates feels it at every step.

CHAPTER XX

SPORT AND GAMES

THE word Sport has been taken into the German language lately, but Germans use it when we should use "hobby." "It is my sport," says an artist when he shows you furniture of his own design. He means that his business in life is to paint pictures, but his pleasure is to invent beautiful chairs and tables. When the talk turns on the absurd extreme to which the Marthas of Germany carry their housekeeping zeal, a German friend will turn to you in defence of his countrywomen. "It is their 'sport,'" says he, and you understand his point of view. Yet another will tell you that the English have only become sportsmen in modern times, and that the Germans are rapidly catching them up; but this is the kind of information you receive politely, disagree with profoundly, and do not discuss because you have not all the facts at your fingers' ends. But you know that the British love of sport, be it vice or virtue, is as ingrained in Britons as their common sense, and as old as their history.

In Germany the country gentleman is a sportsman. He rides, he shoots, he hunts the wild boar which he preserves in his great forests. "You have no country (*Land*)," said a German to me, using the word as opposed to town. In Germany we have country still." He meant that England is thickly populated, and that we have no vast tracts of heath and forest where wild animals live undisturbed. I told him there were a few such places still in Scotland, but that they all belonged to American and Jewish millionaires; however, he would not believe it. He said he had spent a fortnight in England and had not heard of them.

It is not such a matter of course with Germans of a certain class to ride as it is with us. You see a few men, women, and children on horseback in Berlin, but not many; and in most German towns you see no one riding except cavalry officers. I am told that the present Emperor tried to institute a fashionable hour for riding in the Tiergarten, but that it fell through partly because there were not enough people to bring decent carriages and horses. On the great estates in East Prussia the women as well as the men of the family ride, and go great distances in this way to see their friends; but in cities you cannot fail to observe the miserable quality and condition of the horses and the scarcity of private carriages. In fact, the German does not make as much of animals as the Englishman does. If he lives in the country, or if he means to be a man of fashion, he will have dogs and horses, but he will not have one or both, by hook or by crook, whether he is rich or poor, as the Briton does. You see dogs in any German city that remind you of a paragraph that once appeared in an Italian paper, a paragraph about a case of dog stealing. The dog was produced in court, said the paper, and was either a fox terrier or a Newfoundland. But you often see a fine Dachs; in Heidelberg the students are proud of their great boar-hounds, and in the Black Forest there are numbers of little black Pomeranians.

In German towns where there is water, the traffic on it both for business and amusement is as busy as with us, and in some respects better managed. Hamburg life, for instance, is largely on the basin of the Alster; either in the little steamers that carry you from city to suburb, or in the small craft that crowd its waters on a summer night. It is as usual in Hamburg as on the Thames to own boats and understand their management, and there are the same varieties to be seen there: the pleasure boats with people of all ages, the racing outrigger full of strenuous, lightly clad young men, and the little sail boats scurrying across the water before the breeze. On the Rhine the big steamers do a roaring traffic all the summer, and catch the public that likes a good dinner with their scenery; and on the Rhine, as well as on most of the other rivers of Germany, there are a great many swimming baths; for every German who has a chance learns to swim. In Hamburg on a summer evening you meet troops of little boys and girls going to the baths, many of them belonging to the poorer classes; for where there are no swimming baths attached to the school they get tickets free or at a very low rate. About fishing I can only speak from hearsay, for I have never caught a minnow myself, but I have met Germans who are keen anglers, and I have found that they knew every London shop beloved of anglers, and the English name of every fly.

Germans get more amusement out of their waterways in winter than we do, for the winters there are long and hard, so that there is always skating. I have seen the Alster frozen for weeks, and the whole city of Hamburg playing on the ice. It was not what we call good ice, and not what we call good skating. For the most part people were content to get over the ground, to mix with their friends, to have hot drinks at the booths that sprang up in long lines by the chief track, and even to stroll about without skates and watch the fun. All classes, all ages, and both sexes skate nowadays, but some fifty or sixty years ago German ladies were not seen on the ice at all. Skating, like most exercises that are healthy and agreeable, was considered unfeminine, and men had the fun to themselves. In the mountain districts of Germany winter sports are growing in favour every year, and people go to the Riesengebirge or to the Black Forest for tobogganing and ski-ing. The German illustrated papers constantly have articles about these winter pastimes, and portraits of the distinguished men and women who took part in them. The history of cycling in Germany is not unlike its history here. The boom subsided some years ago, but a steady industry survives. In Berlin you see officers in uniform on bicycles, but you see hardly any ladies. That is because the Emperor and Empress disapprove of cycling for women, and their disapproval has made it unfashionable. Ten years ago, two years, that is, after the English boom, no woman on a bicycle had ever been seen in the remoter valleys of the Black Forest. One who ventured there used to be followed by swarms of wondering children, who wished her *All Heil* at the top of their voices. They did not heave bricks at her.

Tennis has not been blighted by the imperial frown, and is extremely popular in Germany. Hockey, as far as I know, is not played yet; certainly not by women. Cricket and football are played, but not very much. An Englishman teaching at a gymnasium, told me that the authorities discouraged outdoor games, as they were considered waste of time. Gymnastics is the form of athletics really enjoyed and practised

by Germans. Every boy, even every girl, begins them
at school, and the boy when he leaves school joins
a *Turnverein*. For wherever Germans foregather,
and whatever they do, you may be sure they have
a *Verein*, and that the *Verein* has feasts in winter
and *Ausflüge* in summer. When a man is young
and lusty, the delights of the *Verein*, the *Ausflug*,
the feast, and the walking tour are often combined.
You meet a whole gang of pleasure pilgrims ascending
the broad path that leads to the restaurant on the
top of a German mountain, or you encounter them
in the restaurant itself making speeches to the honour
and glory of their *Verein*; and you find that they
are the gymnasts or the fire brigade, or the architects or what not of an adjacent town, and that once
a year they make an excursion together, beginning
with a walk or a journey by rail or by steamer, and
culminating in a restaurant where they dine and drink
and speechify. Every age, every trade, and every
pastime has its *Verein* and its anniversary rites. I
was much amused and puzzled in Berlin one afternoon
by a procession that filed slowly past the tram in which
I sat, and was preceded and attended by such a rabble
of sightseers that the ordinary traffic was stopped for
a time. I thought at first it was a demonstration in
connection with temperance or teetotalism, because
there were so many broad blue ribbons about, and
I was surprised, because I know that Germans club
together to drink beer and not to abstain from it,
and that they are a sober nation. At the head of
the procession came a string of boys on bicycles, each
boy carrying a banner. Then came four open carriages
garlanded with flowers. There was a garland round
each wheel, as well as round the horses' necks and
the coachmen's hats, and anywhere else where a

garland would rest. In each carriage sat four damsels robed in white, and they wore garlands instead of hats. After them walked a large, stout, red-faced man in evening dress, and he carried a staff. After him walked the music, men puffing and blowing into brass instruments, and, like their leader, wearing evening dress and silk hats. They were followed by a procession that seemed as if it would stretch to the moon, a procession of elderly, portly men all wearing evening dress, all wearing broad blue ribbons and embroidered scarves, and all marching with banners bearing various devices. The favourite device was *Heil Gambrinus*, and when I saw that I knew that the blue ribbons had nothing to do with total abstention. The next banner explained things. It was the *Verein* of the *Schénkwirte* of Berlin,—the publicans, in fact, of Berlin having their little holiday.

All through the summer the German nation amuses itself out of doors, and leads an outdoor life to an extent unknown and impossible in our damp climate. A house that has a garden nearly always has a garden room where all meals are served. Sometimes it is a detached summer house, but more often it opens from the house and is really a big verandah with a roof and sides of glass. In country places the inn gardens are used as dining-rooms from morning till night, and you may if you choose have everything you eat and drink brought to you out of doors. Most inns have a skittle alley, for skittles are still played in Germany by all classes. The peasants play it on Sunday afternoons, and the dignified merchant has his skittle club and spends an evening there once a week. The favourite card game of Germany is still *Skat*, but bridge has been heard of and will probably supersede it in time. *Skat* is a good game for three players, with a system of

scoring that seems intricate till you have played two
or three times and got used to it. In Germany it is
always *die Herren* who play these serious games, while
the women sit together with their bits of embroidery.
At the Ladies' Clubs in Berlin there is some card
playing, but these two or three highly modern and
emancipated establishments do not call the tune for all
Germany. Directly you get away from Berlin you find
that men and women herd separately, far more than in
England, take their pleasures separately, and have fewer
interests in common. It is still the custom for the
man of the family to go to a beer-house every day,
much as an Englishman goes to his club. Here he
meets his friends, sees the papers, talks, smokes, and
drinks his *Schoppen*. Each social grade will have its
own haunts in this way, or its own reserved table in a
big public room. At the Hof Braühaus in Munich
one room is set apart for the Ministers of State, and
I was told some years ago that the appointments of it
were just as plain and rough as those in the immense
public hall where anyone who looked respectable could
have the best beer in the world and a supper of
sorts.

It is dull uphill work to write about sport and outdoor games in Germany, because you may have been
in many places and met a fair variety of people without seeing any enthusiasm for either one or the other.
The bulk of the nation is, as a matter of fact, not
interested in sport or in any outdoor games except
indifferent tennis, swimming, skating, and in some
places boating. When a German wants to amuse himself, he sits in a garden and listens to a good band; if
he is young and energetic, he walks on a well-made
road to a restaurant on the top of a hill. In winter he
plays skat, goes to the theatre or to a concert, or has

his music at home. Also he reads a great deal, and he reads in several tongues. This, at any rate, is the way of Germans in cities and summer places, and it is a very small proportion of the educated classes who lead what we call a country life. " Elizabeth " knows German country life, and describes it in her charming books ; perhaps she will some day choose to tell us how the men in her part of the world amuse themselves, and whether they are good sportsmen. I must confess that I have only once seen a German in full sporting costume. It was most impressive, though, a sort of pinkish grey bound everywhere with green, and set off by a soft felt hat and feathers. As we were having a walk with him, and it was early summer, we ventured to ask him what he had come to kill. " Bees," said he, and killed one the next moment with a pop-gun.

CHAPTER XXI

INNS AND RESTAURANTS

ENGLISH people who have travelled in Germany know some of the big well-kept hotels in the large towns, and know that they are much like big hotels in other continental cities. It is not in these establishments that you can watch national life or discover much about the Germans, except that they are good hotel-keepers; and this you probably discovered long ago abroad or at home. If you are a woman, you may be impressed by the fineness, the whiteness, the profusion, and the embroidered monograms of the linen, whether you are in a huge caravanserai or a wayside inn. Otherwise a hotel at Cologne or Heidelberg has little to distinguish it from a hotel at Brussels or Bâle. The dull correct suites of furniture, the two narrow bedsteads, even the table with two tablecloths on it, a thick and a thin, the parqueted floor, and the small carpet are here, there, and everywhere directly you cross the Channel.

The modern German tells you with pride that this apparent want of national quality and colour is to be felt in every corner of life, and that what you take to be German is not peculiarly German at all, but common to the whole continent of Europe. This may be true in certain cases and in a certain sense, but there is another sense in which it is never true. For instance,

15

the women of continental nations wear high - necked gowns in the evening. It is only English women who wear evening gowns as a matter of course every day of their lives. I have been told in Germany that, so far from being a sign of civilisation, this fashion is merely a stupid survival from the times when all the women of Europe went barenecked all day. However this may be, there is no doubt that whether the gown be high or low, worn by sunlight or lamplight, you can see at a glance whether the woman who wears it is English, French, or German. Every nation has its own features, its own manners, and its own tone, instantly recognised by foreigners, and apparently hidden from itself. The German assures you that the English manner is quite unmistakable, and he will even describe and imitate for your amusement some of his silly countryfolk who were talking to him quite naturally, but suddenly froze and stiffened at the approach of English friends whose national manner they wished to assume. In England we are not conscious of having a stiff frozen manner, and we never dream that everyone has the same manner. It takes a foreigner to perceive this ; and so in Germany it takes a foreigner to appreciate and even to see the character- istic trifles that give a nation a complexion of its own.

Some of the most comfortable hotels in Germany are the smaller ones supported entirely by Germans. A stray Englishman, finding one of these starred in Baedeker and put in the second class, may try it from motives of economy, but in many of them he would only meet merchants on their travels and the unmarried men of the neighbourhood who dine there. In such establishments as these the *table d'hôte* still more or less prevails, while if you go to fashionable hotels you dine at small tables nowadays and see nothing of your neighbours. The part played during dinner by the hotel proprietor varies considerably. In a big establishment he is represented by the *Oberkellner*, and does not appear at all. The *Oberkellner* is a person of weight and standing; so much so that when you are in a crowded beer garden and can get no one to attend to you, you call out *Ober* to the first boy waiter who passes, and he is so touched by the compliment that he serves you before your turn. But in a real old-fashioned German inn you have personal relations with the proprietor, for he takes the head of his table and attends to the comfort of his customers as carefully as if they were his guests. This used to be a universal custom, but you only find it observed now in the Sleepy Hollows of Germany. I have stayed in a most comfortable and well-managed hotel where the proprietor and his brother waited on their guests all through dinner, but never sat down with them. There were hired men, but they played a subordinate part. In small country inns the host still arrives in the garden when your meal is served, asks if you have all you want, wishes you *guten Appetit*, and after a little further conversation waddles away to perform the same office at some other table. Except in the depths of the country where the inn - keepers are peasants, a German hotel-keeper invariably speaks several languages, and has usually been in Paris and London or New York. His business is to deal with the guests and the waiters, and to look after the cellar and the cigars; while his wife or his sister, though she keeps more in the background than a French proprietress, does just as much work as a Frenchwoman, and, as far as one can judge, more than any man in the establishment. She superintends the chambermaids and has entire care of the vast stock of linen; in many cases she has most of it washed on the premises, and she helps to iron and repair it. She buys the provisions, and sees that there is neither waste nor disorder in the kitchen; she often does a great part of the actual cooking herself. When I was a girl I happened to spend a winter in a South German hotel of old standing, kept for several generations in the same family, and now managed by two brothers and a sister. The sister, a well-educated young woman of twenty-five, used to get up at five winter and summer to buy what was wanted for the market, and one day she took me with her. It was a pretty lesson in the art of housekeeping as it is understood and practised in Germany. All the peasant women in the duchy could not have persuaded my young woman to have given the fraction of a farthing more for her vegetables than they were worth that day, or to take any geese except the youngest and plumpest. She went briskly from one part of the market to the other, seeming to see at a glance where it was profitable to deal this morning. She did not haggle or squabble as inferior housewives will, because she knew just what she wanted and what it was prudent to pay for it. When she got home she sat down to a second breakfast that seemed to me like a dinner, a stew of venison and half a bottle of light wine; but, as she said, hotel keeping is exhausting work, and hotel-keepers must needs live well.

At some hotels in this part of Germany wine is included in the charge for dinner, and given to each guest in a glass carafe or uncorked bottle. It is kept on tap even in the small wayside inns, where you get half a litre for two or three pence when you are out for a walk and are thirsty. If you dislike thin sour wine you had better avoid the grape - growing lands and travel in Bavaria, where every country inn-keeper brews his own beer. Many of these small inns entertain summer visitors, not English and Americans who want luxuries, but their own countryfolk, whose purses and requirements are both small. As far as I know by personal experience and by hearsay, the rooms in these inns are always clean. The bedding all over Germany is most scrupulously kept and aired. In country places you see the mattresses and feather beds hanging out of the windows near the pots of carnations every sunny day. The floors are painted, and are washed all over every morning. The curtains are spotless. In each room there is the inevitable sofa with the table in front of it, a most sensible and comfortable addition to a bedroom, enabling you to seek peace and privacy when you will. If you wander far enough from the beaten track, you may still find that all the water you are supposed to want is contained in a good-sized glass bottle; but if you are English your curious habits will be known, and more water will be brought to you in a can or pail. My husband and I once spent a summer in a Thuringian inn that had never taken staying guests before, and even here we found that the proprietress had heard of English ways, and was willing, with a smile of benevolent amusement, to fill a travelling bath every day. This inn had a summer house where all our meals were served as a matter of course, and where people from a fashionable watering-place in the next valley came for coffee or beer sometimes. The household itself consisted of the proprietress, her daughter, and her maidservant, and during the four months we spent there I never knew them to sit down to a regular meal. They ate anything at any time, as they fancied it. The summer house in which we had our meals was large and pleasant, with a wide view of the hills and a near one of an old stone bridge and a trout stream. The trees near the inn were limes, and their scent while they were in flower overpowered the scent of pines coming at other times with strength and fragrance from the surrounding forest. The only drawback to our comfort was a hornets' nest in an old apple-tree close to the summer-house. The hornets used to buzz round us at every meal, and at first we supposed they might sting us. This they never did, though we waged war on them fiercely. But no one wants to be chasing and killing hornets all through breakfast and dinner, so we asked the maid of the inn what could be done to get rid of them. She smiled and said *Jawohl*, which was what she always said; and we went out for a walk. When we came back and sat down to supper there were no hornets. *Jawohl* had just stood on a chair, she said, poured a can of water into the nest, and stuffed up the opening with grass. She had not been stung, and we were not pestered by a hornet again that summer. I have sometimes told this story to English people, and seen that though they were too polite to say so they did not believe it. But that is their fault. The story as I have told it is true. We found immense numbers of hornets in one wild uninhabited valley where we sometimes walked that summer, but we were never stung.

The proprietress of this inn, like most German women, was a fair cook. Besides the inn she owned a small brewery, and employed a brewer who lived quite near, and showed us the whole process by which he transferred the water of the trout stream into foaming beer. His mistress had no rival in the village, and the village was a small one, so sometimes the beer was a little flat. When *Jawohl* brought a jug from a cask just broached, she put it on the table with a proud air, and informed us that it was *frisch angesteckt*. We once spent a summer in a Bavarian village where a dozen inns brewed their own beer, and it was always known which one had just tapped a cask. Then everyone crowded there as a matter of course. In all these country inns there is one room with rough wooden tables and benches, and here the peasants sit smoking their long pipes and emptying their big mugs or glasses, and as a rule hardly speaking. They do not get drunk, but no doubt they spend more than they can afford out of their scanty earnings.

In the Bavarian village the inns were filled all through the summer with people from Nuremberg, Erlangen, Augsburg, Erfurth, and other Bavarian towns. The inn-keeper used to charge five shillings a week for a scrupulously clean, comfortably furnished room, breakfast was sixpence, dinner one and two-pence, and supper as you ordered it. For dinner they gave you good soup, *Rindfleisch*, either poultry or roast meat, and one of the *Mehlspeisen* for which Bavaria is celebrated, some dish, that is, made with eggs and flour. There was a great variety of them, but I only remember one clearly, because I was impressed by its disreputable name. It was some sort of small pancake soaked in a wine sauce, and it was called *versoffene Jungfern*. Most of these inns kept no servants, and except in the Kurhaus there was not a black-coated waiter in the place. Our inn-keeper tilled his own fields, grew his own hops, and brewed his own beer; and his wife, wearing her peasant's costume, did all the cooking and cleaning, assisted by a daughter or a cousin. When you met her out of doors she would be carrying one of the immense loads peasant women do carry up hill and down dale in Germany. She was hale and hearty in her middle age, and always cheerful and obliging. At that inn, too, we never had a meal indoors from May till October. Everything was brought out to a summer-house, from which we looked straight down the village, its irregular Noah's Ark-like houses, and its background of mountains and forest.

When you first get back to England from Germany, you have to pull yourself together and remember that in your own country, even on a hot still summer evening, you cannot sit in a garden where a band is playing and have your dinner in the open air, unless you happen to be within reach of Earl's Court. In German towns there are always numbers of restaurants in which, according to the weather, meals can be served indoors or out. You see what use people make of them if, for instance, you happen to be in Hamburg on a hot summer night. All round the basin of the Alster there are houses, hotels, and gardens, and every public garden is so crowded that you wonder the waiters can pass to and fro. Bands are playing, lights are flashing, the little sailing boats are flitting about. The whole city after its day's work has turned out for air and music and to talk with friends. And as you watch the scene you know that in every city, even in every village of the empire, there is some such gala going on : in gardens going down to the Rhine from the old Rhenish towns; in the gardens of ancient castles set high above the stifling air of valleys; in the forest that comes to the very edge of so many little German towns; even in the streets of towns where a table set on the pavement will be pleasanter than in a room on such a night as this. You can sit at one of these restaurants and order nothing but a cup of coffee or a glass of beer ; or you can dine, for the most part, well and cheaply. If you order a *halbe Portion* of any dish, as Germans do, you will be served with more than you can eat of it. The variety offered by some of the restaurants in the big cities, the excellence of the cooking, the civilisation of the appointments, and the service, all show that the German must be the most industrious creature in the world, and the thriftiest and one of the cleverest. In London we have luxurious restaurants for people who can spend a great deal of money, but in Berlin they have them for people who cannot spend much. That is the difference between the two cities. How Berlin does it is a mystery. In the restaurants I have seen there is neither noise nor bustle nor garish colours nor rough service nor any other of the miseries we find in our own cheap eating-houses. In one of them the walls were done in some kind of plain fumed wood with a frieze and ceiling of soft dull gold. In another each room had a different scheme of colour.

"So according to your *Stimmung* you will choose your room," said the friends who took me. "To-night we are rather cheerful. We will go to the big room on the first floor. That is all pale green and ivory."

"You have nothing like this in England," said the artist as we went up the lift. "It is terrible in England. When I asked for my lunch at three or four o'clock I was told that lunch was over. *Das hat keinen Zweck*,—I want my lunch when I am hungry."

"But you are terribly behindhand in some ways in Berlin," I said, for I knew the artist liked an argument. "In London you can shop all through the night by telephone. It is most convenient."

"Have you ever done it?"

"I'm not on the telephone, and I am generally asleep at night. But other people . . ."

" *Verrückt*," said the artist. " Who in his senses wants to do shopping at night ? Now look at this room, and admit that you have nothing at all like it."

The first swift impression of the place was that Liberty had brought his stuffs, his furniture, and his glass from London and set up as a restaurateur in Berlin. The whole thing was certainly well done. It was not as florid and fussy as our expensive restaurants. The colours were quiet, and the necessary draperies plain. The glass was thin and elegant; so were the coffee cups ; and the table linen was white and fine. Nothing about it, however, would be worth describing if it had been expensive. But the menu, which covered four closely printed pages, showed that the most expensive dish offered there cost one and three-pence, while the greater number cost ninepence, six-pence, or threepence each. The hungry man would begin with crayfish, which were offered to him prepared in ten various ways ; for the Germans, like the French, are extremely fond of crayfish. He would have them in soup, for instance, or with asparagus, with salad or dressed with dill. Then he would find the week's bill of fare on his card, three or four dishes for each day, some cooked in small casseroles and served so to any guest who orders one. If it was a Friday he could have a ragoût of chicken in the Bremen style, or a slice from a Hamburg leg of mutton with cream sauce and celery salad, or ox-tongue cooked with young turnips. If he was a Catholic he would find two kinds of fish ready for him,—trout, cooked blue, and a ragoût of crayfish with asparagus and baked perch. But these are just the special dishes of the day, and he is not bound to try them. There are seven kinds of soup, including real turtle, and it is not for me to say how real turtle can be supplied in Berlin for 30 pfennig.

There are seven kinds of fish and too many varieties of meat, poultry, salads, vegetables and sweets, both hot and cold, to count. A man can have any kind of cooking he fancies, too ; his steak may be German, Austrian, or French ; he can have English roast beef, Russian caviare, a Maltese rice pudding, apples from the Tyrol, wild strawberries from a German forest, all the cheeses of France and England, a Welsh rarebit, and English celery. The English celery is as mysterious as the real turtle, for it was offered in June. Pheasants and partridges, I can honestly say, however, were not offered. Under the head of game there were only venison, geese, chickens, and pigeons.

I am sorry now that when I dined at this restaurant I did not order real turtle soup, *Roast beef Engl. mit Schmorkartoffeln*, celery, and a Welsh rarebit, because then I should have discovered whether these old British friends were recognisable in their Berlin environment. But it was more amusing at the time to ask for ham cooked in champagne and served with radish sauce, and other curious inviting combinations.

" But at home," I said to the artist,—" at home we just eat to live. We have a great contempt for people who pay much attention to food."

" I stayed in an English house last year, and never did I hear so much about food," said he. " One would eat nothing but grape-nuts and cheese, and another swore by toast and hot water and little *Pastetchen* of beef, and the third would have large rice puddings, and the fourth asked for fruit at every meal, and the fifth said all the others were wrong and that he wanted a good dinner. The poor hostess would have been distracted if she had not been one of those who love a new fad and try each one in turn. Also there were two eminent physicians in the house, and one of these drank champagne every night, while the other would touch nothing but Perrier and said champagne was poison. Directly we sat down we discussed these things, . . . and everyone assured me that if I tried his regime I should improve in health most marvellously."

"Which did you try?" I asked.

"The good dinner and the champagne, of course. But I did not find they affected my health one way or the other."

CHAPTER XXII

LIFE IN LODGINGS

AS rents are high in Germany, it is usual for people of small means to let off one or two rooms, either furnished or unfurnished. But it is not usual to supply a lodger with any meal except his coffee and rolls in the morning. If you wish to take lodgings in a German town, and work through the long list of them in a local paper, you will probably find no one willing to provide for you in the English fashion.

"Cooking!" they say with horror,—"cooking! You want to eat in your room. No. That can we not undertake. Coffee in the morning, yes; and rolls with it and butter and even two eggs, but nothing further. Just round the corner in the *Königstrasse* are two very fine restaurants, where the *Herrschaften* can eat what they will at any hour of the day, and for moderate prices."

If you insist, the most they will promise, and that not willingly, is to provide you with a knife and fork and a tablecloth for a pyramid of courses sent hot from one of the very fine adjacent restaurants for 1 mark or 1 mark 20 pf. Supper in Germany is the easiest meal in the day to provide, as you buy the substantial part of it at a *Delikatessenhandlung*, and find that even a German landlady will condescend to get you rolls and butter and beer. This sounds like the Simple Life, to be sure;

but if you are in German lodgings for any length of time you probably desire for one reason or the other to lead it. The plan of having your dinner sent piping hot from a restaurant in nice clean white dishes rather like monster soufflé dishes is not a bad one if the restaurant keeps faith with you. It is rather amusing to begin at the top with soup and work through the various surprises and temptations of the pyramid till you get to *Biskuit-Pudding mit Vanille Sauce* at the bottom. But in nine cases out of ten the restaurant fails you, sends uneatable food, is absurdly unpunctual or says plainly it can't be bothered. Then you have to wander about and out of doors for your food in all weathers and all states of health. This is amusing for a time, but not in the long run. It is astonishing how tired you can get of the " very fine " restaurants within reach, of their waitresses, their furniture, their menus, and their daily guests. At least, this is so in a small town where the best restaurant is not " very fine," although both food and service will be better than in an English town of the same size. If you are in Berlin and can go to the good restaurants, there you will be in danger of becoming a gourmet and losing your natural affection for cold mutton.

In a university or a big commercial town it is easy to get rooms for less than we pay in England; but in a small *Residenz* I have found it difficult. There were rooms to let, but no one wanted us, because we were not officers with soldier servants to wait on us; nor did we want to engage rooms as the officers did for at least six months. In fact, we found ourselves as unpopular as ladies are in a London suburb where all the lodging-house keepers want " gentlemen in the city " who are away all day and give no trouble. At last, after searching through every likely street in the

town, we found a dentist with exuberant manners, who
said he would overlook our shortcomings, and allow us
to inhabit his rooms at a high price on condition we
gave no trouble. We said we never gave trouble anywhere, and left both hotels and lodging-houses with an
excellent character, so the bargain was concluded. I
saw that his wife was not a party to it, but he over-
ruled her, and as he was a big red-faced noisy man,
and she was a small rat of a woman, I thought he
would continue to do so. One is always making these
stupid elementary mistakes about one's fellow-creatures.
But a little later in the day I had occasion to call at
the rooms to complete some arrangement about luggage,
and then the wife received me alone. I asked her if
she could put a small table into a room that only had
a big one. I forget why I wanted it.

" Table ! " she said rudely. " What can you want
another table for ? Isn't that one enough ? "

" I should like another," I said, " any little one
would do."

" I don't keep tables up my sleeve," said she. " You
see what you can have, . . . just what is there. If it
doesn't suit you . . ."

" But it does suit me," I said hurriedly, for the search
had been long and exhausting, and the rooms were
pleasant enough. I thought we need not deal much
with the woman.

" No meals except coffee in the morning ; you
understand that ? " she said in a truculent tone.

" Oh yes, I understand. We shall go out at midday
and at night. Afternoon tea I always make myself
with a spirit lamp . . ."

Never in my life have I been so startled. I
thought the woman was going to behave like a rat
in a corner, and fly at me. She shook her fist and

shouted so loud that she brought the dentist on the scene.

"*Spiritus*," she screamed. "*Spiritus—Spiritus leid' ich nicht.*"

"Bless us!" I said in English. "What's the matter?"

"*Was ist's?*" said the dentist, and he looked downright frightened.

"*Sie will kochen*," said his wife, shaking her fist at me again. "She has a spirit lamp. She wants to turn my beautiful *bestes Zimmer* into a kitchen. She will take all the polish off my furniture, just as the last people did when they cooked for themselves."

"Cooked!" I said. "Who speaks of cooking?—I spoke of a cup of tea."

"*Spiritus leid' ich nicht*," shrieked the woman.

"No," said the dentist, "we can't have cooking here."

"*Spiritus leid'* . . ."

But I fled. Luckily, we had not paid any rent in advance. I made up my mind that I would never confess to my small harmless Etna in German lodgings again, and would bolt the door while I boiled water for tea in it. We found rooms after another weary search, but they were extremely noisy and uncomfortable. We had to take them for six weeks, and could only endure them for a fortnight, and though we paid them the full six weeks' rent when we left, they charged us for every jug of hot water we had used, and added a *Trinkgeld* for the servant.

"We did not engage to pay extra either for hot water or for *Trinkgeld*," we said, turning, as worms will even in a *Residenz*, where everyone is a worm who is not *Militär*.

"But *Engländer* never give a *Trinkgeld*. That is

why we have put it in the bill. The girl expects it, and has earned it."

" The girl will have it," we said ; " but we shall give it her ourselves. And what have you to say about the hot water ? "

" Without coal it is impossible to have hot water. We let you our rooms, but we did not let you our coal. It is quite simple. Have you any other complaint to make ? "

We had, but we did not make them. We went to one of the big cities, where the civilian is still a worm, but where he has a large number and variety of other worms to keep him company. In Berlin or Hamburg or Leipzig there are always furnished rooms delighted to receive you. There may be a difficulty, however, if you are a musician. The police come in with their regulations ; or your fellow-lodgers may be students of medicine or philosophy, and driven wild by your harmonies. I knew a young musician who always took rooms in the noisiest street in Berlin, and practised with his windows open. He said the din of electric trams, overhead trains, motor cars, and heavy lorries helped his landlady and her family to suffer a Beethoven sonata quite gladly.

One of the insoluble mysteries of German life is the cheapness of furnished lodgings as compared with the high rent and rates. To be sure, the landlady does not cook for you, and the bed-sitting-room is not considered sordid in Germany. In fact, the separate sitting-room is almost unknown, though it is easy to arrange one by shifting some furniture. The pattern of the room and its appointments hardly vary in any part of Germany, though of course the size and quality vary with the price. If you take a small room you have one straight window, and if you take a large one you have several. Or you

16

may have a broad balcony window opening on to a balcony. You have the parqueted or painted floor, the porcelain stove, the sofa, the table, the wooden bed-stead, and the wooden hanging cupboard wherever you are. It is always sensible, comfortable furniture, and usually plain. When people over there know no better they buy themselves tawdry horrors, just as they do here. The German manufacturers flood the world with such things. But people who let lodgings put their treasures in a sacred room they call *das beste Zimmer*, and only use on festive occasions. They fob you off with old-fashioned stuff they do not value, a roomy solid cupboard, a family sofa, a chest of drawers black with age, and a hanging mirror framed in old elm-wood; and if it were not for a bright green rep tablecloth, snuff-coloured curtains, and a wall paper with a brown background and yellow snakes on it, you would like your quarters very well indeed. Rooms are usually let by the month, except in watering-places, where weekly prices prevail. In Leipzig you can get a room for 10s. a month. It will be a parterre or a fourth-floor room, rather gloomy and rather shabby, but a possible room for a student who happens to be hard up. For £1 a month you can get a room on a higher floor, and better furnished, while for £1, 10s. a month in Hamburg I myself have had two well-furnished rooms commanding a fine view of the Alster, and one of them so large that in winter it was nearly impossible to keep warm. Then my Hamburg friends told me I was paying too much, and that they could have got better lodgings for less money. They were nearer the sky than I should like in these days, but the old German system of letting the higher flats in a good house for a low rent benefits people who care about a "select" neighbourhood and yet cannot pay very much. The modern system of lifts will gradually make it impossible to get a flat or lodgings in a good street without paying as much for the fifth floors as for the first.

You do not see much of a German landlady, as she does not cater for you. She is often a widow, and when you know the rent of a flat you wonder how she squeezes a living out of what her lodgers pay her. She cannot even nourish herself with their scraps, or warm herself at a kitchen fire for which they pay. Some of them perform prodigies of thrift, especially when they have children to feed and educate. At the end of a long severe winter, when the Alster had been frozen for months, I found out by chance that my landlady, a sad aged widow with one little boy, had never lighted herself a fire. She let every room of her large flat, except a kitchen and a *Kammer* opening out of it. The little food she needed she cooked on an oil stove, at night she had a lamp, and of course she never by any chance opened a window. She said she could not afford coals, and that her son and she managed to keep warm. The miracle is that they both kept alive and well. Another German landlady was of a different type, a big buxom bustling creature, who spent most of the day in her husband's coal sheds, helping him with his books and taking orders. Although she was so busy she undertook to cook for me, and kept her promise honourably; and she cooked for herself, her husband, and their workpeople. She used sometimes to show me the huge dishes of food they were about to consume, food that was cheap to buy and nourishing to eat, but troublesome to prepare. She did all her own washing too, and dried it in the narrow slip of a room her husband and she used for all purposes. I discovered this by going in to see her when she was ill one day, and finding rows of wet clothes hung on strings right across her bed. I made no comment, for nothing that is an outrage of the first laws of hygiene will surprise you if you have gone here and there in the byways of Germany. An English girl told me that when she was recovering from a slight attack of cholera in a Rhenish *Pension*, they were quite hurt because she refused stewed cranberries. "*Das schadet nichts, das ist gesund*," they said. I could hear them say it. Only the summer before a kindly hotel-keeper had brought me a ragoût of *Schweinefleisch* and vanilla ice under similar circumstances. The German constitution seems able to survive anything, even roast goose at night at the age of three.

A *Pension* in Germany costs from £3 a month upwards. That is to say, you will get offers of a room and full board for this sum, but I must admit that I never tried one at so low a rate, and should not expect it to be comfortable. Rent and food are too dear in the big towns to make a reasonable profit possible on such terms, unless the household is managed on starvation lines. To have a comfortable room and sufficient food, you must pay from £5 to £7 a month, and then if you choose carefully you will be satisfied. The society is usually cosmopolitan in these establishments, and the German spoken is a warning rather than a lesson. It is not really German life that you see in this way, though the proprietress and her assistants may be German. In most of the university towns some private families take "paying guests," and when they are agreeable people this is a pleasanter way of life than any *Pension*.

Before you have been in Germany a fortnight the police expects to know all about you. You have to give them your father's Christian and surname, and tell them how he earned his living, and where he was born; also your mother's Christian and maiden name, and

where she was born.   You must declare your religion,
and if you are married give your husband's Christian
and surname ; also where he was born, and what he
does for a living.   If you happen to do anything yourself, though, you need not mention it.   They do not
expect a woman to be anything further than married
or single.   But you must say when and where you were
last in Germany, and how often you have been, and
why you have come now, and what you are doing, and
how long you propose to stay.   They tell you in London
you do not need a passport in Germany, and they tell
you in Berlin that you must either produce one or be
handed over for inquiry to your Embassy.   Last year
when I was there I produced one twenty-three years
old.   I had not troubled to get a new one, but I came
across this, quite yellow with age, and I thought it
might serve to make some official happy ; for I had
once seen my husband get himself, me, and our bicycles
over the German frontier and into Switzerland, and next
morning back into Germany, by showing the gendarmes
on the bridge his C.T.C. ticket.   I cannot say that my
ancient passport made my official exactly happy.
Twenty-three years ago he was certainly in a *Steckkissen*, and no doubt he felt that in those days, in a
world without him to set it right, anything might happen.

" Twenty-three years," he bellowed at the top of his
voice, for he saw that I was *fremd*, and wished to make
himself clear.   We are not the only people who scream
at foreigners that they may understand.   " Twenty-
three years.   But it is a lifetime."

It was for him no doubt.   I admitted that twenty-
three years was—well, twenty-three years, and explained
that I had been told at a *Reisebureau* that a passport
was unnecessary.

" They know nothing in England," he said gloomily.

" With us a passport is necessary ; but what is a passport twenty-three years old ? "

I admitted that, from the official point of view, it was not much, and he made no further difficulties. As a rule you need not go to the police bureau at all. The people you are with will get the necessary papers, and fill them in for you ; but I wanted to see whether the German jack-in-office was as bad as his reputation makes him. Germans themselves often complain bitterly of the treatment they receive at the hands of these lower class officials.

" I went to the police station," said a German lady who lived in England, and was in her own country on a visit. " I went to *anmelden* myself, but not one of the men in the office troubled to look up. When I had stood there till I was tired I said that I wished someone to attend to me. Every pen stopped, every head was raised, astounded by my impertinence. But no one took any notice of my request. I waited a little longer, and then fetched myself a chair that someone had left unoccupied. I did not do it to make a sensation. I was tired. But every pen again stopped, and one in authority asked in a voice like thunder what I made here. I said that I had come to *anmelden* myself, and he began to ask the usual questions with an air of suspicion that was highly offensive. You can see for yourself that I do not look like an anarchist or anything but what I am, a respectable married woman of middle age. I told the man everything he wanted to know, and at every item he grunted as if he knew it was a lie. In the end he asked me very rudely how long a stay I meant to make in Germany.

" Not a day longer than I can help," I said ; " for your manners do not please me."

All the pens stopped again till I left the office, and

when I got back to my mother she wept bitterly; for she said that I should be prosecuted for *Beamtenbeleidigung* and put in prison.

"But the really interesting fact about the system is that it doesn't work," said a German to me; "when I wanted my papers a little while ago I could not get them. Nothing about me could be discovered. Officially I did not exist."

Yet he had inherited a name famous all over the world, was a distinguished scientific man himself, and had been born in the city where his existence was not known to the police.

"Take care you don't go in at an *Ausgang* or out at an *Eingang*," said an Englishman who had just come back from Berlin. "Take care you don't try to buy stamps at the Post Office out of your turn. Remember that you can't choose your cab when you arrive. A policeman gives you a number, and you have to hunt amongst a crowd of cabs for that number, even if it is pouring with rain. Remember that the police decides that you must buy your opera tickets on a Sunday morning, and stand *queue* for hours till you get them. If you have a cold in your head, stay at home. Last winter a man was arrested for sneezing loudly. It was considered *Beamtenbeleidigung*. The Englishwoman who walked on the grass in the Tiergarten was not arrested, because the official who saw her died of shock at the sight, and could not perform his duty."

Wherever you go in Germany you hear stories of police interference and petty tyranny, and it is mere luck if you do not innocently transgress some of their fussy pedantic regulations. In South Germany I once put a cream jug on my window-sill to keep a little milk cool for the afternoon. The jug was so small and the window so high that it can hardly have been visible from the street, but my landlady came to me excitedly and said the police would be on her before the day was out if the jug was left there.   The police allowed nothing on a window-sill in that town, lest it should fall on a citizen's head.   Each town or district has its own restrictions, its own crimes.   In one you will hear that a butcher boy is not allowed on the side-path carrying his tray of meat.   If a policeman catches him at it, he, or his employer, is fined.   In another town the awning from a shop window must not exceed a certain length, and you are told of a poor widow, who, having just had a new one put up at great expense, was compelled by the police to take the whole thing down, because the flounce was a quarter of an inch longer than the regulations prescribed.   You hear of a poor man laboriously building a toy brick wall round the garden in his *Hof*, and having to pull it to pieces because " building " is not allowed except with police permission.   In some towns the length of a woman's gown is decided in the *Polizeibureau*, and the officers fine any woman whose skirt touches the ground.   In one town you may take a dog out without a muzzle ; in another it is a crime. A merchant on his way to his office, in a city where there was a muzzling order, found to his annoyance, one morning, that his mother's dog had followed him unmuzzled.   He had no string with him, he could not persuade the dog to return, and he could not go back with it, because he had an important appointment.   So he risked it and went on.   Before long, however, he met a policeman.   The usual questions were asked, his name and address were taken, and he was told that he would be fined.   Hardly had he got to the end of the street when he met a second policeman.   He explained that the matter was settled, but this was not the opinion of the policeman   Was the dog not at large, unmuzzled,

on his the policeman's beat? With other policemen he
had nothing to do. The dog was his discovery, the
name and address of the owner were required, and there
was no doubt, in the policeman's mind, that the owner
would have to pay a second fine. The merchant went
his ways, still followed by an unmuzzled unled dog.
Before long he met a third policeman, gave his name
and address a third time, and was assured that he would
have to pay a third time.

" *Dann war es mir zu bunt,*" said the merchant, and
he picked up the dog and carried it the rest of the way
to his office. When he got there he sent it home in a
cab.

CHAPTER XXIII

SUMMER RESORTS

IF you choose to leave the railroad you may still travel by diligence in Germany, and rumble along the roads in its stuffy interior. As you pass through a village the driver blows his horn, old and young run out to enjoy the sensation of the day, the geese cackle and flutter from you in the dust, you catch glimpses of a cobble-stoned market-place, a square church-tower with a stork's nest on its summit, Noah's Ark-like houses with thatched or gabled roofs, tumble-down balconies, and outside staircases of wood. Sometimes when the official coach is crowded you may have an open carriage given you without extra charge, but you cannot expect that to happen often; nor will you often be driven by postillion nowadays. Indeed, for all I know the last one may have vanished and been replaced by a motor bus. You can take one to a mountain inn in the Black Forest nowadays, over a pass I travelled a few years ago in a mail coach. In those times it was a jog-trot journey occupying the long lazy hours of a summer morning. I suppose that now you whizz and hustle through the lovely forest scenery pursued by clouds of dust and offended by the fumes of petrol, but no doubt you get to your destination quicker than you used. The pleasantest way to travel in Germany, if you are young and strong, is on your feet. It is enchanting to walk day after day through the cool scented forest and sleep at night in one of the clean country inns. You must choose your district and your inn, for if you went right off the traveller's track and came to a peasant's house you would find nothing approaching the civilisation of an English farmhouse. But in most of the beautiful country districts of Germany there are fine inns, and there are invariably good roads leading to them. This way of travelling is too tame for English people as a rule. They laugh at the broad well-made path winding up the side of a German mountain, and still more at the hotel or restaurant to be found at the top. From the English point of view a walk of this kind is too tame and easy either for health or pleasure. But the beauty of it, especially in early summer, can never be forgotten; and so it is worth while, even if you are young and cherish a proper scorn for broad roads and good dinners. You would probably come across some dinners that were not good, tough veal, for instance, and greasy vegetables. The roads you would have to accept, and walk them if you choose in tennis shoes. Indeed, you would forget the road and eat the dinner unattending; for all that's made would be a green thought in a green shade for you by the end of the day, and as you shut your eyes at night you would see forest, forest with the sunlight on the young tips of the pines, forest unfolding itself from earth to sky as you climbed hour after hour close to the ferns and boulders of the foaming mountain stream your pathway followed, forest too on the opposite side of the valley, with wastes of golden broom here and there, and fields of rye and barley swept gently by the breeze. You may walk day by day in Germany through such a paradise as this, and meet no one but a couple of children gathering wild strawberries, or an old peasant carrying faggots, or the goose-girl herding her fussy flock. You may even spend your summer holiday in a crowded watering-place, and yet escape quite easily into the heart of the forest where the crowd never comes. The crowd sits about on benches planted by a *Verschönerungsverein* within a mile of their hotel, or on the verandah of the hotel itself. Some of the benches will command a view, and these will be most in demand. Those that are nearly a mile away will be reached by energetic elderly ladies, and at dinner you will hear that they have been to the Rabenstein this morning, and that the *Aussicht* was *prachtvoll* and the *Luft herrlich*, but that they must decline to go farther afield this afternoon as the morning's exertions have tired them. But some of *die Herren* say they are ready for anything, and even propose to scale the mountain behind the hotel and drink a glass of beer at the top. You readily agree to go with them, for by this time you know that even if you are a poor walker you can toddle half way up a German hill and down again; and the hotel itself has been built high above the valley. But after dinner you find that nearly everyone disappears for a siesta, while the few who keep outside are asleep over their coffee and cigar. Even *Skat* hardly keeps awake the three *Herren* who proposed a walk; and your friend the Frau Geheimrath Schultze warns you solemnly against the insanity of stirring a step before sundown; for summer in South Germany is summer indeed. The sun comes suddenly with power and glory, bursting every sheathed bud and ripening crops in such a hurry that you walk through new mown hayfields while your English calendar tells you it is still spring. Later in the year the heat is often intense all through the middle of the day, and the young men who make their excursions on foot start at dawn, so that they may arrive at a resting place by ten or eleven. " For many years our boys have wandered cheaply and simply through their German Fatherland," says a leaflet advertising a society that organises walking tours for girls; Saturday afternoon walks, Sunday walks, and holiday walks extending over six or eight days. " Simplicity, cheerful friendly intercourse, gaiety in fresh air, these are the companions of our pilgrimage. . . . We wish to provide the German nation with mothers who are at home in woods and meadows, who have learned to observe the beauties of nature, who have strengthened their health and their preceptions of everything that is great and beautiful by happy walks. . . . Anyone *wanderfroh* who has been at a higher school or who is still attending one is eligible. The card of membership only costs 3 marks for a single member and 4 marks for a whole family. Some of the excursions are planned to include brother pilgrims, and their character is gay and cheerful, without flirting or coquetry, a genuine friendly intercourse between girls and boys, young men and maidens, a pure and beautiful companionship such as no dancing lesson and no ballroom can create, and which is nevertheless the best training for life." So nowadays gangs of girls, and even mixed gangs of boys and girls, are to swarm through the pleasant forests of Germany, ascend the easy pathways of her mountains, and fill her country inns to overflowing. How horrified the little *Backfisch* would have been at such a suggestion, how unmaidenly her excellent aunt would have deemed it, how profoundly they would both have disapproved of any exercise that heightens the colour or disturbs the neatness of a young lady's toilet. I myself have heard German men become quite violent in their condemnation of Englishwomen who play games or take walks that make them temporarily dishevelled. It never seemed to occur to them that a woman might think their displeasure at her appearance of less account than her own enjoyment. "No," they said, "ask not that we should admire Miss Smith. She has just come in from a six hours' walk with her brother. Her face is as red as a poppy, her blouse is torn, and her boots are thick and muddy."

As a matter of fact, I had not asked them to admire Miss Smith. I knew that the lady they admired was arch, and had a persuasive giggle. Nevertheless I tried to break a lance for my countrywoman.

"You will see," I assured them, "she will remove the torn blouse and the muddy boots; and when she comes down her face will be quite pale."

"But she often looks like that," said one of the men. "At least once a day she plays a game or takes a walk that is more of a strain on her appearance than it should be. A young woman must always consider what effect things have on her appearance."

"Why?"

"Why?——Because she is a woman. There is no sense in a question like that. It goes back to the beginning of all things. It is unanswerable. Every young woman wishes to please."

"But is it not conceivable," I asked, "that a young woman may sometimes wish to please herself even at the expense of her appearance. Miss Smith assures me that she enjoys long walks and games, — oh, games that you have not seen her play here— hockey, for instance, and cricket."

"*Verrückt!*" said the men in chorus. "A young woman should not think of herself at all. The Almighty has created her to please us, and it does not please us when she wears muddy boots and is as red as a poppy; at least, not while she is young. When she is married, and her place is in the kitchen, she may be as red as she pleases. That is a different matter."

"Is it?" I said, and I wanted to ask why again; but I held my tongue. Some questions, as they said, lead one too far afield.

The majority of visitors at a German watering-place take very little exercise of any kind. They sit about the forest as our seaside visitors sit about the sands, and though they cannot fill in their mornings by sea bathing, there are often medicinal baths that take as much time. Then the *Badearzt* probably prescribes so many glasses of water from his favourite spring each day, and a short walk after each glass, and a long rest after the midday dinner. Dinner is the really serious business of the day, and often occupies two hours. Where there is still a *table d'hôte* it is a tedious, noisy affair, conducted in a stuffy room, and even if you are greedy enough to like the good things brought round you wish very soon that you were on a Cumberland fell-side with a mutton sandwich and a mountain stream. You wish it even although you hate mutton sandwiches and like meringues filled with Alpine strawberries and whipped cream; for the clatter and the clack going on around you, and the asphyxiating air, bring on a de-moralising somnolence that you despise and cannot easily throw off. You sit about as lazily as anyone else half through the golden afternoon, drink a cup of coffee at four o'clock, look at mountains of cake, and then start for the restaurant, which is said to be *eine gute Stunde* from the hotel. You find, as you expected, that you saunter gently uphill on a broad winding road through the forest, and that you have a charming walk, but not what anyone in this country would call exercise till they were about seventy. In case you should be weary you pass seats every hundred yards or so, and when you have made your ascent you are received by a bustling waiter or a waitress in costume, who expects to serve you with beer or coffee before you venture down the hill again. By the time you get back to the hotel everyone is streaming in to supper, which is not as long as dinner, but quite as noisy. After supper everyone sits about the verandah or the garden. The men play cards, and smoke and drink coffee and Kirsch, the married women talk and do embroidery, the maidens stroll about in twos and threes or sit down to Halma. There are never many young men in these summer hotels, and the few there are herd with the older men or with each other more than young men do in this country. What we understand by flirtation is not encouraged, unless it is almost sure to lead to marriage; and what the Germans understand by flirtation is justly considered scandalous and reprehensible. For the Germans have taken the word into use, but taken away the levity and innocence of its meaning. They make it a term of serious reproach, and those who dislike us condemn the shocking prevalence of Flirt (they make a noun of the verb) in our decadent society.

The *Pension* price at a German summer hotel varies from four to fifteen marks, according to the general style of the establishment and the position of the rooms engaged. In one frequented by Germans the sitting-rooms are bare and formal, and as English visitors are not expected no English papers are taken. The season begins in June and lasts till the end of September, and you must be a successful hotel-keeper yourself to understand how so much can be provided for so little, miles away from any market. Many of these summer hotels have been built high up in the forest, and with

no others near them. Some are run as a speculation
by doctors. There is hardly a woman or girl in Germany
who has not needed a *Kur* at some time of her life,
or who does not need one every year if she has money
and pretty gowns. The *Badereise* and everything
connected with it serves the German professional
humorist much as the mother-in-law and the drop
too much serve the English one, perennially and
faithfully. For the wife is determined to have her
Badereise, and the husband is not inclined to pay for
it, and the family doctor is called in to prescribe it.
The artifices and complications arising suggest themselves, and to judge by the postcards and farces of
Germany never weary the public they are designed
to amuse.

In Berlin, when the hot weather comes, you see the
family luggage and bedding going off to the sea-coast,
for people who take a house take part of their bedding
with them. There is so little seaside and so much
Berlin that prices rule high wherever there is civilised
accommodation. In Ruegen £1 a week per room
is usual, and the room you get for that may be a very
poor one. In most German watering-places, both on
the coast and in the forest, you can have furnished
rooms if you prefer them to hotel life, but as a rule
you must either cook your own dinner or go out to
a hotel for it. The cooking landlady is as rare in
the country as in the town. Then in some places, at
Oberhof, for instance, high upon the hills above Gotha,
there are charming little furnished bungalows. Friends
of mine go there or to one of the neighbouring villages
every year, and never enter a hotel. They either take a
servant with them, or find someone on the spot to do what
is necessary. When there are no mineral waters or sea
baths to give a place importance, Germans say they

17

have come there to do a *Luftkur*. A delightful Frenchwoman who has written about England lately is amused by our everlasting babble about a "change." This one needs a change, she says, and that one is away for a change, and the other means to have a change next week. So the Germans amuse us by their eternal "cures." One tries air, and the other water, and the next iron, and the fourth sulphur, while the number and variety of nerve cures, *Blutarmut* cures, diet cures, and obesity cures are bewildering. It is difficult to believe that life in a hotel can cure anyone anywhere. However, in Germany, if you are under a capable *Badearzt*, there may be some salvation for you, since he orders your baths, measures your walks, and limits your diet so strictly. At one of the well-known places where people who eat too much all the year round go to reduce their figures, there is in the chief hotels a table known as the *Corpulententisch*, and a man who sits there is not allowed an ounce of bread beyond what his physician has prescribed.

But the German *Luxusbad*, the fashionable watering-place where the guests are cosmopolitan and the prices high—Marienbad, Homburg, Karlsbad, Schwalbach, Wiesbaden—all these places are as well known to English people as their own Bath and Buxton. Homburg they have swallowed, and I have somewhere come across a paragraph from an English newspaper objecting to the presence of Germans there. It is the quiet German watering-place where no English come that is interesting and not impossible to find. During the summer I spent in a Bavarian forest village I only saw one English person the whole time, except my own two or three friends. I heard the other day that the village and the life there have hardly altered at all, but that some English people have discovered the

trout streams and come every year for fishing. In my
time no one seemed to care about fishing. You went
for walks in the forest. There was nothing else to do,
unless you played *Kegel* and drank beer; for it was
only a *Luftkur*. There was no *Badearzt* and no
mineral water. To be sure, there were caves, huge
limestone caves that you visited with a guide the day
after you arrived, and never thought about again.
There were various ruined castles, too, in the neighbourhood that made a goal for a drive in cases where there
was a restaurant attached, and not far off there was a
curious network of underground beer-cellars that I did
not see, but which seemed to attract the men of our
party sometimes. There were several inns in the
straggling village, for the place lay high up amongst
the dolomite hills of Upper Franconia, and people came
there from the neighbouring towns for *Waldluft*. The
summer I was there Richard Wagner passed through
with his family, and we saw him more than once. He
stayed at the Kurhaus, a hotel of more pretentions than
the village inns, for it had a good sized garden and did
not entertain peasants. My inn, recommended by an
old Nuremberg friend, was owned and managed by a
peasant proprietor, his wife, their elderly daughter, and
two charming orphan grandchildren in their early teens.
The peasant customers had as usual a large rough room
to themselves, the town guests had their plain bare
Speisesaal, and we Britishers possessed the summer
house; so we were all happy. The whole glory of the
place was in the forest; for it was not flat sandy forest
that has no undergrowth, and wearies you very soon
with its sameness and its still, oppressive air. It was
up hill and down dale forest, full of lovely glades,
broken by massive dolomite rocks; the trees not set in
serried rows, but growing for the most part as the birds

and the wind planted them; a varied natural forest tended but not dragooned by man. The flowers there were a delight to us, for we arrived early enough in the year to find lilies of the valley growing in great quantities amongst the rocks, while a little later the stream and pathways were bordered by oak and beech fern and by many wild orchises that are rare now with us. It was not here, however, but in another German forest, where, one day when I had no time to linger, I met people with great bunches of the *Cypripedium calceolus* that they had gathered as we gather primroses. At the Bavarian watering-place we had the whole forest as much to ourselves as the summer house, for no one seemed to wander farther than the seats placed amongst the trees by the *Verschönerungsverein.*

> "Warum willst du weiter schweifen
> Sieh das Gute liegt so nah,"

says Goethe, and most Germans out for their summer holiday seem to take his advice in the most literal way, and find their happiness as near home as they possibly can.

When you begin to think about the actual process of travelling in Germany, the tiresome business of getting from the city to the forest village, for instance, you at once remember both the many complaints you have heard Germans make of our system, or rather want of system, and the bitter scorn poured on German fussiness by travelling Britons. The ways of one nation are certainly not the ways of another in this respect. Directly I cross the German frontier I know that I am safe from muddle and mistakes, that I need not look after myself or my luggage, that I cannot get into a wrong train or alight at a wrong station, or suffer any injury through carelessness or mismanagement. Everything is managed for me, and on long journeys in the corridor trains things are well managed. But your carriage is far more likely to be unpleasantly crowded in Germany than in England; and as hand-luggage is not charged for, the public takes all it can, and fills the racks, the seats, and the floor with heavy bags and portmanteaux. In bygone years the saying was that none travelled first class save fools and Englishmen, but nowadays Germans travel in their own first-class carriages a good deal. The third-class accommodation is wretched, more fit for animals than men. In some districts there are fourth-class uncovered seats on the roof of the carriages, but I have only seen these used in summer. When I was last in Germany a year ago there was much excitement and indignation over certain changes that were to make travelling dearer for everyone. All luggage in the van was to be paid for in future, first-class fares were to be raised, and no return tickets issued.

But you must not think that when you have bought a ticket from one place to another you can get to it by any train you please. " I want the 10.15 to Entepfuhl," you say to the nearest and biggest official you can see; and he looks at your ticket.

" *Personenzug*," he says in a withering way,—" the 10.15 is an express."

You say humbly that you like an express.

" Then you must get an extra ticket," he says, " This one only admits you to slow trains."

So you get your extra ticket, and then you wait with everyone else in a big room where most people are eating and drinking to wile away the time. Don't imagine that you can find your empty train, choose your corner, and settle yourself comfortably for your journey as you can in England. You are well looked after, but if you are used to England you never quite lose the impression in Germany that if you are not an official or a soldier you must be a criminal, and that if you move an inch to right or left of what is prescribed you will hear of it.   Just before the train starts the warders open your prison doors and shout out the chief places the train travels to.   So you hustle along with everyone else, and get the best place you can, and are hauled out by a watchful conductor when you arrive. If it is a small station there is sure to be a dearth of porters, but you get your luggage by going to the proper office and giving up the slip of paper you received when it was weighed.   Never forget, as I have known English people do, that you cannot travel in Germany without having your luggage weighed and receiving the *Schein* for it.   If you lose the *Schein* you are undone.   I cannot tell you exactly what would happen, because it would be a tragedy without precedent, but it is impossible that German officials would surrender a trunk without receiving a *Schein* in exchange; at least, not without months of rigmarole and delay.   Even when it is the official who blunders the public suffers for it.   We were travelling some years ago from Leipzig to London when the guard examining our tickets let one blow away.   Luckily some German gentlemen in the carriage with us saw what happened, gave us their addresses, and offered to help us in any way they could.   But we had to buy a fresh ticket and trust to getting our money back by correspondence. Six months later we did get it back, and this is an exact translation of the letter accompanying it :—

" In answer to your gracious letter of the 26th September, we inform your wellbornship, respectfully, that the Ticket Office here is directed, in regard to the ticket by you on the 23rd of September taken, by the guard in checking lost ticket Leipzig-London via Calais 2nd class, the for the distance Hanover to London outpaid fare of 71 m. 40 pf. by post to you to refund."

One must admire the mind that can compose a sentence like that without either losing its way or turning dizzy.

But if you want to see what Germans can give you in the way of order and comfort you must leave the railroad and travel in one of their big American liners. Even if you are not going to America, but only from Hamburg to Dover, it is well worth doing. The interest of it begins the day before, when you take your trunks to the docks and see the steerage passengers assembled for their start. They are a strange gipsy-looking folk, for the most part from the eastern frontier of Germany, bare-footed and wearing scraps of brighter colours than western people choose. When we arrived the doctor was examining their eyes in an open shed, and we saw them huddled together in families waiting their turn. There was no weeping and wailing as there is when the Irish leave their shores. These people looked scared by the bustle of departure, and concerned for the little children with them, and for their poor bundles of clothes; but they did not seem unhappy. In the luggage bureau itself you came across the emigrant upsides with fortune, the successful business German returning to America after a summer holiday in his native land, and speaking the most hideously corrupt and vulgar English ever heard. The most harsh and nasal American is heavenly music compared with nasal American spoken by a German tongue. The great ship was crowded with people of this type, and the resources of Europe could hardly supply them with the luxuries they wanted. We had a special train next day to Cuxhaven, and an army of blue-coated white-gloved stewards to meet us on the platform, and a band to play us on board. Our private rooms were hung with pale blue silk and painted with white enamel and furnished with satin-wood; the passages had marble floors; there were quantities of flowers everywhere, and books, and the electric light. In fact, it was the luxurious floating hotel a modern liner must be to entice such people as those I saw in the luggage bureau to travel in it. The meals were most elaborate and excellent; and I feel sure that any royal family happening to travel incognito on the ship would have been satisfied with them. But my neighbours at table were not. "We shall not dine down here again," said one of them, speaking with the twang I have described. "After to-night we shall have all our meals in the Ritz Restaurant." I looked at her reflectively, and next day after breakfast I stood on the bridge and looked at the other emigrants. The women were singing an interminable droning mass, the men sat about on sacks and played cards, the bare-footed children scuttled to and fro.

"One day some of these people will come back in a *Luxus* cabin," said a German acquaintance to me.

"And they will dine in the Ritz Restaurant, because our dinner is not good enough for them," I prophesied.

Directly we got to Dover every feature of our arrival helped us to feel at home. There was a batch of large good-natured looking policemen, whose function I cannot explain, but it was agreeable to see them again. There was no order or organisation of any kind to protect and annoy you. The authorities had thoughtfully painted the letters of the alphabet on the platform where the luggage was deposited, and you were supposed to find your own trunks in front of your own letter. I, full of German ideas still, waited a weary time near my letter. "You'll never get them that way," said an English friend. "You'd much better go to the end of the platform and pick them out as you can." So I went, and found a huge pile of luggage pitched anyhow, anywhere, and picked out my own, seized a porter, made him shoulder things, and followed him at risk to life and limb. All the luggage leaving Dover was being tumbled about at our feet, and when we tried to escape it we fell over what had arrived. Porters were rushing to and fro with trunks, just as disturbed ants do with eggs, but in this case it was the German passengers who felt disturbed. They were not used to such ways. When they had to duck under a rope to reach the waiting train they grew quite angry, and said they did not think much of the British Empire. But there was worse to come for us all. Breakfast on board had been early and a fog had delayed our arrival. We were all hungry and streamed into the refreshment room. We filled it.

"What is there to eat?" said one.

The young woman with the hauteur and detachment of her calling did not speak, but just glanced at a glass dish under a glass cover. There were two stale looking ham sandwiches.

"Well," says my Englishman, when I tell him this true story—"we are not a greedy nation."

"But how about the trunks that were not under their right letters?" I ask.

"Who in his senses wants to find trunks under letters?" says he. "The proper place for trunks is the end of the platform. Then you can tear out of the train and find yours first and get off quickly. When you are all dragooned and drilled an ass comes off as well as anyone else. You place a premium on stupidity."

"But that is an advantage to the ass," I say; "and in a civilised State why should the ass not have as good a chance as anyone else?"

The argument that ensues is familiar, exhausting, and interminable. "An ass is an ass wherever he lives," says someone at last; and everyone is delighted to have a proposition put forward to which he can honestly agree.

CHAPTER XXIV

PEASANT LIFE

THE peasant proprietors of Southern Germany are a comfortable, prosperous class. "A rich peasant" begins your comic story as often as "a rich Jew." The peasants own their farms and a bit of forest, as well as a vineyard or a hop garden. They never pretend to be anything but peasants; but when they can afford it they like to have a son who is a doctor, a schoolmaster, or a pastor. Unless you have special opportunities you can only watch peasant life from outside in Germany, for you could not stay in a Bauernhaus as you would in a farmhouse in England. At least, you could not live with the family. In some of the summer resorts the peasants make money by furnishing bedrooms and letting them to *Herrschaften*, but the *Herrschaften* have to get their meals at the nearest inn. The inner life of the peasant family is rougher than the inner life of the farmer's family in England, though their level of prosperity is as high, possibly higher. You cannot imagine the English farmer and his wife putting on costly and picturesque mediæval costumes every Sunday and solemnly marching to church in them; but the German Bauer still does this quite simply and proudly. In some parts of the Black Forest every valley has its own costume, so that you know where a man lives by the clothes he wears. There is one valley where all the girls are pretty, and on festive occasions or for church they wear charming transparent black caps with wings to them. There is another valley where the men are big-boned and blackavised, with square shaven chins and spare bodies, rather like our English legal type; and they go to church in scarlet breeches, long black velvet coats, and black three-cornered hats. Their women-folk wear gay-coloured skirts and mushroom hats loaded with heavy poms-poms. In Cassel there are most curious costumes to be seen still on high days and holidays; from Berlin, people go to the Spreewald to see the Wendish peasants, and in Bavaria there is still some colour and variety of costume. But everywhere you hear that these costumes are dying out. The new generation does not care to label itself, for it finds *städtische Kleider* cheaper and more convenient. The Wendish girls seem to abide by the ways of their forefathers, for they go to service in Berlin on purpose to save money for clothes. They buy or are presented with two or three costumes each year, and when they marry they have a stock that will last a lifetime and will provide them with the variety their pride demands. For they like to have a special rig-out for every occasion, and a great many changes for church on Sundays. In Catholic Germany a procession on a saint's day seems to have stepped down from a stained-glass window, the women's gowns are so vivid and their bodies so stiff and angular. But to see the German peasantry in full dress you must go to a *Kirchweih*, a dance, or a wedding.

You can hardly be in Germany in summer without seeing something of peasants' weddings, and of the elaborate rites observed at them. Different parts of the empire have different ways, and even in one district you will find much variety. We saw several peasant weddings in the Black Forest one summer, and no two were quite alike. Sometimes when we were walking through the forest we met a *Brautwagen* : the great open cart loaded with the furniture and wedding presents the bride was taking as part of her dowry to her new home. It would be piled with bedding, wooden bedsteads, chests of drawers, and pots and pans ; and gay-coloured ribbons would be floating from each point of vantage. Sometimes the bridal pair was with the cart, the young husband in his wedding clothes walking beside the horse, the bride seated amongst her possessions. Sometimes a couple of men in working clothes, probably the bridegroom and a friend, were carrying the things beforehand, so that the new home should be ready directly after the wedding. We happened to be staying in the Black Forest when our inn-keeper's daughter was going to marry a young doctor, the son of a rich peasant in a neighbouring valley, and we were asked to the wedding. Our landlord ran two inns, the one in which we stayed and another a dozen miles away, which was managed by his wife and daughters. The wife's hotel was in a fashionable watering-place, and offered a smarter background for a wedding than the one in our out-of-the-world little town. It is the proper moment now for you to object that this could not have been a " peasant" wedding at all, and has no place in a picture of peasant life ; and I concede that the bride and bridegroom, their parents, and certain of their friends all wore *städtische Kleider*. The bride was in black silk, and the bridegroom in his professional black coat. But nearly all the guests were peasants, and wore peasant costume ; and the heavy long-spun festivities were those usual at a peasant's wedding. We started with our bicycles at six o'clock in the morning, and soon found ourselves in a straggling procession of carts and pedestrians come from all the valleys round. The main road was like a road on a fair day. Everyone knew that there was to be a *Hochzeit* at R., a big splendid *Hochzeit*, and everyone who could afford the time and the money was going to eat and drink and dance at it. Everyone was in a holiday mood, and all along the lovely forest road we exchanged greetings with our fellow-guests and gathered scraps of information about the feast we were on our way to join. Every inn we passed had set out extra tables, and expected extra custom that day, and when we got to one within a mile of R. we found the garden crowded. People were ready by this time for their second breakfast, and were having it here before making their appearance at the wedding. We were hungry and thirsty ourselves, so we sat down under the shade of trees and ate *belegtes Butterbrot* and drank Pilsener as our neighbours did. We arrived at R. just in time to remove the dust of the road, and then walk, as we found our hosts expected us to do, in the wedding procession. First came the bride and bridegroom, and then a long crocodile of brides-maids, all wearing the curious high bead wreaths possessed by every village girl of standing in this part of Germany. We witnessed the civil ceremony, but though I have been present at several German civil weddings I remember as little about them as about a visit to the English District Council Office where I have sometimes been to pay taxes. In both cases there is a bare room, an indifferent official, some production of official papers, and the thing is done. When the bride and bridegroom had been made legally man and wife they headed the waiting proces-

sion again, and proceeded to the church for the real,
the religious ceremony. It was packed with people,
and the service, which was Catholic, lasted a long time.
When it was over everyone streamed back to the hotel,
and as soon as possible the *Hochzeitsmahl* began;
but though we were politely bidden to it we politely
excused ourselves, for we knew that the feast would
last for hours and would be more than we could bear.
Till evening, they said, it would last, and there would
be many speeches, and it was a broiling summer day.
The guests we perceived to be a mixed company of
peasants in costume, of inn-keepers and their families
in ordinary clothes, and of university students in black
coats who were removed from the peasantry by their
education, but not by birth and affection. The invited
guests sat down to dinner in the *Speisesaal*, but the
hotel garden was crowded with country people who
paid for what they consumed. The dinner served to
us and to others out here was an unusually good one,
so we discovered that people who attend a wedding
unasked get a spectacle, a dance, and extra fine food
for their money. Towards the end of the afternoon
before we left R. we looked in at the ballroom, where
dancing had begun already.

At another peasant's wedding in the Black Forest
we saw some quaint customs observed that were omitted
at R. In this case the bride and bridegroom were
themselves peasants, and wore the costume of their
valley. The bride was said to be well endowed, but
she was extremely plain. Amongst German peasants,
however, beauty hardly counts. What a woman is
worth to a man, he reckons partly in hard cash and
partly in the work she can do. There were two
charmingly pretty girls in the Bavarian village where
we once spent a summer, but we were told that they

had not the faintest chance of marriage, because, though they belonged to a respectable family, they were orphans and dowerless. Auerbach's enchanting story of *Barfüssele*, in which the village Cinderella marries the rich peasant, is a fairy story and not a picture of real life. The feast at this second wedding we saw must have cost a good deal, for it was prepared at our hotel for a large crowd of guests and lasted for hours. It was an agitating wedding in some of its aspects. The day before we had been startled at irregular but frequent intervals by loud gunshots, and we were told that these were fired in welcome of the wedding guests as they arrived. When the bride appeared with her *Brautwagen* and an escort of young men there was a volley in her honour. We did not go to church to see that wedding, as we were not attracted by the bridal pair; but we watched the crowd from our windows, and as it was a wet day, endured the sounds of revelry that lasted for hours after the feast began. There was no dancing at this marriage, and as each batch of guests departed a brass band just outside our rooms played them a send-off. It was a jerky irritating performance, because the instant the object of their attentions disappeared round the turn of the hill they stopped short, and only began a new tune when there was a new departure. We were rather glad when the day came to an end. In the Black Forest you always know where there is a wedding, because two small fir trees are brought from the forest decked with flying coloured streamers of paper or ribbon, and set on either side of the bride's front door.

The German peasant loves his pipe and his beer, and on a Sunday afternoon his game of *Kegel*; but on high days and holidays he likes to be dancing. He and she will trudge for miles to dance at some distant village inn. You meet them dressed in their best clothes, walking barefoot and carrying clean boots and stockings. How they can dance in tight boots after a long hot walk on a dusty road, you must be a German peasant yourself to understand. The dance I remember best took place in a barn belonging to a village inn in Bavaria. I went with several English friends to look on at it, and the men of our party danced with some of the village girls. The room was only lighted by a few candles, and it was so crowded that while everyone was dancing everyone was hustled. But we were told that anyone who chose could " buy the floor " for a time by giving sixpence or a shilling to the band. Two of the Englishmen did this, and the crowd looked on in solemn approval while they waltzed once or twice round with the pretty granddaughters of our hosts. It was a scene I have often wished I could paint, the crowd was so dense, and the faces, from our point of view, so foreign. The candles only lifted the semi-darkness here and there, but where their light fell it flashed on the bright-coloured handkerchiefs which the women of this village twisted round their heads like turbans, and pinned across their bosoms. I think it is absurd, though, to say that German peasants dance well. They enjoy the exercise immensely, but are heavy and loutish in their movements, and they flounder about in a grotesque way with their hands on each other's shoulders. At a *Kirchweih* they dance in the open air.

A *Kirchweih* is a feast to celebrate the foundations of the village church, and it takes the form of a fair. The preparations begin the day before, when the round-abouts and shooting booths are put up in the appointed field. On the day before the *Kirchweih* in our Bavarian village I found the inn-keeper's wife cooking what we call Berlin pancakes in a cauldron of boiling fat, the

18

like of which I have never seen before or since for size. It must have held gallons. All day long she stood there throwing in the cinnamon flavoured batter, and taking out the little crisp brown balls. They are, it seems, a favourite dainty at a Bavarian *Kirchweih*, and must be provided in large quantities. On the fair field itself the food offered by the stall-keepers seemed to be chiefly enormous slabs of shiny gingerbread made in fanciful shapes, such as hearts, lyres, and garlands, cheap sweetmeats, and the small boiled sausages the artless German eats in public without a knife and fork.

The *Kirchweih* is the chief event of the summer in a German village, and is talked of for weeks beforehand. The peasants stream in from all the villages near, and join in the dancing and the shooting matches. When the day is fine and the fair field has a background of wooded hills, you see where the librettists of pre-Wagnerian days went for their stage effects. All the characters of many a German opera are there correctly dressed, joining in the songs and dances, shooting for wagers, making love, sometimes coming to blows. But you may look on at a *Kirchweih* from morning till night without seeing either horseplay or drunkenness. Not that the German peasant is an opera hero in his inner life. He is a hard-working man, God-fearing on the whole, stupid and stolid often, narrowly shrewd often, having his eye on the main chance. When he is stupid but not God-fearing he dresses himself and his wife in their best clothes, puts his insurance papers in his pockets, sets his thatched house on fire, and goes for a walk. Then he is surprised that he is caught and punished. Fires are frequent in German villages, and in a high wind and where the roofs are of straw destruction is complete sometimes. You often come across the blackened remains of houses, and you always feel anxious about the new buildings that will replace them. It is a good deal to say, but I believe our own jerry-builders are outdone in florid vulgarity by German villadom, and the German atrocities will last longer than ours, because the building laws are more stringent. But the old *Bauernhaus* still to be seen in most parts of the Black Forest is dignified and beautiful. The Swiss chalet is a poor gim-crack thing in comparison. Sometimes the German house has a shingled roof, and sometimes a thatched roof dark with age, and it has drooping eaves and an outside staircase and balcony of wood. It shelters the farm cattle in the stables on the ground floor, and the family on the upper floor, and in the roof there are granaries. But the beautiful old thatched roofs are gradually giving place to the slate ones, because they burn so easily, and fire, when it comes, is the village tragedy. I can remember when a fire in a big German commercial town was proclaimed by a beating drum, the noisy parade of fire-men, the clanging of bells, and all the hullaballoo that panic and curiosity could make. But last year, in Berlin, looking at houses like the tower of Babel, I said something of fire, and was told that no one felt nervous nowadays, the arrangements for dealing with it were so complete.

"People just look out of the window, see that there is a fire next door, or above or beneath them, and go about their business," said my hosts. "They know that the fire brigade will do their business and put it out."

I did not see a fire in Berlin, so I had no opportunity of witnessing the remarkable coolness of the Berliner in circumstances the ordinary man finds trying; but I saw a fire in my Bavarian village, and there were not many cool people there. The summons came in the middle of the night with the hoarse insistent clanging of the church bell, the sudden start into life of the sleeping village, the sounds in the house and in the street of people astir and terrified. Then there came the brilliant reflection of the flames in the opposite windows, and the roar and crackle of fire no one at first knew where. It was only a barn after all, a barn luckily detached from other buildings. Yet when we got into the street we found most of the population removing its treasures, as if danger was imminent. All the beds and chairs and pots and pans of the place seemed to be on the cobble-stones, and the women wailed and the children wept. " But the village is not on fire," we said. " It may be at any moment," they assured us, and were scandalised by our cold-bloodedness. For we had not carted our trunks into the street, but hastened towards the burning barn to see if we could help the men and boys carrying water. The weather was still and the barn isolated, so we knew there was no danger of the fire spreading. But the villagers were too excitable and too panic-stricken to be convinced of this. All their lives they had dreaded fire, and when the flames broke out so near them they thought that their houses were doomed.

Next to fire the German peasant hates beggars and gipsies. We were six months in the Black Forest and only met one beggar the whole time, and he was a decent-looking old man who seemed to ask alms unwillingly. But in some parts of Germany there are a great many most unpleasant-looking tramps. The village council puts up a notice that forbids begging, and has a general fund from which it sends tramps on their way. But it does not seem able to deal with the caravans of gipsies that come from Hungary and Bohemia. In a Thuringian village we came down one morning to find our inn locked and barricaded as if a riot was expected, and an attack. Even the shutters were drawn and bolted. " *Was ist denn los?* " we asked in amazment, and were told that the gipsies were coming.

" But will they do you any harm ? " we asked.

" They will steal all they can lay hands on," our landlady assured us. She was a widow, and her brewer, the only man in her employ, was, we supposed, standing guard over his own house. We thought the panic seemed extreme, but we had never encountered Hungarian gipsies on the warpath, and we did not know how many were coming. So, after assuring our excited little Frau that we would stand by her as well as we could, we went to an upper window to watch for the enemy. Presently the procession began, a straggling procession of the dirtiest, meanest-looking ruffians ever seen. There was waggon after waggon, swarming with ragamuffins of both sexes and all ages. The men were mostly on foot, casting furtive glances to right and left, evident snappers-up of unconsidered trifles, truculent, ragged, wearing evil-looking knives by their sides. During their transit the village had shut itself up, as Coventry did for Godiva's ride. When we all ventured forth again the talk was of missing poultry and rifled fruit trees. The geese had luckily started for their day on the high pastures before the bad folk came ; for in a German village there is always a gooseherd. Sometimes it is a little boy or girl, sometimes an old woman, and early in the morning whoever has the post collects the whole flock, drives it to a chosen feeding ground, spends the day there, and brings it back at night. It must be a contemplative life, and in dry weather pleasant. I think it would suit a philosopher if he could choose his days. In our Franconian village the gooseherd was a little boy, vastly proud of his job. Every morning, long

before we were up, he would stride past our windows
piping the same tune, and at the sound of it every
goose in the village would waddle out from her night
quarters and join the cackling fussy crowd at his heels.
Every evening as dusk fell he came back again, still
piping the same tune, and then the geese would detach
themselves in little groups from the main body and
find their own homes as surely as cows do.

Every rural district of Germany has its own novelist.
Fritz Reuter, Frenssen, Rosegger, Sudermann all write
of country life in the places they know best.   In
Hauptmann's beautiful plays you see the peasant
through a veil of poetry and mysticism.   Auerbach, I
am told, is out of fashion.   His stories end well
mostly, his construction one must admit is childish, and
his characters change their natures with the suddenness
of a thunderbolt to suit his plot.   Yet when I have
Sehnsucht for Germany, and cannot go there in reality,
I love to go in fancy where Auerbach leads.   He takes
you to a house in the Black Forest, and you sit at breakfast with the family eating *Haferbrei* out of one bowl.
You know the people gathered there as well as if you
had been with them all the summer, and you know them
now in winter time when the roads are deep in snow and
a wolf is abroad in the forest.   The story I am thinking
of was published in 1860, and I believe that there are
no wolves now in the Black Forest.   But as far as one
outside peasant life can judge, I doubt whether anything else has changed much.   You hear the history
of the *Grossbauer*, the rich farmer of the district whose
breed is as strong and daring as the breed of the
Volsungs.   Seven years ago the only son and heir of
this forest magnate, Adam Röttman, loved a poor
girl called Martina, and their child Joseph is now six
years old.   Adam is still faithful to Martina, but his

parents will not consent to their marriage, and insists
on betrothing him to an heiress as rich as he will be,
Heidenmüller's Toni. The whole village looks on at
the romance and sides with Martina; for Adam's
mother, *die wilde Röttmännin*, is one of those stormy
viragoes I myself have met amongst German women.
She masters her husband and son with her temper.
She is so rich that she has more *Schmalz* than she can
use, and so mean that she would rather let it go bad
than give it to the poor. At midnight, when the roads
are deep in snow, she sends for the *Pfarrer*, and when
he risks his life and goes because he thinks she is
dying, he finds she is merely bored and wanted his
company; for she has been used to think that she
could tyrannise over all men because she was richer
and more determined than most. Next day she gets
up, orders her husband and son to put on Sunday
clothes, and well wrapped up in *Betten* drives with them
to the *Heidenmühle*, where Adam is formally betrothed
to Toni. The girl knows all about Martina, but she
consents because she would marry anyone to escape
from her stepmother, who treats her cruelly, and in
order to hurt her feelings has given her mother's cup to
the *Knecht*. After the betrothal the two fathers sit
together and drink hot spiced wine, the two mothers
gossip together, and the *Brautpaar* talk sadly about
Martina, who should be Adam's wife, and Joseph who
is his child. At last Adam could bear it no longer.
He would go straight to Martina, he said, and he
would be with Toni again before the Christmas tree
was lighted; and then he would either break with
Toni or feel free to marry her. " The bride stared at
Adam with amazement as he put on his grey cloak
and his fur cap and seized his pointed stick. He
looked both handsome and terrible." For he is one

of the heroes Germans love, a giant who once held a
bull by its horns while Martina escaped from it, who
is called the *Gaul*, because for a wager he once carried
the cart and the load a cart horse should have carried,
and who on this wild winter night meets the wolf in
the forest and kills it with his stick. So you see him
striding through the snow-bound forest to the village
where Martina lives, dragging the wolf after him, as
strong as Siegfried, as credulous as a child, ready to
believe that the voices of his father and his child both
looking for him in the snow are witches' voices. But
when he gets to the village he finds that his child, so
long disowned and disregarded, is really lost, and is
looking for him in the snow. The hatter who tramps
from village to village hung with hats met him, and
tried to turn him back. But the child said he had
come out to find his father, and must go on. Then
every man in the village assembles at the *Pfarrhaus*,
and, led by the *Pfarrer's* brother-in-law (an eventual
husband for Heidenmüller's Toni), sets out to find
Joseph in the snow. Before they start Adam vows
before the whole community that whether the child is
alive or dead nothing shall ever part him again from
Martina, and when he has made this vow you see the
whole company depart in various directions carrying
torches, ladders, axes, and long ropes. Meanwhile the
child, after some alarms and excursions, meets three
angels (children masquerading), who take him with
them to the mill where Toni has just lighted the
Christmas tree. She rescues Joseph from *die wilde
Röttmännin*, and that same night, her father dying of
his carouse, she becomes a rich heiress and free of
her wicked stepmother. Joseph's hostile grandfathers,
after a fight in the snow, make friends, the obliging
Pfarrer marries Adam and Martina at midnight, and

soon after the *wilde Röttmännin* who will not be reconciled leaves this world. So everyone who deserves happiness gets it. But though you only half believe in the story you have been in the very heart of the Black Forest, the companion of its people, the observer of their most intimate talk and ways. You have heard the women gossip at the well, you have made friends with Leegart the seamstress, who believes that quite against her will she is gifted with supernatural powers. There is Häspele, too, who made Joseph his new boots, and would marry Martina if he could; and there is David, the father of Martina, who was hardly kept from murdering his daughter when she came home in disgrace, and whose grandson becomes the apple of his eye. The whole picture of these people is vivid and enchanting, touched with quaint detail, veined with the tragedy of their lives, glowing with the warm human qualities that knit them to each other. The South German loves to tell you that his country is *ein gesegnetes Land*, a blessed country, flowing with milk and honey; and whether you are reading Auerbach's peasant stories or actually staying amongst his peasant folk, you get this impression of their natural surroundings. Nature is kind here, grows forest for her people on the hill-tops, and wine, fruit and corn in her sheltered valleys, ripens their fruit in summer, gives them heavy crops of hay, and sends soft warm rain as well as sun to enrich their pastures.

In the eastern provinces of Germany the conditions of life amongst the poor are most unhappy. Here the land belongs to large proprietors, and until modern times the people born on the land belonged to the landlords too. No man could leave the village where he was born without permission, and he had to work for his masters without pay. Even in the memory of living men the whip was quite commonly used. In her most interesting account of a Silesian village,[1] Gertrud Dyhrenfurth says that the present condition of the peasantry in this region compares favourably with former times, but she admits that they are still miserably overworked and underpaid. They are no longer legally obliged to submit to corporal punishment, nor can they be forced to live where they were born, and as they emigrate in large numbers, scarcity of labour has brought about slightly improved conditions for those remaining. But a man's wage is still a mark a day in summer and 90 pf. in winter. A woman earns 60 pf. in summer and 50 pf. in winter. Besides receiving these wages, a family regularly employed lives rent free and gets a fixed amount of coal, and at harvest time some corn and brandy. You cannot say the family has a house or cottage to itself, because the system is to build long bare-looking barracks in which numbers of working families herd like rabbits in a warren. In modern times each family has a kitchen to itself, so there is one warm room where the small children can be kept alive. In former times there was a general kitchen, and in the rooms appointed to each family no heating apparatus; therefore, if the children were not to die of cold, they had to be carried every morning to the kitchen, where there was a fire. The present plan has grave disadvantages, as in one room the whole family has to sleep, eat, wash, and cook for themselves and for the animals in their care. The furniture consists of two or three bedsteads with straw mattresses and feather plumeaux, shelves for pots and pans, a china cupboard with glass doors, a table in the window, and wooden benches with backs. This installation is

[1] *Ein schlesisches Dorf und Rittergut*, von Gertrud Dyhrenfurth. Leipzig, Duncker und Humblot.

quite luxurious compared with that of a milkmaid's or a stablemaid's surroundings sixty or seventy years ago. " Her home consisted of a plank slung from the stable roof and furnished with a sack of straw and a plumeau. Her small belongings were in a little trunk in a wooden niche, her clothes in a chest that stood in the garret." Here is the life history of an unmarried working woman of eighty-six born in a Silesian village. When she left school she was apprenticed to a thrasher, with a yearly wage of four thalers, besides two chemises and two aprons as a Christmas present. Even in those days this money did not suffice for clothing, although even in winter the women wore no warm under-garments. Quite unprotected, they waded up to the middle in snow. . . . In summer the girl was in the barn and at work by dawn ; in winter they threshed by artificial light. A bit of bread taken in the pocket served as breakfast. The first warm meal was taken at midday. When the farm work was finished there was spinning to do till 10 o'clock."

This woman " bettered herself" as she grew older till she was earning 35 thalers (£5, 5s. 0d.) a year ; she accustomed herself to live on this sum, and when wages increased, to put by the surplus. So in her old age she is a capitalist, has saved enough for a decent funeral, for certain small legacies, and for such an amazing luxury as a tin foot-warmer. The family she faithfully served for so many years allows her coal, milk and potatoes, and when necessary pays for doctor and medicine. Her weekly budget is as follows—

							Pf.
Rent	.	.	.	.	,	.	50
Bread	.	.	.	.	,	.	25
Rolls	.	.	.	.	.	.	5
			Carried forward	.		.	80

	Brought forward .	.	Pf. 80
¼ lb. butter	. . . .	.	25
¼ lb. coffee and chicory	. . .	.	25
Sugar . . .	. .	.	15
1 lb. flour .	. .	.	.14
Salt . .	. . .	.	1
Light . .	. .	.	10
Washing . .	. .	.	5

1m. 75

Meat is of course out of the question, and in discuss-
ing another budget Fräulein Dyhrenfurth shows that
a family of eight people could only afford three
quarters of a pound a week. Their yearly expenses
amounted to 455 m. 26 pf., so each one of the eight
had to be fed and clothed for about 1s. 1d. a week.
Women are still terribly overworked in the fields.
They used to begin at four o'clock in the morning, and
go on till nine at night,—a working day, that is, of
seventeen hours for a wife and the mother of a family.
When the family at the mansion had the great half-
yearly wash, the village women called in to help began
at midnight, and stood at the washtub till eight o'clock
next evening, twenty hours, that is, on end. In 1880
the working day was shortened, and only lasts now
from five in the morning till seven at night, with a
two hours' pause for dinner and shorter pauses for
breakfast and vesper. But, on the other hand, women
do work now that only men did in former times. The
threshing of corn has fallen entirely into their hands,
and they follow a plough yoked with oxen. Both
kinds of work are heavy and unpleasant. But women
are glad to get the threshing in winter time when
other work fails, and it is often on this account that
the proprietors do not introduce threshing machines.
At certain times of the year Poles swarm over the

frontier into the eastern provinces of Germany, but Fräulein Dyhrenfurth says that they do not work for lower wages. The women have no house-keeping to do, and can therefore give more hours to field labour. One woman prepares a meal for a whole gang of her country people, and they live almost entirely on bread, potatoes, and brandy. They do not mix with the Germans, but spend their evenings and Sundays in playing the harmonium, dancing, and drinking. They return every year, are always foreigners in Germany, and are very industrious, religious, contented, and cheerful, but inclined to drink and fight.

CHAPTER XXV

HOW THE POOR LIVE

POVERTY in German cities puts on a more respectable face than it does in London or Manchester. It herds in the cellars and courtyards of houses that have an imposing frontage; and when it walks out of doors it does not walk in rags. But you only have to look at the pinched faces of the children in the poorer quarters of any city to know that it is there. They are tidier and cleaner than English slum children, but they make you wish just as ardently that you were the Pied Piper and could pipe them all with you to a land of plenty. It would require more experience and wider facts than I possess to compare the condition of the poor in England and Germany, especially as the professed economists and philanthropists who make it their business to understand such things disagree with each other about every detail. If you talk to Englishmen, one will tell you that the German starves on rye bread and horse sausage because he is oppressed by an iniquitous tariff; and the next will assure you that the German flourishes and fattens on the high wages and prosperous trade he owes entirely to his admirable protective laws. If you talk to the Anglophobe, he will tell you that the dirt, drunkenness, disease, and extravagance of the English lower classes are the sin and scandal of the civilised world; that it is useless for you to ask where the poor live in Berlin, because there are no poor. Everyone in Germany is clean, virtuous, well housed, and well-to-do. If you talk to an honest, reasonable German, he will recognise that each country has its own difficulties and its own shortcomings, and that both countries make valiant efforts to fight their own dragons. He will tell you of the suffering that exists amongst the German poor crowded into these houses with the imposing fronts, and of all that statecraft and philanthropy are patiently trying to accomplish. Doctor Shadwell, in his most valuable and interesting book *Industrial Efficiency*, says that the American has to pay twice as much rent as the English working man, and that rents in Germany are nearer the American than the English level. As wages are lower in Germany than in England, and as meat and groceries are decidedly dearer, it is plain that the working man cannot live in clover. Doctor Shadwell gives an example of a smith earning 1050 marks, and having to pay 280 for rent. He had a wife and two children, and Doctor Shadwell reckoned that the family to make two ends meet must live on 37 pf. per head per day; the prison scale per head being 80 pf. I know a respectable German charwoman who earns 41 marks a month, and pays 25 marks a month for her parterre flat in the *Hof*. She lets off all her rooms except the kitchen, and she sleeps in a place that is only fit for a coal-hole. A work-girl pays her 6 marks a month for a clean tidy bedroom furnished with a solid wooden bedstead, a chest of drawers, a sofa, and a table. This girl works from 7.30 to 6 in a shop, she pays the charwoman 10 pf. for her breakfast, 10 pf. weekly for her lamp, and another 10 pf. for the use and comfort of the kitchen fire at night. Her dinner of soup, meat, and vegetables the

girl gets at a *Privatküche* for 40 pf. So the workgirl's
weekly expenses for food, fire, and lodging are 5 marks
20 pf., but this does not give her an evening meal or
afternoon coffee. The charwoman reckoned that she
herself only had 15 marks a month for food, fire, light,
and clothes; but she got nearly all her food with the
families for whom she worked. She was a cheerful,
honest body, and though she slept in a coal-hole was
apparently quite healthy. She looked forward to her
old age with tranquillity, because before long she would
be in receipt of a pension from the State, a weekly sum
that with her habits of thrift and industry would enable
her to live.

A German lady who chooses to teach in a *Volks-
schule*, because she thinks the *Volk* more interesting
than Higher Daughters, described a home to me from
which one of her pupils came. The parents had eight
children, and the family of ten lived in two rooms.
That is a state of things we can match in England,
unhappily. But my friend described this home, not on
account of its misery, but for the extraordinary neatness
and comfort the mother maintained in it. "Every
time I go there," said my friend, who lived with her
father and sister in a charming flat,—"every time I go
there I say to the woman, if only it looked like this in
my home"; and there was no need for me to see the
rooms to understand what she meant; for I know the
air of order and even of solidity with which the poorest
Germans will surround themselves if they are respectable. They have very few pieces of furniture, but those
few will stand wear and tear; they prefer a clean
painted floor to a filthy carpet, and they are so poor
that they have no pence to spend on plush photograph
frames. I cannot remember what weekly wage this
family existed on, but I know that it seemed quite

inadequate, and when I asked if the children were healthy as well as clean and tidy, my friend admitted that they were not. In spite of the brave struggle made by the parents, it was impossible to bring up a large family on such means, and the maladies arising from insufficient food, fire, and clothing afflicted them. The case is, I think, a typical one. English people are always impressed when they visit German cities by the tidy clothes poor people wear, and if they are shown the right interiors, by their clean tidy homes. But you need most carefully and widely collected facts and figures to judge how far the children of a nation are suffering from poverty. It was found, for instance, in one German city, that out of 1472 children examined in the elementary schools, 63 per cent. of the girls and 60 per cent. of the boys were *nicht völlig normal.*

Moreover, there are whole classes of poor people in Germany whose homes are not tidy and comfortable, who are crowded into cellars and courtyards, and who have neither time nor strength for the decencies of life. The "Sweater" flourishes in Berlin as well as in London, and his victims are as overworked as they are here. He is usually a Jew, it is said in Berlin, but I will not guarantee the truth of that, for I have not observed that the Jew is anywhere a harder task-master than the Christian. As Berlin grew, these spiders of society increased in numbers, finding it easy and profitable to employ home workers and spare themselves the expenses of factories and of insurance. Women who could not go out to work were tempted by the chance offered them of earning a trifle at home, and woman-like never paused to reckon whether it was worth earning. As the city gets larger every evil connected with the system increases. The worst paid are naturally the incompetent rough peasant

women who swarm into Berlin from the country
districts, because they think that it will be easier
to sit at a machine than to labour in the fields.
These people have to buy their machines and their
cotton at high prices from their employers, and then
they get 10 pf. for making a blouse. A lady who
spends her life in working amongst poor people told
me that many of them worked for nothing in reality,
because the trifle they earned only just paid the
difference between the food they had to buy ready
cooked and the food they might with more leisure
prepare at home. They pay high rents for wretched
homes, £15, for instance, for a kitchen and one room in
a dark courtyard. Under £13 it is impossible to get
anything in the poorest quarter of Berlin.

"The house itself looked respectable enough from
outside," says Frau Buchholz, when she went to see a
girl who had just married a poor man ; "but oh ! those
steep narrow stairs that I had to mount, those wretched
entrances on each floor, the miserable door handles, the
sickly bluish-grey walls, the shaky banisters ! It was
easy to see that the outside had been devised with a
view to investors, and the inside for poverty." In houses
of this class there are often three courtyards, one behind
each other, all noisy and badly kept. The conditions
of life in such circumstances are no better than in our
own notorious slums, but a slum seven storeys high, and
presenting a decent front to the world, does not suggest
the real misery behind its regular row of windows, nor
does the quiet well-swept street give any picture of the
rabbit warren in the courtyards at the back. In the
enormous " confection " trade of Berlin the home-workers
are nearly all widows and mothers of families, as the
unmarried girls prefer to go to factories. A skilled
hand can earn a fair wage at certain seasons of the year,

as the demand for skilled work in this department always exceeds the supply. But the average wage of the unskilled worker is only 10 marks a week, while it sinks as low as 4 marks for petticoats, aprons, and woollen goods. A corset maker, who has learned her trade, can only make from 8 to 10 marks a week in a factory, while a woman who sits at home and covers umbrellas gets 1 mark 50 pf. *a dozen* when the coverings are of stuff, and slightly more when they are of silk. The extreme poverty of these home-workers is a constant subject of inquiry and legislation, but for various reasons it is most difficult to combat. The market is always overcrowded, because, badly paid as it is, the work is popular. Women push into it from the middle classes for the sake of pocket-money, and from the agrarian classes because they fancy a city life. Efforts are being made to organise them, and especially to train the daughters of these women to more healthy and profitable trades. I went over a small *Volksküche* in Berlin, and was told that there were many like it established by various charitable agencies, and that the effect of them was to make the children ready to go into service; a life that has some drawbacks, but should at any rate be wholesome and civilising,—a better preparation for marriage, too, than to sit like a slattern over a machine all day, and buy scraps of expensive ready-made food, because both time and skill are wanting for anything more palatable. In the kitchen I visited there were sixteen children from the poorest families in the neighbourhood, and, assisted by a superintendent and two teachers, they were preparing a dinner that cost 30 pf. a head for 250 people. The rooms were clean and plainly furnished. A small laundry business was run in connection with the kitchen, so that the girls should be thoroughly trained to wash and iron as well as to cook. Of late years the working

classes of Berlin have adopted what they call *Englische
Tischzeit*, and no one who knows the ways of the English
artisan will guess that the German means *late dinner*.
He now does his long day's work, I am told, on bread
alone, and has the one solid meal in the twenty-four
hours when he gets home at night. *Durch Arbeiten*, he
calls it, and people interested in the welfare of the poor
say it is bad for all concerned, but especially bad for
the children, who come in too exhausted to eat, and
for the women, who have to cook and clean up when
the day's business should be nearly done. It is quite
characteristic of some kinds of modern Germans that
they should in a breath condemn us, imitate us, and
completely misunderstand our ways.

The business women of Germany have organised
themselves. *Der Kaufmännische Verband für Weibliche
Angestellte* was founded by Herr Julius Meyer in 1889,
and, beginning with 50 members, numbered 17,000 in
1904. Its aim has been to improve the conditions of
life for women working in shops and businesses, to carry
on their education, and to help them when ill or out of
work. It began by opening commercial schools for
women, where they could receive a thorough training
in book-keeping, shorthand, typewriting, and other
branches of office work. These have been a great
success, have been imitated all over Germany, and have
led to an expansion of the law enforcing on girls attendance at the State continuation schools. The society
was founded to remedy some crying abuses amongst
women employed in shops and offices, a working day of
seventeen hours, for instance, dismissal without notice,
no rest on Sundays, no summer holiday, and not only
a want of seats but an actual prohibition to sit down
even when unemployed. All these matters the society,
which has become a powerful one, has gradually set

right. A ten-hours' day for grown-up women, and eight hours for those under age, the provision of seats, an 8 o'clock closing rule, a month's notice on either side, some hours of rest on Sunday, and a summer holiday are all secured to members of the organisation. The system of " living in " does not obtain in Germany. Shops may only open for five hours on Sundays now, and large numbers do not open at all. They may only keep open after ten on twenty days in the year. Other reforms the society hopes to bring about in time ; and meanwhile it occupies itself both in finding work for members who are out of place, and in protecting those who are sick and destitute.

The ladies of Germany have taken to philanthropic work with characteristic energy and thoroughness. There is one society in Berlin that has 700 members, some of whom devote their whole time to their poor neighbours. I am not going to give the name of the society, so I may describe one of its secretaries, who personified the best modern type of German woman. She was about 27, a dark-haired, slim, serious-looking person with delicate Jewish features and beautiful grey eyes ; a girl belonging to the wealthy classes, and able if she had chosen to lead a life of frivolity and pleasure. But she had chosen instead to give herself to the sick, the afflicted, the needy, and even to the sinning ; for she was a moving spirit of the organisation that dives down into the depths of the great city, and rescues those who have gone under. Her society also does a great deal for the children of the very poor, not only for babies in crêches, but for those who go to school. The members help these older ones with their school work, and when the children are free teach them to wash, cook, and sew, and to play open-air games. They teach the blind, they look after the deserted families of men in prison, and the older members act as guardians to illegitimate children; for in Germany every illegitimate child must have a guardian, and women are now allowed to act in this capacity. The secretary said they found no difficulty in getting both married and single women to take up these good works.

"What do the parents say when their daughters take it up?" I asked, for I could not picture the German girl as I had always known her going out into the highways and byways of the city, leaving her cooking, her music, her embroidery, and her sentiment, and battling with the hideous realities of life amongst the sick, the poor, and the more or less wicked of the earth.

"The parents don't like it," my girl with the honest eyes admitted. "When girls have worked for us some time they often refuse to marry; at least, they refuse the arranged marriages proposed to them. But we cannot stop on that account. If a girl does not wish to marry in this way it is better that she should not. No good can come of it."

Then she went on to tell me how well it was that a child born to utmost shame and poverty should have a woman of the better classes interested from the beginning in its welfare, and responsible for its decent upbringing. It implied contact with various officials, of course, but she said that the ladies who took this work in hand met with courtesy and support everywhere.

You have only to place this type of young woman beside the *Backfisch*, who represents an older type quite fairly, to understand how far the modern German girl has travelled from the traditional lines. If you can imagine the *Backfisch* married and mentally little altered in her middle age, you can also imagine that she would find a daughter with the new ideas upsetting.

At present both types are living side by side, for there are still numbers of women of the old school in Germany, women who passively accept the life made for them by their surroundings, whether it suits their needs or not; and who would never strike out a path for themselves, even if by doing so they could forget their own troubles in the troubles of others.

The State and Municipal establishments for the poor and sick have been so much described lately, that everyone in England must be acquainted with all that Berlin does for its struggling citizens.   There are, of course, large hospitals and sanatoriums for consumption; and the admirable system of national insurance secures help in sickness to every working man and woman, as well as a pension in old age. "The club doctor and dispensary as we have them here do not exist," say the Birmingham Brassworkers in their pamphlet.   " In their stead leading doctors and specialists (with very few exceptions) are at the service of the working man or woman."

"Yes," said a leading doctor to me when I quoted this; "we get about three half-pence for a consultation, and we find them the most impossible people in the community to satisfy.   As they get medical advice for nothing they run from one doctor to another, and consult a dozen about some simple ailment that a student could set right.   We all suffer from them." So that is the other side of the question.

But Berlin certainly manages its Submerged Tenth both more humanely and more wisely than we manage ours.   It begins, as one thinks any civilised country must, by separating those who will not work from those who cannot.   The able-bodied beggar, the drunkard, and other vagrants are sent to a house of correction and made to work.   The respectable poor are not driven to herd with these people in Germany. They receive shelter and assistance at institutions reserved for the deserving. In one of these old married people who cannot support themselves are allowed to spend the evening of their lives together. Anyone desiring to know more about the charitable institutions of Berlin will find a most interesting account of them in the pamphlet written by the Birmingham Brassworkers, and published by P. S. King & Son. The bias of the authors is so strongly German that when you have read to the end you begin to lean in the opposite direction, and look for the things we manage better over here. " In 1900," they say, " there was such a shortage of houses (in Berlin) that 1500 families had to be sheltered in the Municipal Refuge for Homeless People." That is surely a worse state of affairs than in London. But when you walk through London or a London suburb in winter, and are pestered at every crossing and corner by able-bodied young beggars of both sexes, you begin to agree with the brassworkers. Berlin is clear of beggars and crossing-sweepers all the year round, and you know that as far as possible they are classified and treated according to their deserts. It is not possible for the individual bent on his own business to know at a glance whether he will encourage vice by giving alms or behave brutally to a deserving case by withholding them. The decision should never be forced upon him as it is in England every day of his life.

CHAPTER XXVI

BERLIN

ONCE upon a time a German got hold of Aladdin's lamp, and he summoned the Djinn attendant on the lamp. " Build me a city of broad airy streets," he bade him, " and where several streets meet see that there is an open place set with trees and statues and fountains." All the houses, even those that the poor inhabit, are to be big and white and shining, like palaces; but the real palaces where princes shall live may be plain and grey. There are to be pleasure grounds in the midst of the city, but they are to be woods rather than parks, because even you and the lamp cannot make grass grow in this soil and climate. In the pleasure grounds, and especially on either side of one broad avenue, there are to be sculptured figures of kings and heroes, larger than life and as white as snow. The Djinn said it would be easy to build the city in a night as the German desired, but that the sculpture could not be hurried in this way, because artists would have to make it, and artists were people who would not work to order or to time. The German, however, said he was master of the lamp, and that the city must be ready when he wanted it early next morning. So the Djinn set to work and got the city ready in a night, sculpture and all. But when he had finished he had not used half the figures and garlands and other stone ornaments he had made. If he had been in England he might have reduced them in size,

and given them to an Italian hawker to carry about
on his head on a tray. But he knew that hawkers
would not be allowed in the city he had built. So,
as he was rather tired and anxious to be done, he
quickly made one more long, broad street stretching
all the way from the pleasure ground in the centre
of the city to the forest that begins where the city
ends; and on every house in the street he put figures
and garlands and gilded balconies and ornamental
turrets, as many as he could. The effect when he
had finished pleased him vastly, and he said it was
the finest street in the city, and should be called the
Kurfürstendamm. His master and all the Germans
who came to live in it agreed with him. They gave
large rents for a flat in one of the houses, and when
they went to London and saw the smoky dwarfish
houses there they came away as quickly as possible
and rubbed their hands and were happy, and said
to each other, " How beautiful is our *Kurfürstendamm*.
We have as many turrets as we have chimneys, and
we have garlands on our balconies of green or gilded
iron, and some of us have angelic figures made of red
brick, so that the angelic faces are checked with white
where the bricks are joined together."

" But it does not become anyone from England to
criticise the architecture and sculpture of a foreign
country," I said to the artist who told me the story
of the lamp. " Our own is notoriously bad."

" It is not you who will criticise ours," he answered.
" By your own confession, you know nothing whatever
of architecture and sculpture, and when people know
nothing they should either keep silence or ask for
information in the best quarter. You have my authority
for saying that the architects and sculptors of Berlin
would have been better employed building dog-kennels."

" But I rather like your wide cheerful streets," I objected, " and your tall clean houses. Our houses . . ."

" Your houses are little black boxes in which people eat and sleep. They do not pretend to anything. Ours pretend to be beautiful, and are ridiculous. Moreover, in England there are men who can build beautiful houses. You do not employ them much. You prefer your ugly little boxes. But they are there. I know their names and their work."

" But what do you think of our statues ? " I asked him

" I don't think of them," he said ; " I prefer to think of something pleasant. When I am in London I spend every hour I have at the docks."

" I like the *Sieges-Allee*," I said boldly,—" it is so clean and cheerful."

" It was made for people who look at sculpture from that point of view," said my friend.

I hardly know where an artist finds inspiration in the streets of Berlin. It really makes the impression of a city that has sprung up in a night, and that is kept clean by invisible forces. The great breadth of the streets, the avenues of trees everywhere, and the many open places make it pleasant ; but you look in vain for the narrow lanes and gabled houses still to be found in other German towns, and you are not surprised when Americans compare it with Chicago, because it is so new and busy. It is indeed the city of the modern German spirit, and what it has of old tradition and old social life lies beneath the surface, hidden from the eye of the stranger. There is Sans-Souci, to be sure, and Frederick the Great, and the Grosser Kurfürst. There is the double line of princes on either side of the *Sieges-Allee*. But modern Berlin dates from 1870, and so do all good Berliners, whatever their age may be. They are proud of their young empire and of

their big city, and of doing everything in the best possible way. There is unceasing flux and growth in Berlin,
so that descriptions written a few years ago are as
out of date as these impressions must be soon. For
instance, I had counted steadfastly on finding three
things there that I cannot find at home : first and
second-class cabs, hordes of soldiers everywhere, and
policemen who would run a sword through you if you
looked at them ; and of all these I was more or less
disappointed.

I did get hold of a second-class cab on my arrival in
Berlin, but it nearly came to pieces on the way, and I
never saw another during my stay there. The cabs
are all provided with the taximeter now, so that the fare
knows to a fraction what is due to the driver ; and the
drivers are of the first class, and wear white hats. Anyone who wished to see a second-class cab would have
to make inquiries, and find a stand where some still
languish, but before long the last of them will probably
be preserved in a museum. Cabs are not much used in
Berlin, because communication by the electric cars is
so well organised. The whole population travels by
them, the whole city is possessed by them. If it is to
convey a true impression, a description of Berlin should
run to the moan of them as they glide everlastingly to
and fro. You can hardly escape their noise, and not
for long their sight. Even the Tiergarten, the Hyde
Park of Berlin, is traversed by them, which is as it
should be in a municipal republic. This is what the
Germans call their city, for they are not conscious
themselves of living under an autocracy or of being in
any sense of the word less free than, let us say, the
English, a point of view most puzzling to an English
person, who is conscious from the moment he crosses
the German frontier of being governed for his good.

But it is pleasant on a summer morning to be carried through the shady avenues of the Tiergarten in an open car, whether it is an autocracy or are public that arranges it for you; and you reflect that in this and a thousand other ways Germany is an agreeable country even if it is not a free one; especially for " the people " who have small means, and are able to drive through the chief pleasure ground of their city for a penny. The conductors of the cars are obliged to announce the name of the next halting-place, so that passengers alighting may get up in time and step off directly, but on no account before the car stops. Nothing is left to chance or muddle in Berlin, and unless you are a born fool you cannot go astray. If you are a born fool you ask a policeman, as you would at home, and find another dear illusion shattered. He does not draw his sword, he is neither gruff nor disobliging. He greets you with the military salute, and calls you gracious lady. Then he answers your question if he can. If not he gets out the little guide book he carries, and patiently hunts up the street or the building you want. He is usually a good-natured rosy faced young man with a fair moustache, and he will do anything in the world for you except control the traffic. That with the best will in the world he cannot do. So he stands in the midst of it and smiles. Sometimes he sits amidst it on a horse and looks solemn. But he never impresses himself on it. There is a story of a policeman who went to London to learn from our men what to do, and who bemoaned his fate when he got back. " I hold up my hand in just the same way," he said, "and then the people run and the horses run, and there's a smash and I get put in prison." The Berliners themselves say that they are not accustomed yet, as we have been for years, to regard the police as their well-liked and trusted servants, and to obey their directions willingly. However this may be, there is at present only one safe way of getting to the opposite side of a busy street in Berlin, and that is to wait till a crowd gathers and charges across it in a bunch like a swarm of bees.

Berlin is never asleep, and it is as light by night as by day. It is much pleasanter for a woman without escort to come out of the theatre there than in London. She will find crowds of respectable people with her, and they will not depart in their own cabs and carriages. They will crowd into the electric cars, and she must know which car she wants and crowd with them. The worst that can happen to her will be to find her car overcrowded, and in that case she must not expect a man to give her his seat. I have seen a young German lady make an old lady take her place, but I have never known men yield their seats to women. You do not see as many private carriages in Berlin in a week as you do in some parts of London in an hour. Even in front of the Opera House very few will be in waiting; and there is no fashionable hour for riding and driving in the Tiergarten. I know too little about horses to judge of those that were being ridden, or driven in private carriages; but the miserable beasts in cabs and carts force the most ignorant person to observe and pity them. They look as if they were on their way to the knacker's yard, and very often as if they must sink beneath the load they are compelled to carry. It is comforting to reflect that horses will doubtless soon be too old-fashioned for Berlin, and that all the cabs and vans of the future will be motors. The cars run early enough in the morning for the workmen, and late enough at night for people who have had supper at a popular restaurant after the theatre or a glass of beer

at one of the *Zelten*, the garden restaurants that in the
time of Frederick the Great were really tents, and
where the Berliners flocked then as they do now to
hear a band, look at the trees of the Tiergarten, and
enjoy light refreshments. When you get back to your
house from such gaieties you find it locked and in
darkness, but though there is a "portier" you do not
disturb him by calling out your name as you would in
Paris. In modern houses there is electric light outside
each floor that you switch on for yourself, and you have
a race with it that you lose unless you are active; but
you soon learn to feel your way up to the next light
when you are left in darkness. The Berlin "portier"
is not as much in evidence as the Paris concierge. He
opens the door to strangers, but if you stay or live in
the house you are expected to carry two heavy keys
about with you, one for the street door and one for
the flat. The modern doors have some machinery by
which they shut themselves noiselessly after you. You
hear a great deal more said about "nerves" in Germany
than in England, and yet Germans seem to be amaz-
ingly indifferent to noise. They will not tolerate the
brass bands and barrel-organs that pester us, but
that is because they are fond of music. Screaming
voices, banging doors, and the clatter of kitchens and
business premises seem not to trouble them at all.
Most houses in Berlin are five or six storeys high, and
are built round the four sides of a small paved court.
No one who has not lived in such a house, and in a
room giving on the court, can understand how every
sound increases and reverberates. Footsteps at dawn
sound as if the seven-leagued boots had come, and were
shod with iron. You whisper that the kitchen on a
lower floor in an opposite corner looks well kept, and
the maid hears what you say and looks at you smiling.

I knew that the back premises of these big German
hives might harbour any social grade and almost any
industry, and for a long time I vowed that some one
must live in our court whose business it was to hammer
tin, and that he hammered it most late at night and
early in the morning.   I had not heard anything like
the noise since I had lived in a high narrow German
street paved with cobble-stones, and occupied just
opposite my windows by a brewer whose vans returned
to him at daybreak and tumbled empty casks at his
door. . But I never discovered my tin merchant in
Berlin, and in time I had to admit that my hosts were
right.   The noise I complained of was made by the cook
washing up in the opposite kitchen.   I should not have
noticed it if I had been a sensible person, and slept
with my curtains drawn and my double windows tight
shut.

Of course, there are some quiet streets in Berlin, and
there are charming homes in the "garden-houses."
Some of the quadrangles are built round a garden
instead of a paved yard, and then you can get a quiet
pleasant flat with a balcony that looks on a garden
instead of a street.   The traditional plan of a Berlin
flat is most inconvenient and unpractical.   In old-
fashioned houses, and even in houses built sixteen
years ago or less, you find that one of the chief rooms
is the only thoroughfare between the bedrooms near
the kitchen premises and the rooms near the front door.
Anyone occupying one of these back rooms, which are
often good ones, can only get to the front door by way of
this thoroughfare, where he will usually find the family
gathered together ; the maid, too, must pass through
every time the door bell rings, and when she goes about
her business in the front regions her brooms and pails
must pass through with her.   The window of this room,

which is known as a *Berliner Zimmer*, is always in
one corner and lights it insufficiently. The Berliners
themselves recognise its disadvantages, but I like to
describe it, because I observe amongst the Germans
of to-day a fierce determination to destroy and deny
everything a foreigner might call a little absurd, even
if it is characteristic ; so I feel sure that if I go to
Berlin a few years hence there will not be a *Berliner
Zimmer* left in the city, and no Berliner will ever
have seen or heard of one ; nor will the flat doors have
the quaint little peepholes through which the maid's
eye may be seen appraising you before she lets you in.
The newest houses, those in the *Kurfürstendamm*, for
instance, have every " improvement "—central heating,
lifts, gas cooking stoves, sinks for washing up, and
bathrooms that are a reality and not a mere appearance.
These bathrooms, I am assured, can be used without
several hours' notice and the anxious superintendence
of the only person, the head of the family as a rule,
who understands the heating apparatus. Berlin, like
Mr. Barrie's Admirable Crichton, has found out how
to lay on hot and cold. It has found out about electric
light too, and it might teach London how to use the
telephone. Berlin talks to its friends by telephone
as a matter of course, asks them how they are, if they
enjoyed the *Fest* last night, whether if you call
on Tuesday they will be at home. Perhaps when Mr.
Wells goes to Berlin he will forsee a reaction, a revolt
against the incessant insistent bell that respects no
occupation and allows no undisturbed rest. It is a
hurried generation that uses the telephone so much, for
the letter boxes are emptied eighteen times in twenty-
four hours, and if the post is not quick enough or a
telegram too expensive for all you want to say you can
send a card by the tube post.

Berlin is not the city of soldiers that the English fancy pictures it. English people, English little boys, for instance, who would like to see all their lead soldiers come to life, must go to one of the smaller garrison towns, where in every street and every square they will watch men on the march and at drill. In those quarters of Berlin not occupied by barracks the population is civilian. You see the grey and the dark blue uniforms everywhere, but not in masses and not at work. The people rush like children to follow the guard changed at the Schloss every day; just as they might in London, where soldiers are a rare spectacle. In a smaller town the army is more evidently in possession. It fills the restaurants, occupies the front row of the stalls at the opera, prevails in public gardens, and holds the pavement against the world. But Berlin to all appearances belongs to its citizens, and provides for their profit and convenience. They fill its multitude of houses. They say they make its laws and order its progress. At any rate they live in an agreeable, well-managed city, full of air and light, and kept so clean that most other cities seem slovenly and grimy by comparison. To go suddenly from Berlin to Hamburg, for instance, gives you a shock; though Hamburg is incomparably more attractive and delightful. But in Hamburg you may see bits of paper lying about, and dust on the pavement. In Berlin there is no dust, and no one has ever seen an untidy bit of paper there. It is to be hoped that no one ever travels direct from Berlin to London. What would he think of Covent Garden Market? There are markets in Berlin, at least a dozen of them, but by midday they are swept and garnished. You would not find a leaf of parsley or an end of string to tell you where one had been.

CHAPTER XXVII

ODDS AND ENDS

THE most amusing columns in German daily papers are those devoted to family advertisement. There you find the prolix intimate announcements of domestic events compared with which the first column of the *Times* is so bare, so *nichtssagend*.

> "The birth of a second son is announced with joy by Dr Johann Weber and Wife Martha, born Hansen."—Dresden, 22 May 1907."

> "Emil Harzdorf and wife Magdalene, born Klaus, have the honour to announce the birth of a strong girl."—Hamburg, 26 May 1907."

Boy babies are nearly always *stramm*, the girl babies are *kräftig*, and the parents are *hocherfreut*, as they should be. Engagements and marriages are advertised more simply, and your eye is not caught by them as it is by the big black bordered paragraphs that inform the world that someone has just left it.

> "To-day, in consequence of a stroke of apoplexy, my deeply loved husband, our dear father, grandfather, father-in-law, brother, and uncle fell asleep. In the name of the survivors, Olga Wagner, born Richter.—Leipzig, 23 May 1907."

This is a curt announcement compared with many. When the deceased has occupied any kind of official post, or has been an employer of labour, a long register of his many virtues accompanies the advertisement of his death. " He who has just passed away was an exemplary chief, a fatherly friend and adviser, who by his benevolence erected an everlasting monument to himself in the hearts of his colleagues and subordinates." He who had just passed away had been the head of a small soap factory, and this advertisement was put in by the factory hands just beneath the one signed by all the family. Another advertisement on the same page expresses thanks for sympathy, " on the death of my dear wife, our good mother, grandmother, mother-in-law, aunt, sister-in-law, and cousin, Frau Angelika Pankow, born Salbach."

A German friend who had to undergo an operation last year wrote just before to tell me she expected to come through safely. " If not," she said, " you'll receive a card like this "—

" Yesterday passed away
        Adelaide Deminski, born Weigert,
          Her heart-broken

                    Husband
                    Grandmother
                    Father
                    Mother
                    Sons
                    Daughters
                    Sons-in-law
                    Daughters-in-law
                    Brothers
                    Sisters
                    Brothers-in-law
                    Sisters-in-law
                    Uncles
                    Aunts
                    Cousins " ;

for Germans themselves laugh at these advertisements, and assure the inquiring foreigner that their vogue has had its day. But if the inquiring foreigner looks at the right papers he will find as many as ever. You will also find matrimonial advertisements in papers that are considered respectable.

But when you turn to the news columns for details of some event that is startling the world, whether it is a crime, an earthquake, a battle, or a royal wedding, you find a few lines that vex you with their insufficiency. Our English papers have pages about a German coronation, German manoeuvres, German high jinks at Köpenick. But when I wanted to see what happened in London on our day of Diamond Jubilee I found five lines about Queen Victoria having driven to St. Paul's accompanied by her family and some royal guests. I was in a country inn at the time, and the paper taken there was one taken everywhere in the duchy. It is a great mistake to think that German newspaper hostility to England dates from the Transvaal War. The same journal that spared five lines to the Jubilee gave a column to a question asked by one of our parliamentary cranks about the ill-treatment of natives by Britons in India. The question was met by a complete and convincing denial, but we had to turn to our English papers to find that recorded. The —— *Tageblatt* printed the question with comments, and suppressed the denial. As long ago as 1883, when there was cholera in Egypt, a little Thuringian paper we saw weekly had frenzied articles about the evil English who were doing all they could to bring the scourge to Germany. I think we had refused some form of quarantine that modern medical science considers worse than useless. The tone of the press all through the Transvaal War did attract some attention in this country, and since then from time to time we are presented with quotations from abusive articles about our greed, our perfidy, and our presumption. I am not writing as a journalist, for I know nothing whatever of journalism; but as a member of the general public I believe that we are inclined to overrate the importance of these amenities, because we overrate the part played by the newspaper in the average German household. One can only speak from personal experience, but I should say that it hardly plays a part at all. Whatever Tageblatt is in favour with the *Hausherr* comes in every morning, and is stowed away tidily in a corner till he has time to look at it while he drinks his coffee and smokes his cigar. If the ladies of the household are inclined that way they look at it too. But there really is not much to look at as a rule. These paragraphs about the wicked British that seem so pugnacious when they are printed on solid English paper in plain English words, are often in a corner with other political paragraphs about other wicked nations. At times of crisis, when the leading papers are attacking us at great length, the Germans themselves will talk of *Zeitungsgeschrei* and shrug their shoulders. It is absurd to deny the existence of Anglophobia in Germany, because you can hardly travel there without coming across isolated instances of it. But these isolated instances will stand out against a crowded background of people from whom you have received the utmost kindness and friendship; and of other people with whom your relations have been fleeting, but who have been invariably civil. Unfortunately the German Anglophobe is a creature of the meanest breed, and he impresses himself on the memory like a pain; so that one of him looms larger than fifty others, just as the moment will when you had your last tooth out, and not the summer day that went before and after. The

truth is, that we are on the nerves of certain Germans.
You may live for ever in an English family and never
hear a German mentioned. You would assuredly not
hear the nation everlastingly discussed and scolded.
As far as we are concerned, they are welcome to their
own manners, their own ways, and their own opinions.
If they would only take their stand on these and leave
ours alone we could meet on equal terms. But that is
the one thing this particular breed of German cannot
do. He must be always arguing with you about the
superiority of his nation to yours, and you soon think him
the most tiresome and offensive creature you ever met.
In private life you can usually avoid him and seek out
those charming German people who, even if their
Tageblatt teaches them that they should hate England,
will never extend their hatred to the English stranger
within their gates, and who will admit you readily and
kindly to their pleasant unaffected lives. Germany is
full of such people, whatever the German newspapers
are saying.

Presumably every country has the press that suits it,
and in one respect German journalism is more dignified
and estimable than our own. It does not publish
columns of silly society gossip, or of fashions that only a
duchess can follow and only a kitchen-maid can read.
Nor would the poorest, smallest provincial Tageblatt
descend to the depths of musical criticism in which one
of our popular dailies complacently flounders all through
the London season.

"I cannot tell you much about last night's Wagner
opera, because to my great annoyance the auditorium
was dark nearly all the time. Once when we were
allowed to see each other for a moment I noticed that
the Duchess of Whitechapel was in her box, looking so
lovely in cabbage green. Mrs. 'Dicky' Fitzwegschwein

was in the stalls with a ruby necklace and a marvellous coat of rose velours spangled in diamonds, and on the grand tier I saw Lady 'Bobby' Holloway, who is of course the daughter-in-law of Lord Islington, in black net over silver, quite the dernier cri this season, and looking radiant over her sister Lady Yolande's engagement to the Duke of Bilgewater. Richter conducted with his usual brilliance, and the new Wotan sang with great élan, although he was obviously suffering from a cold in his head."

It is impossible to imagine Berlin waking some winter morning to find such a "criticism" as this on its breakfast table. In Germany, people who understand music write about music, and people who understand about fashions write about fashions, and the two subjects, both of them interesting and important, are kept apart. Society journalists who write about Lady Bobbies and Mrs. Fitzwegschweins do not exist yet in Germany, and so far the empire seems to worry along quite comfortably without them. I once asked a well-known English journalist who is of German birth, why one of our newspaper kings did not set up a huge, gossipy, frivolous paper in Berlin, and it was explained to me that it would be impossible, because the editor and his staff would probably find themselves in prison in a week. What we understand by Freedom of the Press does not exist there.

On the other hand, books and pamphlets are circulated in Germany that would be suppressed here; and the stage is freer than our own. *Monna Vanna* had a great success in Berlin, where Mme. Maeterlinck played the part to crowded audiences. *Salome* is now holding the stage both as a play and with Richard Strauss' music as an opera; Gorky's *Nachtasyl* is played year after year in Berlin. Both French and

German plays are acted all over Germany that could not be produced in England, both because the censor would refuse to pass them and because public opinion would not tolerate them, unless, to be sure, they were played in their own tongues. It is most difficult to explain our attitude to Germans who have been in London, because they know what vulgar and vicious farces and musical comedies pass muster with us, and indeed are extremely popular. It is only when a play touches the deeps of life and shows signs of thought and of poetry that we take fright, and by the lips of our chosen official cry, "This will never do." Tolstoy, Ibsen, Gorky, Bernard Shaw, Oscar Wilde, Hauptmann, and Otto Ernst are the modern names I find on one week's programme cut from a Berlin paper late in spring when the theatrical season was nearly over. Besides plays by these authors, one of the State theatres announced tragedies by Goethe, Schiller, and a comedy by Molière. The *Merchant of Venice* was being played at one theatre and *A Midsummer Night's Dream* at another; there were farces and light operas for some people, and Wagner, Gluck, and Beethoven at the Royal Opera House for others. The theatre in Germany is a part of national life and of national education, and it is largely supported by the State; so that even in small towns you get good music and acting. The Meiningen players are celebrated all over the world, and everyone who has read Goethe's Life will remember how actively and constantly he was interested in the Weimar stage. At a *Stadt-Theater* in a small town two or three operas are given every week, and two or three plays. Most people subscribe for seats once or twice a week all through the winter, and they go between coffee and supper in their ordinary clothes. Even in Berlin women do not wear full dress at any theatre.

In the little towns you may any evening meet or join the leisurely stream of playgoers, and if you enter the theatre with them you will find that the women leave their hats with an attendant. You are in no danger in Germany of having the whole stage hidden from you by flowers and feathers.

Shakespeare is as much played as Goethe and Schiller, and it is most interesting and yet most disappointing to hear the poetry you know line upon line spoken in a foreign tongue. Germans say that their translation is more beautiful and satisfying than the original English; but I actually knew a German who kept Bayard Taylor's *Faust* by his bedside because he preferred it to Goethe's. I think there is something the matter with people who prefer translated to original poetry, but I will leave a critic of standing to explain what ails them. I have never met a German who would admit that Shakespeare was an Englishman. They say that his birth at Stratford-on-Avon was a little accident, and that he belongs to the world. They say this out of politeness, because what they really believe is that he belongs to Germany, and that as a matter of fact Byron is the only great poet England has ever had. I am not joking. I am not even exaggerating. This is the real opinion of the German man in the street, and it is taught in lessons in literature. An English girl went to one of the best-known teachers in Berlin for lessons in German, and found, as she found elsewhere, that the talk incessantly turned on the crimes of England and the inferiority of England.

"You have had two great names," said the teacher, —"two and no more. That is, if one can in any sense of the word call Shakespeare an English name . . . Shakespeare and Byron, . . then you have finished.

You have never had anyone else, and Shakespeare has always belonged more to us than to you."

The English girl gasped, for she knew something of her own literature.

" But have you never heard about Chaucer," she asked, " or of the Elizabethans, or of Milton, Keats, Shelley, Wordsworth . . . ? "

" *Reden Sie nicht, reden Sie nicht !* " cried the teacher, —" I never allow my pupils to argue with me. Shakespeare and Byron . . . no, Byron only, . . . then England has done."

You still find Byron in every German household where English is read at all, and no one seems to have found out what fustian most of his poetry really was. Ruskin and Oscar Wilde are the two popular modern authors, and the novel-reading public chooses, so several booksellers assured me, Marion Crawford and Mrs. Croker. I could not hear a word anywhere of Stevenson or Rudyard Kipling, but I did come across one person who had enjoyed *Richard Feverel.*

" Your English novels are rather better than they used to be, are they not ? " said a lady to me in good faith, and I found it a difficult question to answer, because I had always believed that we had a long roll of great novelists; but then, I had also thought that England had a few poets.

The most popular German novels are mostly translated into English, and all German novels of importance are reviewed in our papers. So English people who read German know what a strong reaction there is against the moonshine of fifty years ago. The novels most in vogue exhibit the same coarse, but often thoughtful and impressive, realism that prevails on the stage and in the conversation and conduct of some sets of people in the big cities. The *Tagebuch einer*

Verlorenen has sold 75,000 copies, and it is the story of a German *Kamelliendame* compared with whom Dumas' lady is moonshine. It is a haunting picture of a woman sinning against the moral and social law, and no one with the least sense or judgment could put it on the low level of certain English novels that sell because they are offensive, and for no other reason in the world. *Aus guter Familie*, by Gabrielle Reuter, is another remarkable novel, and I believe it has never been translated into English. It presents the poignant tragedy of a woman's life suffocated by the social conditions obtaining in a small German town where a woman has no hope but marriage, and if she is poor no chance of marriage. It is one of the most sincere books I ever read. *Das Tägliche Brot*, Klara Viebig's story of servant-life in Berlin, is another typical novel of the present day, and that has been translated for those amongst us who do not read German. I choose these three novels for mention because they are written by women, and because they are brilliant examples of the modern tone amongst women. If you want the traditional German qualities of sentiment, poetry, formlessness, and dreamy childlike charm, you must read novels written by men.

I have said very little about music in Germany, because we all know and admit that it reaches heights there no other nation can approach. An Englishman writing about Germany lately says that you often hear very bad music there, but I think his experience must have been exceptional and unfortunate. I am sure that Germans do not tolerate the vapid dreary drawing-room songs we listen to complacently in this country; for in England people often have beautiful voices without any musical understanding, or technical facility without charm. I suppose such cases must occur amongst Germans too, and in the end one speaks of a foreign nation partly from personal experience, which must be narrow, and partly from hearsay. I have met Germans who were not musical, but I have never met any who were pleased with downright bad music. On the whole, it is the art they understand best, the one in which their instinctive taste is sure and good. You would not find that the Byron amongst composers, whoever he may be, was the one they set up for worship. Nor do you find the street of a German city or suburb infested with barrel-organs. There is some kind of low dancing saloon or *café chantant* called a Tingl-Tangl where I imagine they have organs and grama-phones and suchlike horrors, but then unless you chance to pass their open windows you need not endure their strains. In England, even if we are fond of music, and therefore sensitive to jarring sounds and maudlin melodies, yet in the street we cannot escape the barrel-organ nor in the house the drawing-room songs. As if these were not enough, we now invite each other to listen to the pianotist and the pianola.

"I will explain my country to you," said the artist one day when I had expressed myself puzzled by the curious gaps in German taste, and even in German knowledge ; by their enthusiasm for the second rate in poetry and literature, and by their amazing uncertain mixture of information and blank complacent ignorance. For when an Englishman says " Goethe ! Schiller !— Was is das ? " you are not surprised. It is just what you expect of an Englishman, and for all that he may know how to build bridges and keep his temper in games and argument. But when a German teacher of literature tells you Byron is the only English poet, and when the whole nation neglects some of our big men but runs wild over certain little ones, you listen eagerly for any explanation forthcoming. " We have *Wissen*," said the artist, "we have *Kunst*; but we have no *Kultur*."

I did not recover from the shock he gave me till the evening, when I saw the professor of philosophy and æsthetics.

"The artist says that you have no *Kultur*," I told him ; for I wanted to see how he received a shock.

"The artist speaks the truth," said the professor calmly. I have never met anyone more civilised and scholarly then he was himself; and I set a high value on his opinion.

"What is *Kultur ?*" I asked.

"One result of it is a fine discrimination," he replied, "a fine discrimination in art, in conduct, and in manner."

"Are you not the most intellectual people in the world ?" I said reproachfully.

He seemed to think that had nothing to do with it.

"Are you still worrying your head about *Kultur ?*" said the artist next time I saw him. "Then I will explain a little more to you. I, as you know, am extremely *anti-Semit*."

"I am sure that is not a proof of *Kultur*," I said hurriedly.

"It is not a proof of anything. It is a result. Nevertheless I perceive that if it were not for the Jews there would be neither art nor literature in Germany. They create, they appreciate, they support, and although we affect to despise them we invariably follow them like sheep. What they admire we admire ; what they discover we see to be good. But. . . I told you I was *anti-Semit*, . . . though they have most of the brains in the country, they have little *Kultur*. One of us who is as stupid as an ox, . . . most of us are as stupid as oxen, . . . may have more, . . . but because he is stupid he cannot impose his opinion on the multitude."

" Do you mean that the Jews set the fashion in art and literature, and that they sometimes set a bad one ? " I asked.

" That is exactly what I mean."

It was a curious theory, and I will not be responsible for its truth.   But there is no doubt that in every German town artistic and literary society has its centre amongst the educated Jews.   They are most generous hosts, and it is their pleasure to gather round them an aristocracy of genius.   The aristocracy that is perfectly happy without genius would as a rule not enter a Jew's house; though the poorer members of the aristocracy often marry a Jew's daughter.   Where there is inter-marriage some social intercourse is presumably inevit-able.   But the social crusade against Jews is carried on in Germany to an extent we do not dream of here. The Christian clubs and hostels exclude them, Christian families avoid them, and Christian insults are offered to them from the day of their birth.   "What do you use those long lances for ? " said the wife of a Jewish professor to a young man in a cavalry regiment. " *Damit hetzen wir die Juden,*" said he, with the snarl of his kind ; and he knew very well that the lady's husband was a Jew.   I have been told a story of a Jewish girl being asked to a Court ball by the Emperor Frederick, and finding that none of the men present would consent to dance with her.   I have heard of girls who wished to ask a Jewish schoolmate to a dance, and discovered that their Christian friends flatly refused to meet anyone of her race.   How any Christians contrive to avoid it I do not understand, for wherever you go in Germany some of the great scholars, doctors, men of science, art, and literature, are men of Jewish blood.   The press is almost entirely in their hands, and when there is a scurrilous artist or a coarse picture your friends explain it by saying that the tone of that special paper is *jüdisch*. The modern campaign against Jews began nearly thirty years ago, when a Court chaplain called Stöcker startled the world by the violence of his invective. But the fire he stirred to flame must have been smouldering. He and his followers gave the most ingenuous reasons for curtailing Jewish rights and privileges in Germany, one of which was the provoking fact that Jewish boys did more brilliantly at school than Christians. The subject bristles with difficulties, and no one who knows the German Jew intimately will wish to pose him as a persecuted saint. The Christian certainly makes it unpleasant for him socially, but in one way or the other he holds his own. I have seen him vexed and offended by some brutal slight, but his keen sense of humour helps him over most stiles. So no doubt does his sense of power. " They will not admit me to their clubs or ask my daughters to their dances," said a Jewish friend, " but they come to me for money for their charities." And I knew that half the starving poor in the town came to his wife for charity, and that she never sent one empty away.

When a very clever, sensitive, numerically small race has lived for hundreds of years cheek by jowl with a dense brutal race that has never ceased to insult and humiliate it, you cannot be surprised if those clever but highly sensitive ones become imbued in course of time with a painful undesirable conviction that the brutes are their superiors. So you have the spectacle in Germany of Jews seeking Christian society instead of avoiding it; and you hear them boast quite artlessly of their *christlicher Umgang*. They would really serve their people and even themselves more if they refused all *christlicher Umgang* until the Christians had learned to behave themselves. An Englishwoman living in Berlin told me that once as she came out of a concert hall an officer standing in the crowd stared at her and said, so that everyone could hear: " At last ! a single face that is not a *jüdischer Fratz*." The concert, you will understand, must have been a good one, and therefore largely attended by a Jewish audience. Possibly the officer who so much disliked his surroundings had married a Jewish heiress and was waiting for his wife. Such things happen. During the worst times of Stöcker's campaign a woman with Jewish features could hardly go out unescorted ; and even now, though it is not openly expressed, you can hardly fail to catch some note of sympathy with the Russian persecution of the Jews. The deep helpless genuine horror felt in England at the pogroms is felt in a fainter way in Northern Germany.

Meanwhile the Jewish woman of the upper classes takes her revenge by knowing how to dress. In German cities, when you see a woman who is " exquisite," slim that is and graceful, dainty from head to foot and finely clad, then you may vow by all the gods that she has Jewish blood in her.

INDEX

Home Life in Holland. By D. S. Meldrum

With Sixteen Illustrations. $1.75 net; by mail, $1.85

In this volume the author's object is to show that present-day Holland is exceedingly "modern," and at the same time how in its manifestations of this there is displayed the individualism which explains those ancient survivals that preoccupy the stranger. The reader is therefore introduced to the classes on the land and shown old-fashioned conditions of life and industry existing among them alongside of much "up-to-date" enterprise, and also to the highly educated and progressive classes in the towns, who nevertheless retain the character and many of the customs of the old Dutch. It is in this odd contrast of old and new that the author sees the characteristic and significant features of the home life of Holland.

Home Life in America. By Katherine G. Busbey

With Twelve Illustrations. $2.00 net; by mail, $2.12

In "Home Life in America," the daily routine of the American family is shown. For the greater part it is the family of the city, but Mrs. Busbey enters the country too. The book should be not only of interest, but of real service, for domestic budgets are given which should be of value to prospective emigrants to the New World.

"A vital, vivid, lively, and always readable human account of a nation which is nothing if not vital and vivid in its personality." — *Daily Chronicle.*

"A collection of shrewd, intelligent observations by an educated woman, and is a distinct contribution to the literature of American life and customs." — *Standard.*

"The best book on its particular subject that exists at the present time." — *Globe.*

"The work is admirably done, being based upon intimate first-hand knowledge." — *Morning Post.*

"A delightful book which gives in a most vivid and intelligent manner an intimate insight of American life." — *Sphere.*

Home Life in France. By Miss Betham-Edwards

With Twenty Illustrations. $1.75 net; by mail, $1.85

This work, the result of over twenty-five years' close acquaintance with all sorts and conditions of men over the water, informs us how our near neighbors and friends manage their households, incomes, holidays, children, recreations, and routine of daily existence, and what are the average standards and ideals of the great middle classes.

"This charming book is as original as it is fascinating. The reader who knows it will know French ways as a Frenchman does." — *Daily Telegraph.*

"A sympathetic study of contemporary France, written from a genuine knowledge of its national life." — *T. P.'s Weekly.*

"Miss Betham-Edwards writes with knowledge on a subject she may be said to have made her own, and she writes sympathetically. The book will be read with interest and profit." — *Athenæum.*

THE MACMILLAN COMPANY

Publishers   **64–66 Fifth Avenue**   **New York**

Home Life in Italy. By Lina Duff Gordon. Second Edition
(Mrs. Aubrey Waterfield)

With Twenty-eight Illustrations. $1.75 net; by mail, $1.85

In this book the author has carefully avoided anything in the nature of a treatise, but has sought to describe simply the life of the people; bourgeois, artisan, and peasant. In order to make the picture of the people more vivid, and to enable the reader to understand what makes the charm of living among Italians who have been unspoilt by the advent of foreigners, she has dealt with the subject in a personal way, making the interest centre round a sixteenth-century castle, and the little town below. She describes, among other things, feasts, fairs, old customs and beliefs, and the country life of the day.

"Agreeable and graceful from beginning to end. This sunny book should make English readers know Italians better." — *Spectator.*

"A charming book, written in a natural and engaging style, and admirably illustrated." — *Globe.*

"By her sympathetic observation of the people, her delightful manner of recording the result of her observations, Mrs. Waterfield wins and holds our attention with her engaging book." — *Daily Telegraph.*

Home Life in Russia. By Dr. Angelo S. Rappoport

With Twelve Illustrations. $1.75 net; by mail, $1.85

Dr. Rappoport gives a popular account of the various classes of Russian society, the country squire, the peasant, the clergyman, the professional man, and the tradesman, and of the various institutions which distinguish Russia from Western Europe. It is, however, the pictures of the Russian Home that he especially gives us in the present book. Whilst describing the Russians at School, in the University, and in business, he shows us the Russians as they really are, how they talk and behave, how they play and work. As a native of the country, the author has had many opportunities to watch and study all those trifles which make up the round of life.

Home Life in Spain. By S. L. Bensusan

With Twelve Illustrations. $1.75 net; by mail, $1.85

The presentation of the Spanish man and woman as they are at school and in college, in the kitchen, the drawing-room, and the patio, in the cathedral and the market-place, in the heart of the town and the depths of the country, is made by Mr. S. L. Bensusan in this volume. Here will be found the intimate personal details that can only be gathered by those who have resided in the country, and while there, have not been entirely dependent upon the big hotels, which, as Mr. Bensusan remarks, have nothing more Spanish about them than a French chef and an English scale of charges.

"At once a book of reference of high value and a descriptive work of the most charming kind. We have seldom been so well entertained and so vividly informed in a single volume." — *Standard.*

THE MACMILLAN COMPANY
Publishers   64-66 Fifth Avenue   New York

ILLUSTRATED DESCRIPTIONS OF AMERICAN PLACES AND PEOPLE

BOSTON: THE PLACE AND THE PEOPLE

By M. A. DeWolfe Howe.

With over one hundred illustrations including many from pen drawings executed especially for this volume by L. A. Holman.

Travel series, decorated cloth, boxed, $2.00 net, by mail, $2.20

CHARLESTON: THE PLACE AND THE PEOPLE

By Mrs. St. Julien Ravenel.

Illustrated from photographs and from drawings by Vernon Howe Bailey.

Travel series, decorated cloth, boxed, $2.00 net, by mail, $2.20

NEW ORLEANS: THE PLACE AND THE PEOPLE

By Grace King.

With eighty-three illustrations from drawings by Frances E. Jones.

Travel series, decorated cloth, boxed, $2.00 net, by mail, $2.20

PHILADELPHIA: THE PLACE AND THE PEOPLE

By Agnes Repplier.

With eighty-two illustrations from drawings by Ernest C. Peixotto.

Travel series, decorated cloth, boxed, $2.00 net, by mail, $2.20

STAGE COACH AND TAVERN DAYS

By Mrs. Alice Morse Earle.

With over one hundred and fifty illustrations.

Travel series, decorated cloth, boxed, $2.00 net, by mail, $2.20

TARRY AT HOME TRAVELS

By Dr. Edward Everett Hale.

With over two hundred fine illustrations from interesting prints, photographs, etc., of his own collection.

Travel series, decorated cloth, boxed, $2.00 net, by mail, $2.20

THE MACMILLAN COMPANY

PUBLISHERS, 64-66 FIFTH AVENUE, NEW YORK